LAURENCE KELLY is the editor of the Traveller's Companion series. Born in Brussels and educated at New College, Oxford, where he read history, he joined the Life Guards in 1950 and served in the Foreign Office. He is the son of a former British ambassador to Russia.

Other titles in the Traveller's Companion series
(Series Editor Laurence Kelly)

A TRAVELLER'S COMPANION TO
MOSCOW

EDITED AND INTRODUCED BY

Laurence Kelly

Interlink Books

An imprint of Interlink Publishing Group, Inc.
Northampton, Massachusetts

This edition first published in 2005 by

INTERLINK BOOKS
An imprint of Interlink Publishing Group, Inc.
46 Crosby Street, Northampton, Massachusetts 01060
www.interlinkbooks.com

Published simultaneously in the UK by Constable & Robinson Ltd

ISBN 1-56656-576-6

Printed and bound in the EU

To request our complete 40-page full-color catalog, please call us toll free at 1-800-238-LINK, visit our website at www.interlinkbook.com, or write to
Interlink Publishing
46 Crosby Street, Northampton, Massachusetts 01060
e-mail: info@interlinkbooks.com

For my parents,
who first showed me Moscow

Contents

BEYOND THE KREMLIN

THE RED SQUARE

LIFE, CUSTOMS AND
MORALS IN MOSCOW

Illustrations

Maps
Map of eighteenth-century Moscow, from *Moscow, An Architectural History* by Kathleen Berton

Part Title Illustrations
The coronation of Tsar Nicholas I; lithograph by L. Courtin and V. Adam, 1828. (*Courtesy of the Novosti Press Agency, London*)

The Red Square in the nineteenth century; lithograph of a painting by Cadolle. (*Courtesy of Agnew & Son*)

The Troitsko-Sergievo Monastery, at Zagorsk; by K.F. Yuon. (*Courtesy of the Novosti Press Agency, London*)

Peter the Great's mummery, 1722; by N. Surikov, (*Courtesy of the Novosti Press Agency, London*)

Plates

The surrender and evacuation of the Kremlin by the Poles in 1612; by Lissner. (*Courtesy of the Novosti Press Agency, London*)

Ivan the Terrible shows his treasures to the English Ambassador; by A. Litovtchenko. (*Courtesy of the Mansell Collection*)

Dmitry, the 'false' Tsar and his Polish bride, Marina Mniszek; from the collection of the Grand Duke Sergey Alexandrovitch. (As reproduced in *Moscow in Her Past and Present*, edited by I. Zabyelin, Moscow, no date)

The riot of the *streltsy*, 1682. (*Courtesy of the Novosti Press Agency, London*)

The great bell of Moscow; engraving by André Durand. (*Courtesy of the Ashmolean Museum, Oxford*)

Peter the Great's mass torture and execution of the *streltsy*, 1698. (*Courtesy of the Novosti Press Agency, London*)

The great fire of 1812; artist unknown. (*Courtesy of the Novosti Press Agency, London*)

The Kremlin seen across the River Moskva: an eighteenth-century view. (*Courtesy of the Novosti Press Agency, London*)

The Chapel of the Iverian Mother of God; artist unknown, 1850. (*Courtesy of the Novosti Press Agency, London*)

Gilliardi's Moscow University; by K.F. Yuon

The Moscow Theatre burns to the ground, 1853. (*Courtesy of the Novosti Press Agency, London*)

Acknowledgements

I should like to thank again – as I did in the companion volume to this, *St Petersburg: a traveller's companion* – George Vasiltchikov and my wife Linda for excellent suggestions. For their help in translations from French or Russian original texts, I am grateful to my mother Marie Noële Kelly, Marina Berry and Sophie Lund, who worked hard and to excellent effect. Maria Ellis and Gay Renault saw to the typing with great patience and accuracy. Prudence Fay, my editor, solved various problems of chronology and arrangement with adroit tact and sure judgement. The history of Moscow is, after all, some six centuries longer than that of St Petersburg.

I also wish to make acknowledgement to the following for extracts used from their editions, translations, or where copyright permission was needed:

William Collier and Frank Cass for *A Tour of Russia, Siberia and the Crimea, 1792–1794*, by John Parkinson; Dr A. Lentin and Cambridge University Press for *On the*

Corruption of Morals in Russia by Prince Shcherbatov; Chatto and Windus and the translator's literary estate for *My Past and Thoughts, Memoirs of Alexander Herzen*, translated by Constance Garnett, edited and revised by Humphrey Higgens; Hamish Hamilton for *The Memoirs of Catherine the Great* by Dominique Maroger, translated by Moura Budberg; M. Victor Alexandrov and Allen and Unwin for *The Kremlin*; Macmillan Publishing Co, New York, for Kathleen Berton's *Moscow, An Architectural History*; Adam B. Ulam and Secker and Warburg for *Lenin and the Bolsheviks*; Stanford University Press for *The Travels of Olearius in Seventeenth Century Russia*, translated and edited by Samuel H. Baron; Oxford University Press for *Pushkin* by Ernest J. Simmons, and for Chekhov's *A Nervous Breakdown* from *The Oxford Chekhov*, Volume 4, *Stories 1888–1889*, translated and edited by Ronald Hingley; Cassel Collier Macmillan for *The Memoirs of General de Caulaincourt, Duke of Vicenza, 1812–1813*, edited by Jean Hanoteau, translated by Hamish Miles; Mrs David Magarshack for her late husband's *Chekhov, a Life*; Sir Charles Johnston for his translation of Alexander Pushkin's stanzas about the Petrovsky Castle, in *Eugene Onegin*; the Marquess of Londonderry and H. Montgomery Hyde for *The Russian Journals of Martha and Catherine Wilmot 1803–1808*; C.E. L'Ami and A. Welikotny and the University of Manitoba Press for their translations of Lermontov's poetry in *Michael Lermontov*; Princess Zinaïda Shakhovskoye for *La Vie Quotidienne à Moscou au XVIIe Siècle*; A. Haskell and Gollancz for *Diaghileff: his artistic and private life*; and J. Thomas Shaw and the University of Wisconsin for *The Letters of Alexander Pushkin*.

All the extracts have been reprinted as they originally appeared in English, which accounts for any apparent discrepancies in spelling.

My thanks also go to the following, who either obtained for me pictures or made pertinent suggestions; and, where appropriate, to the Keepers and Institutes which they represent:

Mrs S. Alford, Novosti Press Agency (APN); Mr M. Higgins and the staff of the London Library; Mr J.S.G. Simmons; HBM Ambassador in 1982 in Moscow, Sir Curtis Keeble, his Minister, Mr A. Brooke-Turner, and his Cultural Attaché, Mr T. Sandell: Sir Geoffrey Agnew for his generosity in providing photos from an Agnew's exhibition; the Ashmolean Museum with their unrivalled Taylor collection; Vice-President A. Sorokin and Vneshtorgizdat, and the Museum for the History and Reconstruction of Moscow, for Chernetsov's painting of the Kremlin in 1839; and the Mansell Collection in London. The generosity of the Macmillan Publishing Co in New York for permission to use the maps of Moscow from Kathleen Berton's *Moscow, An Architectural History* should be especially mentioned.

Readers may notice that, unlike *St Petersburg, Moscow* contains some biographical details about the contributors to the Anthology. This excellent suggestion was made by Edward Crankshaw, reviewing *St Petersburg* in the *Observer*. There remain, however, some extracts with no explanatory note: the reason in those cases is either that no biographical details could be found at all (e.g., for George Carrington or Sutherland Edwards); that the contributor is a writer or biographer of our times (e.g. K. Waliszewski, E. Schuyler); or that the contributor is well known for his other activities or writings (e.g. Stanislavsky, Stendhal).

L.K.

Map of the city locating the places described

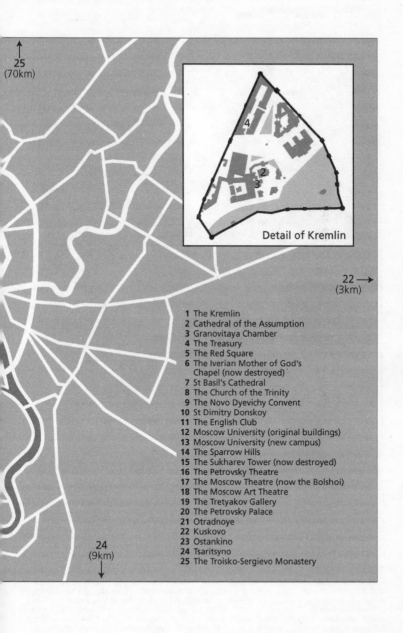

Detail of Kremlin

25
(70km)

22 →
(3km)

24
(9km)

1 The Kremlin
2 Cathedral of the Assumption
3 Granovitaya Chamber
4 The Treasury
5 The Red Square
6 The Iverian Mother of God's
  Chapel (now destroyed)
7 St Basil's Cathedral
8 The Church of the Trinity
9 The Novo Dyevichy Convent
10 St Dimitry Donskoy
11 The English Club
12 Moscow University (original buildings)
13 Moscow University (new campus)
14 The Sparrow Hills
15 The Sukharev Tower (now destroyed)
16 The Petrovsky Theatre
17 The Moscow Theatre (now the Bolshoi)
18 The Moscow Art Theatre
19 The Tretyakov Gallery
20 The Petrovsky Palace
21 Otradnoye
22 Kuskovo
23 Ostankino
24 Tsaritsyno
25 The Troisko-Sergievo Monastery

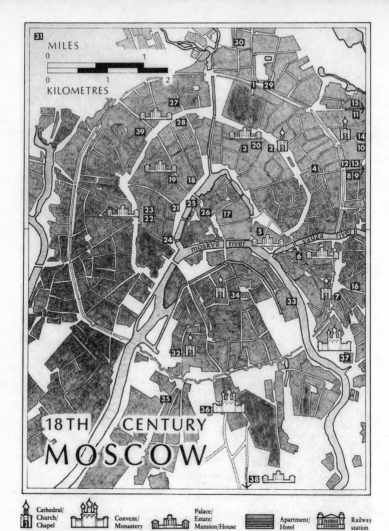

MILES

KILOMETRES

18TH CENTURY
MOSCOW

Cathedral/ Church/ Chapel   Convent/ Monastery   Palace/ Estate/ Mansion/House   Apartment/ Hotel   Railway station

1 Sukharev Tower 1692–1701 (now demolished) 2 Church of the Archangel Gabriel (Menshikov Tower) 1705–7, rebuilt in 1780 3 Rostopchin House, first half of the 18th century 4 Apraksin House, 1760s 5 Foundling Home, 1764–70 6 Batashov House, now a hospital, end of 18th century 7 St Martin the Confessor, 1782–93 8 Dvortsovy Most, 1779–81 9 Razumovsky House, now the Institute of Physical Culture 1790–93 10 Demidov House, 1779–91 11 Musin-Pushkin House, end of the 18th century 12 The Military Hospital, 1798–1802 13 The Catherine Palace, 1773–96 14 St Nikita the Martyr, 1751 15 Preobrazhenskoe Cemetery, Old Believers 16 Rogozhskoe Cemetery, Old Believers 17 Gostiny Dvor, 1790–1805 18 The Dolgoruky House, latter Nobles' Club, now House of Unions, 1784 19 Chernyshevsky House, now Mossoviet, 1782–84, almost totally rebuilt in the 1940s 20 Yushkov House, 1780s 21 The University Old Buildings and Chapel, 1786–93 22 Talyzin House, now the Museum of Russian Architecture, 1787 23 Sheremetiev House, 1780 24 Pashkov House, now Old Building of the Lenin Library, 1784–6 25 The Arsenal, 1701–36 26 The Senate, 1776–87 27 The Gagarin House or Catherine Hospital, 1786–90 28 The Gubin House, 1780s 29 The Sheremetiev Hospital, now Skliforovsky Institute, 1791–1807 30 Church of Filip the Metropolitan, 1777–88 31 Petrovsky Zamok, the Peter Palace, 1775–82 32 Ioanna Voina, St John the Warrior, 1709–13 33 Kriegskommissariat, 1778–80 34 St Klimenta, 1740s, 1770s 35 Golitsyn Hospital, 1796–1801 36 Gate Bell-tower of the Donskoi Momastery, 1730–50 37 Bell-tower of the Novospassky Convent, 1759–62 38 Tsaritsyno, 1775–97 39 The English Club, 1780

Introduction

Moscow 'is neither Europe nor Asia: it is Russia – and it is Russia's heart.' Marquis de Custine, 1839.

St Petersburg: a traveller's companion, published in 1981, was selected and edited on principles which have again been applied to the tumultuous, often sanguinary, and always enthralling life of Moscow, synonymous for most of her history with the amazing growth of the Muscovite Tsardom. It is an anthology that seeks to describe the literary and historical perspectives of the city, and is intended to complement rather than replace the excellent guide-books currently available. The aim is to let Moscow speak for herself through the voices of participants, both native and foreign, in her life, or, in default of this, through the liveliest authority on the period. Due place has been given to literature, whether poems, ballads, or novels, so often in Russian history the only authentic incarnations of *vox populi*; while there are echoes of *vox dei* in the witness of such writers of genius as Pushkin, Lermontov and Herzen. The material is arranged by place and chronologically, and a section on Moscow manners and morals seeks to capture the 'physiology' (as Balzac would have called it) of the city. Napoleon's capture of Moscow and the great fire of 1812 merit a special section.

The difficult decision has been taken, as in *St Petersburg*, to conclude the story in 1918, with the triumph of the Soviet State, and in Moscow's case, the arrival of Lenin in the Kremlin. To cover his reign, and its aftermath – the tortured days of the thirties; the desperate struggle for the city in the Second World War, when Nazi tanks were at its gates; the death of Stalin; the fall and arrest of Beria, and the Kruschev 'thaw'; the hundred Committees and Ministries – would demand and justify a further volume.

The interest of the present volume for the traveller, it is hoped, lies in the discovery of how much of the legacy of medieval and Imperial Muscovy survives today, both on the ground and in the manners and morals of its citizens. It is no accident that Ivan the Terrible was one of Stalin's favourite models, that Kutuzov's character was upheld as an ideal in 1941, or that Soviet schoolchildren are taught to regard Lermontov's *Borodino* as the quintessence of patriotism. The exploration of the past provides unexpected ways to understanding today's Muscovite. Heredity must count for something.

'A miracle! A small town, scarcely known before the fourteenth century, long called from contempt for its insignificance "Village Kutchkovo", raised its head, and saved the fatherland. Honour and glory to Moscow!' – Nicholas Karamzin.

Yuri Dolgoruky, Prince of 'Suzdalia',* had other hunting-camps and fortified settlements ('Kremlins') as well as the one he built in AD 1147–56 where the rivers Neglinnaya and

* J. Fennell's phrase. See his *The Emergence of Moscow 1304–1359*, London 1968. It covered the principalities of Rostov, Suzdal and Vladimir.

Moskva meet. It was not long before this conveniently placed township between Rostov and Vladimir, a link to the rivers Volga and Oka, acquired a pre-eminent place among them. The Moskva River was the trade artery of medieval Russia. Between 1237 and 1241, however, Moscow's evolution was arrested when Khan Baty of the Golden Horde sacked the town, burnt the modest wooden Kremlin, and laid down the rules of survival for all the princes of old 'Rus', of Kiev, Suzdal, Vladimir, Tver, Novgorod: a pilgrimage of homage to his tents thousands of miles away on the lower Volga at Saray, or even to the Great Khan at Karakorum in Mongolia; the right to rule under his patent auctioned off to the highest bidder; annual tribute in money and recruits. The Khan of Kipchak was Moscow's first Tsar, and so called by the Russians. 'Divide and rule' was his precept. Moscow's princes were but the harassed agents of exceptionally greedy principals, whose totalitarian society and empire was to provide their political, fiscal, and military education. It was the wily Ivan I (1325–41)* who knew the rules of this 'glib and oily art' so well that he outdistanced his rivals of Tver, Novgorod, or Suzdal, in Karl Marx's words, as 'the Tartar's hangman, sycophant and slave in chief'. He even married the Khan's sister. In 1328 Ivan I received the Khan's patent (*yarlyk*) as Great Prince of Vladimir, first amongst his peers by Tartar appointment, and their chosen bulwark against the menace of Lithuania. The Khan endorsed Ivan's will leaving all his patrimony to his sons, and issued the *yarlyk* to his son Semen as Great Prince of Vladimir, an unprecedented act.

Shaking off the Khans, their tribute, and the odious task of being their toadying fiscal inquisitor took another hundred and forty years. Under Dmitry Donskoy, victor of the battle of Kulikovo over Khan Mamai and the Horde (1380), the principality of Moscow became that of Vladimir *and* Moscow. The Golden Horde, after their 'Time of Troubles' in the 1350s, had been effectively dispersed by Timurlane in

* Ivan I was nicknamed 'Kalita', or 'Money-Bags'.

1389–95, but it took nearly another century before the Moscow Princes dared to default finally with the tribute (1480). Only after 1472 did Ivan III (1462–1505), emboldened by his marriage to the obese heiress Sophia of the Byzantine Paleologues, adopt the bicephalous eagle for his arms. Only after 1486 did the ruler's title ring sonorously with the word 'Autocrat' of all the Russias. It had been an education of nearly three centuries in deceit, humiliation, treachery to one's own brothers, and collaborationist book-keeping under the eye of Mongol inspectors in the heart of their own Kremlin. These lessons fashioned the character of Moscow and her rulers for all time.

Ivan Kalita's Kremlin was destroyed in 1365 by fire. It was, of course, built of wood. Fire proved a worse enemy to Moscow over the centuries than the sword. She might be ravished by the Crimean Tartars, Poles, Cossacks, or the French; and finally in 1941 Germans might seek to defile her. But it was fire that swept Moscow away a score of times. Amongst the worse years were 1547, 1571, 1595, 1612, 1701, 1712 and 1737. Moscow was more grandly reborn each time, the phoenix of the world's great cities. This act of faith was made possible because of the Tsar's total power over bodies, souls and goods of his subjects, not only as ruler but actual proprietor of his domain. The first two stone cathedrals in the Kremlin (1326), those of the Assumption and the Archangel Michael, were both built in the fourteenth century. The Kremlin's famous white stone walls twice saw off the Lithuanians; they were begun in 1367. Ivan the Terrible, after the holocaust of 1547, proved himself a mighty builder. *Ukazes* decreed that open spaces should be left between courtyards and households, and between the Kremlin and the adjoining settlements so that – as Lord Carlisle noted in 1688 – the hellish flames should consume themselves and not buildings. Brick or stone building was encouraged. It was a merchant who built Moscow's first domestic stone house in 1471. The Kremlin's walls were of white limestone by the end of the fourteenth century, then brick, as we see them today. The main settlement, the

Kitaigorod, east of the Kremlin, was by 1534–38 endowed with massive stone walls along which a carriage and pair could drive. Tsar Alexis Mikhailovitch (1645–1676) gave Moscow her first stone bridge in 1643, that endured until 1819. Peter the Great did endanger the principle when he gave exclusivity to his new city on the Neva to have stone and brick materials, leaving a problem for the Empress Anne when she tried to restore Moscow in the 1730s. In fact, in the fire of 1712 more than 3,000 houses and 500 shops were destroyed, 2,700 people burnt, and a quarter of the city charred to ashes. (Peter did, however, order streets to be straight, seeking a symmetry unknown to medieval Moscow, whose crooked lanes are realistically reproduced in Vasnetsov's paintings.) Despite the creation yet again of a new city after the great fire of 1812, it was calculated in 1860 that some 9,800 houses out of 14,900 were still in wood.

White stone and brick instead of wood might have defeated the fires which God sent to chastise his sinners. But it was remarkable how, after every fire, where there had been one church before, two would replace it. The proverb indeed said that Moscow had 'forty times forty' churches. Whole districts boasted of a fortified convent, monastery or major church as its most beautiful landmark: the Andronikov on the Yauza (1359), the Simonov ('the sentinel of the city', 1405), the Rojdestvensky (1501–5), or those jewels of the Orthodox tiara saved for today's tourist, the Novo-Dyevichy Convent (1524) and the Donskoy Monastery (1591). Here were tangible proofs of the artistic intelligence and adaptive genius of Moscow's architects, masons and icon-painters, fusing the styles of Pskov and Vladimir with those of Byzantium or Renaissance Italy, later creating Moscow's own enchanting version of Baroque, and later still, of Russian Gothic. It is noteworthy that the amazing, mysterious and triumphalist St Basil (1555–60), built to Ivan the Terrible's orders and celebrating his conquest of Kazan, was the work of *Russian* architects.

The Russian Orthodox Church had greatly prospered under the Khans, exempt from the tribute if it prayed for them and their families, and subject itself to the need for a *yarlyk*. The Metropolitans, formerly of Kiev and Vladimir, had since 1328 chosen the Prince of Moscow as the protector who would finesse the Khans or Tartars, either in battle (as at Kulikovo) or in diplomacy, more adroitly than other princes of ancient Russia, and grant them substantial estates. They ratified his power as God-given and without appeal.

The cross of orthodoxy in Ivan the Great's bell tower, so proudly standing above that of lesser churches, reminded Muscovites that they were living under a totalitarian theocracy. Church land – after the overthrow of the Khans – required the Tsar's confirmation, though administered by a Metropolitan or Abbot. Basil III had deposed a Metropolitan in 1521. There was no Patriarch until 1589. Peter the Great abolished the office. In the seventeenth century the inevitable happened: an outstanding Patriarch (Nikon, 1605–1681) tried to promote reforms of ritual and doctrine which led to dissidence, schism, and social disorder intolerable even for his erstwhile protector, the Tsar Alexis Mikhailovitch. The Tsar broke the Patriarch. Henceforth 'Russia no longer had a Church; it had a religion of state'.* Any hope, therefore, that the Tsar's servants and slaves might have had that the church would – as in Europe – balance the power of the ruler were pure fantasy. As an early theologian, Joseph of Volok, wrote, 'In his mortal form the Tsar resembles all men, but in his power he is like unto Almighty God.'†

The Orthodox ritual did provide key concepts that might make the people's life a little more tolerable. The Churches themselves were the most beautiful places which they could enter and use as of right. The doctrine of resignation to this world's evils was obviously attractive; that of humility suited a totalitarian society; so did acceptance of suffering. The Church's leaders *might* even influence the rulers to soften individuals' fates. Monasteries and convents were

* R. Pipes, *Russia under the Old Regime* quoting Pierre Pascal, *Awakum et les débuts de Raskol*, Paris, 1938.
† *The Russian Tradition*, Tibor Szamuely, London, 1974.

retreats, however spartan, from the troubles of daily life. And an important ingredient of the Faith was the fanatic belief that Moscow had become God's holiest city after the fall of Constantinople in 1453, arrogant bearer of the burden of the Third Rome.

Where fire, Tartars and invaders failed, Stalin and his metro-builders in the thirties (and fifties) succeeded. For they swept away much of medieval Moscow, including the famous towers and chapel protecting the holy icon of the Iverian Mother of God at the entrance to the Red Square (to be replaced by Lenin in his Pantheon) and the massive presence of the Cathedral of the Redeemer, built after 1812 to thank God for delivering Moscow from the French, which had dominated Moscow's skyline for over a century.

After Ivan the Terrible's conquest of Kazan (1553), of Astrakhan, and of Siberia, his writ ran over a staggering 5.4 million kilometres, whereas his grandfather, Ivan III, in the 1460s had only controlled 430,000. The Tsars took good care to monopolize all profitable raw materials, and trade in them. (Moscow's 'merchants' were more like Imperial factors than Elizabethan adventurers, in contractual partnership with their Sovereign.) The Tsar had mastered every possible element in society that might stand against his will, militarily and economically. As a result there was a reservoir of labour to build Moscow, and foreign or native architects were given resources beyond their dreams to beautify the Kremlin and Moscow. From Yuri Dolgoruky's one-hectare Kremlin in 1156, Moscow grew to cover an area of 17,685 hectares, housing 1.6 million inhabitants by 1917.

The Tsars took care that their praetorian guard, whether Ivan the Terrible's fiendish servants (the *opritchniki*) or Alexis Mikhailovitch's musketeers (*streltsy*), were within easy riding distance of the Kremlin, in barracks occupying whole quarters of Moscow. (One should not forget that in the sixteenth and seventeenth centuries Moscow was the headquarters of a standing army of 65,000 men, where in Europe 18,500 men, mustered once by the Holy Roman Emperor against the Turks (1467), was considered a prodigy.) Such was the origin of the Konyushennaya ('equerries') district, or opposite the Kremlin over the river, of the Zamoskvorechiye. Their captains on a grace and favour basis were well looked after. As a clerkly caste – in effect the Tsar's bureaucracy – expanded with the growth of the Tsardom, so they, too, received land on an appropriate scale (the *pomestiye*) near the Kremlin.

Such hired men earned notorious reputations, especially under Ivan the Terrible. The name of Maliuta-Skuratov, in every sense his chief hatchet-man, can still conjure up a *frisson* in Russia.

Beyond these estates of the Tsars' servants, whose stone walls (in the case of the richest) encompassed spacious orchards, falconries, cattle-byres, and carp-ponds, criss-crossing Moscow's twenty or more rivers and streams, there stretched the *slobodi*, the trading and craftsmens' settlements, and the home in future of Moscow's merchants. There market-gardens and grazing-fields were attached to the two-storey houses of richer boyars and merchants, to provide a necessary cottage economy and the Tsar's vegetables and fruit. Initially these had been the camps of traders from Novgorod, Tver, Smolensk, but they were expanded by function: the armourers' district (*bronnaya*), the weavers (*khamovniki*). In the seventeenth century an opulent ghetto sprang up to quarantine fortune-hunting foreigners whose technical skills were unavoidably needed, whether to set a Jacobean clocktower athwart the existing Spasskoye Gate into Red Square (made by one Christopher Galloway in 1624–5) or to teach courtiers how to act Molière and Racine in a makeshift theatre hall. This was the *Nemetskaya sloboda* (1652), whose German and Swiss ladies were to provide sexual solace for Peter the Great in his salad days.

Conditions beyond the Kremlin were primitive. Distinguished foreigners noted how log rafts had to be flung as bridges over the mud seas that passed for streets; how cows grazed everywhere in summer; how most of the wooden cottages had no glass windows; how poor families all slept on top of their single stove. And what of the *narod*, the 'black' people, servants and slaves, ants milling around the Red Square outside the Kremlin, over the hundreds of booths, stalls, shops, and wharves along the River Moskva? The heart of popular Moscow adjoined the Kremlin in an epidemic-prone, unsalubrious, and stench-laden quarter (the Zaryad), redolent of 'perfumed Russian leather, spirituous liquors, sour beer, cabbages, grease of Cossacks' boots, . . . and of musk, and ambergris', whose undrained cesspits gave rise to 'mephitic air'.* Apart from breeding plagues, this bazaar-land could easily spawn rioting crowds and conceal criminals.

The Red Square† was their *agora*. There, until Peter the Great, they had their trading booths. But there also their bodies might be impaled, knouted, broken on the wheel, or simply quartered, and from the torturers' tower‡ along the Kremlin wall, they could hear the screams and groans of suspects. There stalked rumour and gossip. (Had Tsar Boris Godunov really murdered the Tsarevitch Dmitry at Uglitch?) There they heard the Tsar's decrees, read out by his ever interfering '*pristavi*' or bureaucrats. However cruel, corrupt, or even evil their Autocrat might be, his power had been vested in him, without appeal, by God. Occasionally, the latter would allow His people a brief and bloody say – for example, during the Salt or Copper riots (1662), or when Moscow's women took arms to kill Poles. Sometimes the people helped disaffected ruling clans to make history by killing a false Pretender, by acclaiming in a 'popular' election Boris Godunov or the new Romanov Tsar preselected for them by the boyars, or by defenestrating unpopular boyars such as the Naryshkins. But always the *narod* would be scattered back into its ant-heap. The Tsar, abetted by his familiars, would resume his divine and proprietory rule, taking care to satiate his slaves with such bread and gory circuses as they enjoyed. Executions, especially those of such great threats to the Sovereign as Stenka Razin and

* Marquis de Custine.
† Until St Basil was built, it was called Troitskaya (Trinity) Square.
‡ Konstantino-Yeleninskaya Tower.

Pugachev, were exemplary. Reigns of terror were familiar to Muscovites.

'Progress', in its Victorian meaning, had much to over-come in Moscow. Ivan the Terrible's printers in the 1560s were accused of witchcraft, and despite his protection had to flee to Latvia to escape burning. The founder of the Russian language, Lomonosov, and his contemporary Kantemir, learnt their Greek and Latin at a Kiev-inspired seminary founded in Moscow only in the 1680s. The *Vedomosti*, Russia's first newspaper, did not appear until 1703. Even trade had to overcome the medieval legacy of no less than sixteen customs' barriers into Moscow. They were still there in the 1730s, and the principle was only abolished in 1753. Moscow had no geodesic plan until 1739, and this was the first shaky attempt to plan Moscow's future. Her first bank (which failed) was started only in 1753, under the Empress Anne. The first permanent attempt at the art of town planning came under Catherine the Great's Commission in 1775, established for both capitals. Moscow University was founded in 1755–7, but on the initiative of a private individual (I. I. Shuvalov). The Renaissance, indeed, came late to Moscow.

In the eighteenth century Moscow suffered the greatest blow to her pride in all her history. She had to absorb the painful and violent upheaval caused in 1703 by Peter the Great's creation of his northern capital, St Petersburg. Though Peter had 'cut his window into Europe' on the Baltic, though by smashing the Swedish threat he had assured his country its future as the Russian Empire and not as a Muscovite Tsardom, this stupendous act had an unexpected result. The Court moved in 1712, and Russia henceforth would enjoy two capitals: Moscow, the legatee of her medieval and Asiatic history, would still be witness to the anointing of Tsars in the Kremlin Cathedral, but – as Dostoevsky put it – 'to the overwhelming majority of the Russian people the significance of Petersburg is confined to the fact that the Tsar resides there.' Pushkin caught the new relationship:

> Old Moscow's paled before this other
> metropolis: it's just the same
> as when a widowed Empress Mother
> bows to a young Tsaritsa's claim.*

The contrast between the two capitals fascinated and often obsessed Russia's greatest writers, whose golden age was beginning: Pushkin, Lermontov, Herzen, Byelinsky, Gogol. From the 1800s onwards, the shifts in the relationship between Moscow and a courtly Petersburg are often best captured in their pages. Herzen, Russia's most inspired polemicist and a brilliant 'political' journalist of the nineteenth century, pointed out that Peter the Great's humiliation of Moscow in the 1700s had been turned into triumph for her by Napoleon, an unexpected saviour. By occupying Russia's holiest shrine, namely the Kremlin, and by being forced to leave Moscow in a catastrophic retreat, Napoleon had again made of Moscow – in the century of nationalism – *the* national capital of Russia. And Herzen continued:

> In the reign of Catherine, the court and the Guards really did include all that was cultured in Russia: and this continued more or less until 1812. Since then Russian society has taken terrific strides; the war evoked consciousness, and consciousness evoked the Fourteenth of December.† Society was divided in two from within; it was not the best part that remained on the side of the Court; some were estranged by the executions and savage punishments, others by the new tone prevailing. Alexander had carried on the cultural traditions of the reign of Catherine: under Nicholas the worldly aristocratic tone was replaced by one of dry formality and insolent despotism on the one hand, and absolute servility on the other – a blend of the abrupt and boorish manner of Napoleon with the soullessness of bureaucracy. A

---

* *The Bronze Horseman*, by A.S. Pushkin, translated by Sir Charles Johnston in *Talk about the Last Poet*, London, 1981.
† That is, the failed rebellion against Tsar Nicholas I in St Petersburg in 1826.

new society rapidly developed, the centre of which was in
Moscow.*

This 'new society' chose as its battlefield Moscow's literary
salons, and University platforms. There, 'political questions
being impossible, literary ones became the problem of life'.
Thinly disguised as a literary-historical debate, the war of
ideas between the 'Westerners' and the Slavophiles raged.
The 'Westerners', Byelinsky and Herzen in the lead, could
quote Pushkin's Voltairean gibe at Moscow's traditions:
'How sick and tired I am of Moscow and its Tartar non-
entity!'.† They and their élite sought to imbibe the intoxicating draughts of Western thought, 'forcing itself towards
freedom, the idea of intellectual independence, and the
struggle for it'. Their case was weakened by having to
accept that Peter's window allowed much in from the West
that was – at least in the eyes of Petersburg authorities –
immoral, subversive, or both. Where to draw the line, about
those Jacobin nonsenses of 1789, 1830, and 1848?

To the Slavophiles, Moscow represented romantic values of
piety and of purity, national honour, and the 'imperishable
bodies' of Moscow's saints in the Kremlin. The Kremlin
became a fashionable reminder to them of their forefathers'
belief in Providence which had designated Russia as the
'chosen instrument of her inscrutable designs'. 'Surrounded
here by the holiness of Russia,' – 'inexpressibly tranquil' – they
only heard 'the call of silver-tongued bells', and the 'language
of heaven floating through the skies'.‡ In his time, Dostoevsky
was to revive this nostalgia into the Slavic Gospel of *gesta Dei
per Russos*. Firstly, he rejected the 'Tartar hypothesis' that
Moscow represented only brutal and barbaric Asiatic creeds.
Secondly, he argued that the Russians had a brotherly love of
all peoples, and an urge to render universal service to humanity. (Dostoevsky in the same paragraph defined 'humanity' to

* *My Past and Thoughts*, by A. Herzen, London, 1968.
† Letter of A. Pushkin to E.M. Khitrovo, February 1831.
‡ That lively historian K. Waliszewski, had other words to describe the
Kremlin: 'a crypt, seraglio and gaol in one'.

include only the Aryan races.) This was 'the Russian idea', which 'closer intercourse with Europe' might corrupt; a concept natural to Muscovites, who had always resented and isolated foreigners. And Dostoevsky concluded, 'This is how I understand the Russian mission *in its ideal* . . . the unification of the whole of Slavdom, so to speak, under Russia's wing.'* Not, he hastened to add, for the sake of usurpation but for spiritual regeneration. For him, Moscow, 'this centre of the great Russians, is designed to live long . . . and has not been the third Rome', but the fifteenth-century prophecy that 'there shall be no fourth Rome' must be fulfilled. God's truth was only fully preserved in Orthodoxy.

All this was stuff too heady for the general run of Moscow society, in Catherine the Great's phrase, the 'seat of sloth', a society more interested in breakfast, dinner and tea, name-days and balls, than in dangerous post-Decembrist controversies. Tolstoy's Count Rostov, fussing about Bagration's dinner-party at the English Club, epitomizes his kind. In Byelinsky's phrase, the essence of Moscow was comfortable 'patriarchal domesticity', dissected forever by Griboyedov in *Woe from Wit*. This was a *pritchudlivy gorod*, a town of gossipy, eccentric and whimsical landowners whose idleness was supported by substantial wealth, innumerable servants and serfs.† They had a certain insouciance *vis à vis* new men in St Petersburg rising painfully up the Petrine rungs. (Indeed, great men there usually took good care to have a palace and a country estate or two in and around Moscow; examples included the Sheremetyevs, Orlovs and Potemkin.) In Moscow you would be asked what you did; in the northern capital, where you served. Your Moscow squire thought of himself as open to debate, even-tempered, careless of time, hospitable. He belonged to a society of independent people. His Petersburg counterpart would be worried as to his prospects of promotion, careful not to criticize his superiors, would practise an ironic air to mask

---

* *The Diary of a Writer*, Feodor Dostoievski, London.
† Count P.B. Sheremetyiev (1713–1788) was estimated to own 160,000 souls.

disappointment and the blows of fortune. No wonder the former had a ruddy glow, the latter – according to Byelinsky – an unfortunate 'haemorrhoidal pallor'.* St Petersburg was the GHQ of an Empire; Moscow had now become only its unmilitary and somewhat dishevelled relation, sporting long hair, civilian moustaches and laughable costumes.

It was easy for Herzen and Byelinsky, both liberals, 'Westerners', haters of the autocracy in Petersburg, to endow *their* capital with the monopoly of patriotic virtues. 'Moscow, apparently so drowsy and apathetic, so absorbed in scandal and piety, weddings, and nothing at all, always wakes up when it is necessary, and is equal to the occasion when a storm breaks over Russia. In 1612 she was joined in blood-stained nuptials with Russia, and their union was welded in fire in 1812.'† This heroic myth of Moscow, the true bride of Russia, was further propagated by Gogol who argued that whilst Russia was necessary to St Petersburg, Moscow was necessary to Russia. Byelinsky had the last word by reminding his readers that this judgement, though witty, was untrue: Russia, though rooted in the legacy of Muscovy's Tsardom, henceforth could not escape the constant impact of innovative ideas through Peter's window. Peter's new imperialism, extended so ruthlessly by Catherine, Alexander I and Nicholas I, gave both capitals the necessary security to develop their different ways.

In a gallery of Muscovite types, the leading place has obviously been given to Tsar and Patriarch and their clerks and slaves, inevitably resembling the cast-list of an opera about medieval Moscow by Mussorgsky or Glinka. To enrich the flavour of medieval Muscovy, one could throw in the extras from Pushkin's play *Boris Godunov*: 'The People, Boyars, a Wicked Monk, Abbot of the Chudov Monastery, two courtiers, Hostess, two officers, the Czarevna's Nurse, a Poet, a Cavalier, Serving-women, Russian, Polish and German troops, a Saintly Idiot, a Beggar, a Guard, three Soldiers'. There is a certain familiarity, too, about the eighteenth- and nineteenth-century landowners,

* *Sobraniye Sotehineniya*, V.G. Byelinsky, St Petersburg, 1911.
† A. Herzen, op. cit.

the freedom-thirsting students or the literary intelligentsia, so well-known to us through Russian literature.

It is time, however, to salute an order of mankind also at the heart of Moscow: the order of the merchant. After all, the very survival of the city had once depended on the trade routes meeting there from all corners of Russia, Asia and the south, and linking the Baltic to the Caspian Sea. Yesterday's prince today might find himself in trade, or be tied to a merchant's daughter as his wife and financial salvation. As the perceptive J.G. Kohl observed in the 1840s, Moscow 'is so decidedly first' in respect of manufacturing that 'no other city in the Empire can be compared with it'. Twenty thousand inhabitants of Moscow lived by commerce and industry then. And so Moscow had 'an important voice in the administration', a voice 'seldom loud' but 'listened to, and respected'. In fact, Petersburg would never dare appoint a German to be Moscow's Governor-General, only a Russian, 'because Moscow would endure no other'.*

Strongly Orthodox, bearded, inclined to *kaftans* and *khalats* and similar oriental fancies instead of Petersburgian frock-coats, the Moscow merchant of the Zamoskvorechiye district would cover his portly better half in pearls, and entertain his men friends to gluttonous feasts at the Slavyansky Bazar. Whereas the architectural unity of Petersburg depended on the will of seven or eight Tsars or Tsarinas, determining its public and private character within the short space of perhaps 130 formative years, Moscow's capricious, sprawling, thrust outwards from the Kremlin was spread over 700 years. Despite the Tsars' ownership of all (at least until the eighteenth century), no single will had directed its growth. The merchants made their contribution to this diversity; in Zamyatin's words, 'men who had made their fortunes somewhere in the backwoods of the Urals or in Old Believers' monastery villages along the Volga, would settle in Moscow and build their homes in accordance with the notions of style brought from their home regions'.†

* *Russia*, J.G. Kohl, London, 1842.
† *A Soviet Heretic*: essays by Yevgeny Zamyatin, transl. by Mirra Ginsburg, Chicago, 1970.

In the extraordinary industrial development of Moscow
and Russia (based first and foremost on the arrival of the
railways after 1840), foreigners led the way. A few Russians
followed, and such men deserved their rewards as risk-
takers and capital creators. Their ranks were constantly
renewed by eager candidates rising from the pool of the
meshchantstvo, the wealth-hungry, hard-working, hard-
reading and often unscrupulous clerks, shopkeepers, and
undercapitalized traders, more familiar from the pages of
Saltykov-Shchedrin and Dostoevsky than those of Tolstoy.
At the end of the century a miracle happened. These somewhat porcine-faced and stout burghers, descendants of
Moscow's medieval guildsmen, turned into true merchant
princes, the patrons of Vrubel and Vasnetsov, of Chaliapin
and Diaghilev, of Chekhov and the Moscow Art Theatre.
Such were the Savva Mamontovs and Tretyakovs. Byelinsky's prophecy that Moscow would incorporate in herself
Oxford, Manchester and Rheims had come true – at least in
the context of nineteenth-century Moscow.

With the return to Moscow of the *dominium*, and its
unparalleled extension since 1917, the meaning of the
Slavophile message echoes in familiar cadences, though
now secular and not religious ones. The brotherhood of
man, the unity of Slavs with Aryans, Moscow a third Rome?
Moscow was fated not to remain, as Byelinsky saw her, a
university seat, a manufacturing mart, and a cathedral town.
One of H.G. Wells's novels* is partly set in Moscow, and as
its hero stares out at the city, he muses that 'away from here
to Vladivostok is Russia and all Asia. North, west, east and
south there is limitless land . . . Here one feels the land
masses of the earth.'

The history and traditions of Moscow explain the appeal
today to her inhabitants of the red stars over the Kremlin,
the power they symbolize, stars which dominate Orthodoxy's crosses. She leaves her visitors in no doubt at all that
she relishes once again being a 'ruling Tsaritsa'.

* *Joan and Peter, the Story of an Education*, H.G. Wells, London, 1918.

THE KREMLIN

[1] The legend of its foundation; from *The Kremlin* by Victor Alexandrov.

The story of the Kremlin begins [*c.* 1147 AD] with this legend from an ancient Russian anthology:

'It was a dark, stormy night when the boyar Stephen, son of Ivan Kuchka, came upon a thicket near the River Yauza, a tributary of the Moskva. The boyar and his followers spent the night in a hunting-lodge. The following morning, when the sun was beginning to gild the tops of the birches and the fir-trees, Kuchka had his horns sound the boar-hunt. The huge, savage boar suddenly appeared. The hunters were about to flee, when they saw a bird come out of the sky and swoop down upon the beast. It was a bird of prey of strange shape, having apparently two heads. Its claws and its two beaks reminded one of a fork. The boyar and his men became more afraid of this monster than of the boar. They immediately called off the hunt. The bird pounced upon the boar, seized it in its powerful claws and set it down on the hill which overlooks the Moskva and its tributary the Neglinnaya. Followed by his men, Stephen Kuchka went up to the top of the hill and there found the mangled remains of the boar.

'Very much impressed by this occurrence, the boyar decided to build a hunting-village on this hill and call it Kuchkovo.'

It was this village of Kuchkovo or Kutzkovo that was to become the town of Moscow. On top of the hill where the two-headed bird, the ancestor of the Russo-Byzantine double eagle,* had left the mangled boar, the Kremlin† was later erected.

---

* Two Soviet scholars, V.A. Alexandrov and A.A. Zimin, have collected this legend. In their view, it is steeped in Byzantinism, in that Byzantinism of the time of Ivan III, the Muscovite Grand Duke who married Sophia Zoë Paleolog and adopted as his coat of arms the double-headed eagle of the Emperor of Byzantium. Alexandrov and Zimin have unearthed another, very similar, text of still earlier date, which also treats of this bird of prey with the huge head and strange shape.

† *Kreml*, in Russian, means 'fortress' generally. Every fortified Russian town had its Kremlin.

Whether eagle, falcon or hawk, the bird of the legend had chosen a good spot to appear. Indeed, the place where the boyar Kuchka saw it for the first time is almost in the exact geographical centre of European Russia. It was surrounded on all sides by forests and peat-bogs, being thus provided with effective protection against enemies from outside. The Moskva, which wound its way through the settlement, could be used from the beginning of the first 'Muscovite era' as a link between the Volga and the Oka, both these great rivers rising near it.

The boyar Kuchka had no idea of the consequences of his historical action when he went after the boar and the double-headed bird.

The legend continues:

'When evening came, the bag was so impressive that his servants found it very difficult to set out the slaughtered animals. The forest teemed with nocturnal birds and rats with handsome reddish fur, now extinct. There were also at that time foxes in great number, more plentiful than dogs (if an old twelfth-century Russian manuscript can be believed) and bears, wolves, lynxes, civet-cats, all lying in wait for their prey.

'Stephen Kuchka gave orders for a sort of trench to be dug quite close to the Neglinnaya and disguised with leafy branches and tree-trunks. The trench was dug and trees were cut down. In the middle of a patch of grass* a temporary wooden hut was built.

'So, Stephen Kuchka, happy at having laid the foundations of the future Kuchkovo, went to sleep on the hill, after drinking many glasses of *braga*† with his friends.

'A strong wind was blowing over the hill that night. The smell of the dismembered boar mingled with the scent of the berries and the fir-trees. Kuchka's sleep was disturbed by a troublesome nightmare, in which he saw a huge town built on the site of the settlement; a magnificent fortress with

* This grass-plot was given the name of Kuchkovo Field in the fifteenth century and retained it until the nineteenth century.
† A Russian drink resembling beer.

white battlements stretched away as far as the Neglinnaya. This fortress had a strange appearance; its roofs resembled those to be seen in the lands of the Bassurmans.*

'Many tents and wonderful gold-domed churches stretched down to the Moskva. Thousands of human creatures were being brought in chains to the white walls and while the church bells were sounding the tocsin their decapitated bodies were flung into the pits. Men, bound hand and foot, crawling along on their knees and wailing in front of a huge gallows, were begging mercy of a tall, gaunt skeleton of a man. The sun was already well up when the boyar awoke. He summoned his friends and servants to him and urged them to continue with the hunting, which he desired to be a joyful occasion. But he could not manage to regain his customary calm; there was sadness in his heart.'

[2] The Byzantine connection and the lifting of the Tartar yoke; from *The Kremlin* by Victor Alexandrov.

Sophia Paleolog arrived in Moscow in 1472 with a large body of retainers. She was a woman who weighed about twenty-five stone. According to the *letopis*' [chronicle], she was 'very ugly, intelligent and scheming'. On the night of her arrival in Moscow the magnificent bed of the grand duchesses of Moscow broke down under her weight. During an intimate talk with Prince Odoevsky, Ivan III expressed doubts of his ability to father a child of the huge Byzantine princess, but as he already had several children by his first wife the problem was of secondary importance. The marriage was solemnized without delay.

The new Grand Duchess had brought with her from Rome some architects: Fioravanti, Aleviso, Giuliani and Masconi. It was they who built in the Kremlin the Grand Duke's new palace of brick and stone instead of the usual

* In old Russian the word *Bassurman* means 'Infidel', i.e. 'Moslem'.

wooden palace. They also constructed the new cathedrals of Blagoveschensky, Uspensky, Arkhangelsk, and the Palace of Facets, the place where foreign ambassadors were received.

After his marriage to Sophia, Ivan III devised a new coat of arms, with the Byzantine double-headed eagle and the addition of the figure of St. George slaying the dragon.

The new Grand Duchess asked Ivan III to be rid of the Volga khan with all speed. Ivan, supported by Menghli-Girey, the Crimea khan, declared war on Akhmet Khan, nicknamed *Trusishka* ('the timid one'). The latter and his army were camped for more than a month by the Ugra, a tributary of the Oka, waiting for the attack to come from the Russian force on the opposite bank. Neither side was eager to open the fighting. One morning, at dawn, a host of birds came screaming out of the dense fog. Each of the two armies imagined that the other was launching an attack and took to flight, the Tartars making for the Volga and the Russians for the Moskva. So, in the most incredible fashion, was lifted the Tartar yoke that had bound Russia for more than 200 years.

[3] Of Mosco the chief Citie of the kingdome and of the Emperour thereof [Ivan the Terrible], by Richard Chancellor; from *Voyages and Documents of Richard Hakluyt, 1553.*

(Richard Chancellor took part in an expedition to find a northern sea-route to China in 1553; his ship made harbour in the White Sea, and this led to his visiting Moscow and establishing a trade agreement with Ivan the Terrible. In 1555, following Chancellor's return to England, the famous Muscovy (later the Russia) Company was founded. Chancellor was drowned during the disastrous voyage home after his second visit to Russia, in 1556.)

It remaineth that a larger discourse be made of Mosco, the principall Citie of that Countrey, and of the Prince also, as before we have promised. The Empire and government of the king is very large, and his wealth at this time exceeding great. And because the citie of Mosco is the chiefest of al the rest, it seemeth of it selfe to challenge the first place in this discourse. Our men say, that in bignesse it is as great as the Citie of London, with the suburbes thereof. There are many and great buildings in it, but for beautie and fairenesse, nothing comparable to ours. There are many Townes and Villages also, but built out of order, and with no hansomnesse: their streetes and wayes are not paved with stone as ours are: the walles of their houses are of wood: the roofes for the most part are covered with shingle boords. There is hard by the Citie a very faire Castle, strong, and furnished with artillerie, whereunto the Citie is joyned directly towards the North, with a bricke wall: the walles also of the castle are built with bricke, and are in breadth or thickenesse eighteene foote. This Castle hath on the one side a drie ditch, on the other side the river Moscua, whereby it is made almost inexpugnable. The same Moscua trending towards the East doth admit into it the companie of the river Occa.

In the Castle aforesaide, there are in number nine Churches, or Chappels, not altogether unhansome, which are used and kept by certaine religious men, over whom there is after a sort, a Patriarke, or Governour, and with him other reverend Fathers, all which for the greater part, dwell within the Castle. As for the kings Court and Palace, it is not of the neatest, onely in forme it is foure square, and of lowe building, much surpassed and excelled by the beautie and elegancie of the houses of the kings of England. The windowes are very narrowly built, and some of them by glasse, some other by lettisses admit the light: and whereas the Palaces of our Princes are decked, and adorned with hangings of cloth of gold, there is none such there: they build and joyne to all their wals benches, and that not onely in the Court of the Emperour, but in all private mens houses.

Nowe after that they had remained about twelve dayes in the Citie, there was then a Messenger sent unto them, to bring them to the Kings house: and they being after a sort wearied with their long stay, were very ready, and willing so to doe: and being entred within the gates of the Court, there sate a very honorable companie of Courtiers, to the number of one hundred, all apparelled in cloth of golde, downe to their ankles: and therehence being conducted into the chamber of presence, our men beganne to wonder at the Majestie of the Emperour: his seate was aloft, in a very royall throne, having on his head a diademe, or Crowne of golde, apparelled with a robe all of Goldsmiths worke, and in his hand hee held a Scepter garnished, and beset with precious stones: and besides all other notes and apparances of honour, there was a Majestie in his countenance proportionable with the excellencie of his estate: on the one side of him stood his chiefe Secretarie, on the other side, the great Commander of silence, both of them arayed also in cloth of gold: and then there sate the Counsel of one hundred and fiftie in number, all in like sort arayed, and of great state. This so honorable an assemblie, so great a Majestie of the Emperour, and of the place might very well have amazed our men, and have dasht them out of countenance: but notwithstanding Master Chanceler being therewithall nothing dismaied saluted, and did his duetie to the Emperour, after the manner of England, and withall, delivered unto him the letters of our king, Edward the sixt. The Emperour having taken, & read the letters, began a little to question with them, and to aske them of the welfare of our king: whereunto our men answered him directly, & in few words: hereupon our men presented some thing to the Emperour, by the chiefe Secretary, which at the delivery of it, put of his hat, being before all the time covered: and so the Emperour having invited them to dinner, dismissed them from his presence: and going into the chamber of him that was Master of the Requests to the Emperour, & having stayed there the space of two howres, at the last, the Messenger commeth, and calleth them to dinner: they goe, and being conducted into the golden Court, (for so they call it, although not very faire) they finde the Emperour sitting upon an high and stately seate, apparelled with a robe of silver, and with another Diademe on his head: our men being placed over against him, sit downe: in the middes of the roome stoode a mightie Cupboord upon a square foote, whereupon stoode also a round boord, in manner of a Diamond, broade beneath, and towardes the toppe narrowe, and every steppe rose up more narrowe then another. Upon this Cupboorde was placed the Emperours plate, which was so much, that the very Cupboord it selfe was scant able to sustaine the waight of it: the better part of all the vessels, and goblets, was made of very fine gold: and amongst the rest, there were foure pots of very large bignesse, which did adorne the rest of the plate in great measure: for they were so high, that they thought them at the least five foote long. There were also upon this Cupboard certaine silver caskes, not much differing from the quantitie of our Fyrkins, wherein was reserved the Emperours drinke: on each side of the Hall stood foure Tables, each of them layde and covered with very cleane table clothes, whereunto the company ascended by three steps or degrees, all which were filled with the assemblie present: the ghests were all apparelled with linnen without, and with rich skinnes within, and so did notably set out this royal feast. The Emperour, when hee takes any bread or knife in his hand, doth first of all crosse himselfe upon his forehead: they that are in speciall favour with the Emperour sit upon the same bench with him, but somewhat farre from him: and before the comming in of the meate, the Emperour himself, according to an ancient custome of the kings of Moscovy, doth first bestow a piece of bread upon every one of his ghests, with a loud pronunciation of his title, and honour, in this manner: The great Duke of Moscovie, and chiefe Emperour of Russia, John Basiliwich (& then the officer nameth the ghest) doth give thee bread. Whereupon al the ghests rise up, and by & by sit downe againe. This done, the Gentleman Usher of the Hall comes in, with a notable company of servants, carying the dishes, and having done his reverence to the Emperour, puts a young Swanne in a golden platter upon the table, and immediately takes it thence againe, delivering it to the Carver, and seven other of his fellowes, to be cut up: which being perfourmed, the meate is then distributed to the ghests, with the like pompe, and ceremonies. In the meane time, the Gentleman Usher receives his bread, and tasteth to the Emperour, and afterward, having done his reverence, he departeth. Touching the rest of the dishes, because they were brought in out of order, our men can report no certaintie: but this is true, that all the furniture of dishes, and drinking vessels, which were then for the use of a hundred ghests, was all of pure golde, and the tables were so laden with vessels of gold, that there was no roome for some to stand upon them.

We may not forget, that there were 140. servitors arayed in cloth of gold, that in the dinner time, changed thrise their habit and apparell, which servitors are in like sort served with bread from the Emperour, as the rest of the ghests. Last of all, dinner being ended, and candles brought in, (for by this time night was come) the Emperour calleth all his ghests and Noble men by their names, in such sort, that it seemes miraculous, that a Prince, otherwise occupied in great matters of estate, should so well remember so many and sundry particular names. The Russes tolde our men, that the reason thereof, as also of the bestowing of bread in that manner, was to the ende that the Emperour might keepe the knowledge of his owne houshold: and withal, that such as are under his displeasure, might by this meanes be knowen.

[4] Witches foretell the death of Ivan the Terrible in 1584; he shows his treasure to the English Ambassador; his death, and the accession of Tsar Feodor Ivanovitch; from *A Relacion or Memoriall Abstracted out of Sir Jerom Horsey His Travels Imploiements Services and Negociacions.*

(Sir Jerome Horsey first went to Russia in 1573 as a clerk in the service of the Russia Company and returned to England in 1580 with a commission from Ivan the Terrible to purchase munitions. He spent the next ten years in Russia,

making further trips to England and gaining special privileges for the Company; but left Russia under accusation of
fraud in 1591. He spent the next thirty years of his life in
Buckinghamshire and was knighted in 1604. He died in
1627.)

The Kinge in furie, much distracted and douptinge, caused
many witches magicians presently to be sent for owt of the
North, wher ther is store between Collongorod and Lappia.
Threscore wear brought post to the Musquo, placed and
garded, and dailie dieted and daily vissited and atended one
by the Emperors favorett, Bodan Belskoye, who was only
trusted by the Emperor to receave and bringe from them
their divelinacions or oracles upon the subjects that was
geaven them in charge. This favoret was now revolted in
fathe to the Kinge, wholly sekinge now and servinge the
turns of the sonn risinge, wearied and tired with the divelsh
tiranicall præctices, horrable influencis and wicked devices,
of this Helligabelous. The sowthsaiers tell him that the best
signes 'constellacions' and strongest plannetts of heaven was
against the Emperower, which would produce his end by
such a daye; but he durst not to tell him so; he fell in rage,
and told them they wear veri likly to be all burnt that daye.
The Emperowr began grivously to swell in his coddes, with
which he had most horrablie offended above 50 years
together, bostinge of thowsand virgens he had deflowred
and thowsands of children of his begettinge distroied.

Carried everie daye in his chair into his treasurie. One
daye the prince beckoned to me to follow. I stode emonge
the rest venturously, and hærd him call for som precious
stones and jewells. Told the prince and nobles present before
and aboute him the vertue of such and such, which I
observed, and do pray I maye a littell degress to declare
for my own memorie sake.

'The load-stone you all know hath great and hidden
vertue, without which the seas that compas the world ar
not navigable, nor the bounds nor circle of the earth cannot
be knowen. Mahomett, the Percians proffit, his tombe of

steel hangs in their Rapatta at Darbent most miracously.' –
Caused the waiters to bringe a chaine of nedells towched by
this load-stone, hanged all one by the other. – 'This faire
currell [coral] and this faire turcas you see; take in your
hand; of his natur arr orient coullers; put them on my hand
and arm. I am poisned with disease: you see they shewe their
virtue by the chainge of their pure culler into pall: declares
my death. Reach owt my staff roiall; an unicorns horn
garnished with verie fare diomondes, rubies, saphiers, emer-
alls and other precious stones that ar rich in vallew; cost 70
thowsand marckes sterlinge of David Gower, from the
fowlkers of Ousborghe. Seeke owt for som spiders.' Caused
his phiziccians, Johannes Lloff, to scrape a circle therof upon
the tabell; putt within it one spider and so one other and
died, and some other without that ran alive apace from it. –
'It is to late, it will not preserve me. Behold these precious
stones. This diomond is the orients richest and most precious of all other. I never affected it; yt restreyns furie and
luxurie and abstinacie and chasticie; the least parcell of it in
powder will poysen a horss geaven to drinck, much more a
man.' Poynts at the ruby. 'O! this is most comfortable to the
hart, braine, vigar and memorie of man, clarifies congelled
and corrupt bloud.' – Then at the emorald. – 'The natur of
the reyn-bowe; this precious stone is an enemye to un-
cleannes. Try it: though man and wiff cohabitt in lust
together, havinge this stone aboute them, yt will burst at
the spendinge of natur. The saphier I greatlie delight in; yt
preserves and increaseth courage, joies the hart, pleasinge to
all the vitall sensis, precious and verie soveraigne for the eys,
clears the sight, takes awaye bloud shott, and streingthens
the mussells and strings thereof.' – Then takes the onex in
hand. – 'All these ar Gods wonderfull guifts, secreats in
natur, and yet revells [reveals] them to mans use and
contemplacion, as frendes to grace and vertue and enymies
to vice. I fainte, carie me awaye till an other a tyme.'

In the afternone peruseth over his will and yet thinckes
not to die: he hath ben bewitched in that place, and often
tymes unwiched againe; but now the divell faiells. Co-

maunds the master of his oppathicke and phizicians to prepare and atend for his solace and bathinge; loeks for the goodnes of the signe; send his favorett to his witches againe to know their calculacions. He coms and tells them the Emperor will burry or burn them all quicke for their fals illucions and lies. The daye is come; he is as hartt holl as ever he was. 'Sir, be not so wrathfull. You know the daie is com and ends with the setting of the sun.' – He hasts him to the Emperor: made great preparacion for the bathe. About the third hower of the daye the Emperor went into it, sollaced himself and made merie with pleasant songs as he useth to doe: came owt about the 7th hower wæll refreshed; brought forth, setts him downe upon his bead; calls Rodovone Bœrken, a gentilman whome he favored, to bringe the chess board. He setts his men;* his chieff favorett and Boris Fedorowich Goddonove and others about him. The Emperor in his lose gown, shirtt and lynnen hose, faints and falls backward. Great owt-crie and sturr; one sent for aqua vita, another to the oppatheke for 'marigold and' rose water, and to call 'his gostlie father and' the phizicions. In the mean he was strangled and stark dead. Som shew of hope was made for recoverie to still the owt-crie. The said Bodan Belskoie and Boris Fedorwich, unto whom the Emperor had bequeathed, the first of fower other noblemen, and brother to this Emperor Feodor Ivanowich his wiff and Emporis that must now succed, the government of all, goe owt upon the tarras, acompaned so suddenly at hand with so many, and other multitudes of the nobillite his famillier frends, as it was strainge to behold. Cried owt to the captaines and gonnors to kepe their gard stronge and the gaetts shure aboute the pallace, with their peces and matches lighted: the gaetts of the castell presently shutt and wæll watched. I offered myself, men, powder and pistolls, to atend the prince protector: he accepted me amonge his famillie and servants, passinge by with a chearfull countenance upon me 'said:' – 'Be faithfull and fear not.'

* All savinge the kinge, which by no means he could not make stand in his place with the rest upon the plain board.

[5] Of the manner of crowning or inauguration of the Rus emperors (1584); from *Of the Russe Common wealth* by Giles Fletcher the Elder.

(Giles Fletcher (1546–1611) was a noted classical scholar and linguist, which allowed him to acquire a competent knowledge of Russian. Elizabeth I sent him to Russia in 1588, where he engaged in complex negotiations with Tsar Feodor and Boris Godunov to re-establish trading privileges for the Muscovy (Russia) Company. His book was published in 1591.)

The solemnities used at the Rus emperor's coronation are on this manner. In the great church of Prechistaia,* or Our Lady, within the Emperor's castle, is erected a stage, whereupon standeth a screen that beareth upon it the imperial cap and robe of very rich stuff. When the day of the inauguration is come, there resort thither, first, the Patriarch with the metropolitans, archbishops, bishops, abbots, and priors, all richly clad in their *pontificalibus*. Then enter the deacons with the choir of singers, who, so soon as the Emperor setteth foot into the church, begin to sing, 'Many years may live noble Fedor Ivanovich, etc.' Whereunto the Patriarch and metropolite with the rest of the clergy answer with a certain hymn in form of a prayer, singing it all together with a great noise. The hymn being ended, the Patriarch with the Emperor mount up the stage, where standeth a seat ready for the Emperor. Whereupon the Patriarch willeth him to sit down and then, placing himself by him upon another seat provided for that purpose, boweth down his head toward the ground and sayeth this prayer, 'O Lord God, King of kings, Lord of lords, which by Thy prophet Samuel didst choose Thy servant David and anoint him for king over Thy people Israel, hear now our prayers and look from Thy sanctuary upon this Thy servant Fedor, whom Thou hast chosen and exalted for king over these Thy holy nations;

* Probably the Uspenskii (Cathedral of the Assumption) in the Moscow kremlin.

anoint him with the oil of gladness; protect him by Thy power, put upon his head a crown of gold and precious stones; give him length of days; place him in the seat of justice; strengthen his arm; make subject unto him all the barbarous nations. Let Thy fear be in his whole heart; turn him from an evil faith and from all error; and show him the salvation of Thy holy and universal Church, that he may judge the people with justice and protect the children of the poor and finally attain everlasting life.' This prayer he speaketh with a low voice and then pronounceth aloud: 'All praise and power to God the Father, the Son, and the Holy Ghost.' The prayer being ended, he commandeth certain abbots to reach the imperial robe and cap, which is done very decently and with great solemnity, the Patriarch withal pronouncing aloud: 'Peace be unto all.' And so he beginneth another prayer to this effect: 'Bow yourselves together with us and pray to Him that reigneth over all. Preserve him, O Lord, under Thy holy protection; keep him that he may do good and holy things; let justice shine forth in his days, that we may live quietly without strife and malice.' This is pronounced somewhat softly by the Patriarch, whereto he addeth again aloud: 'Thou art the King of the whole world, and the savior of our souls, to Thee, the Father, Son, and Holy Ghost, be all praise forever and ever. Amen.' Then, putting on the robe and cap, he blesseth the Emperor with the sign of the cross, saying withal, 'In the name of the Father, the Son, and the Holy Ghost.' The like is done by the metropolites, archbishops, and bishops, who all in their order come to the chair and one after another bless the Emperor with their two forefingers. Then is said by the Patriarch another prayer that beginneth, 'O most Holy Virgin, Mother of God, etc.' After which a deacon pronounceth with an high loud voice, 'Many years to noble Fedor, good, honorable, beloved of God, great duke of Vladimir, of Moscow, emperor and monarch of all Russia, etc.' Whereto the other priests and deacons, that stand somewhat far off by the altar or table, answer singing, 'Many years, many years to the noble Fedor.' The same note is taken up by the priests and deacons that are placed at the right and left side of the church, and then all together they chant and thunder out singing, 'Many years to the noble Fedor, good, honorable, beloved of God, great duke of Vladimir, Moscow, emperor of all Russia, etc.' These solemnities being ended, first cometh the Patriarch with the metropolites, archbishops, and bishops, then the nobility and the whole company in their order, to do homage to the Emperor, bending down their heads and knocking them at his feet to the very ground.

[6] The attack on Moscow by the Khan of the Crimea, Devlet Girei, during the reign of Ivan the Terrible, 1571; from *A Relacion or Memoriall . . . of Sir Jerom Horsey.*

Yt was God, that suffereth this wicked people, whoe live, flow and wallowe, in the verie hight of their lust and wickednes of the crienge Sodomiticall sines, to be thus justly punished and plaged with the tirranie of so bloudye a kynge: God, I say, hath now appointed a tyme, and prepared owt of his great justice a fearfull reveng and spectacle to all generacions, both for prince and people. The Sithian Emperowr takes the oportunitie, enters the confines of Russia, stands with an army of 200 thowsand soldiers, all horsmen, within 50 miells compas upon the rivers sied Ocka, facinge the Emperowr Ivan Vazilewich his army of 100 thowsand gallant generalls and souldiers, whoe kepe the phords and passages very stronge with great artillarie, municion, suplie of men and arms, vittualls, and all other provicion plentifull. Upon hoep and secreat intelligence they ar incouraged, and ventur to swyme and pass the particion river without repuls. The Emperors army dare not (it is death to excead their comission) sturs not beyond their bounds of 25 miells compas to defend the enymies approach, upon what advantage soever. The enemye being

come a this side the river have noe lett, but speed towards
Musco, but 90 miells of, wher the Emperor thincks himself
secure. But the enime approaching the great cittie Musco,
the Russ Emperor flies, with his two sonns, treasur, hows-
hold, servants, and personall guard of 20 thowsand gonnors, towards a stronge monesterie, Troietts, 60 miells of,
upon Assencion daye. The enyme fiers St Johns church high
stepll: at which instant happened a wounderfull stormye
wynd, through which all the churches, howses and palaces,
within the cittie and suberbs 30 miells compas, built most of
firr and oak tymber, was sett one fier and burnt within six
howers space, with infinit thowsands men, weomen, and
children, burnt and smothered to death by the fierie eyre,
and likwise in the stone churches, monestaries, vaults, and
sellors; verie fewe escapinge both without and within the
three walled castells. The rever and ditches about Musco
stopped and filled with the multituds of people, loaden with
gold, silver, jewells, chains, earrings, brasletts and treasur,
that went for succer eaven to save their heads above water.
Notwithstandinge, so many thowsands wear ther burnt and
drowned, as the river could not be ridd nor clensed of the
dead carcasses, with all the means and industrye could be
used in twelve monneths after; but those alive, and many
from other towns and places, every daie wear occupied
within a great circuat to search, dregg, and fish, as it wear,
for rings, jewells, plate, baggs of gold and silver, by which
many wear inriched ever after. The streets of the cittie,
churches, sellors and vauts, laye so thicke and full of dead
and smothered carcasses, as noe man could pass for the
noisom smells and putrifection of the ear [air] longe after.
The Emperowr of the Crimes and his armye beheld this
goodly fier, lodged and solaced himself in a fare monues-
tarie by the river sied, fower miells of the cittie, called
Symon monesterie; toke the wælth and riches they had.

[7] The 'Troubled Times' (*Smutniye Vremena*), 1598–1613: introductory note, from notes to *Feodor Dostoievsky 1877, The Diary of a Writer*.

The Troubled Epoch in Russia (1598–1613). Following the death of Czar Fiódor Ioánnovich (1584–1598), the son of Czar Iván the Terrible the Zemsky Sobor elected Boris Godunóv, a favorite of Czar Ivan, and the late Czar Fiódor's brother-in-law, to the throne of Russia. But it was persistently rumored that Godunóv had been instrumental in the assassination, in May, 1591, of the young Czarévich Dmitry, Iván's youngest son and Czar Fiódor's only brother. Besides, Godunóv was of humble Tartar descent, and therefore quite unpopular among the ancient Russian boyard families. Godunóv was an enlightened ruler, and his early legislation proves that he was an able statesman. However, suspicious of boyard intrigues, he began to persecute the nobles and thus aroused among them great indignation. In 1601 Russia began to suffer from a dreadful famine which was followed by an equally devastating plague. Popular discontent grew to a high pitch. Hunger-stricken peasants and all sorts of rebellious elements began to plunder the boyards' estates. Highway robberies spread all over Russia. In the presence of these political and social conditions, it was comparatively easy for an impostor to challenge the authority of Boris Godunóv. Such an impostor appeared in the person of a young man (exact date of birth is unknown) Grigóry Otrépiev who is supposed to have been the son of a government official. In the latter part of the XVIth Century he settled in Moscow, where he took religious orders, and shortly thereafter he began to spread the rumor that he was Czarévich Dmítry, miraculously saved from the hands of Godunóv's assassins. Realizing the danger of such propaganda, the Czar ordered Otrépiev to be seized. But he managed to escape, fled across the Lithuanian border and proceeded to Poland, where he enlisted in the service of a Polish magnate Wisznewézki. He convinced the latter as well as the Sandomir Waýwode Mníszek that he was the son of Czar Iván the Terrible. Having embraced Roman Catholicism, Otrépiev, with the aid of the Jesuits, succeeded in securing formal recognition by King Sigismund of Poland of his status as lawful pretender to the Russian throne. Some 1500 Polish adventurers joined his ranks. He crossed the Russian border and the Cossacks and robbers' bands gave him active support. In April, 1605, Godunóv died, and in June of the same year, Dmítry the Impostor triumphantly entered Moscow at the head of his rebel army. He ascended the Throne, but his avowed pro-Polish sympathies and the fact that he had married Marína Mníszek, a Roman Catholic, caused widespread discontent. Taking advantage of this situation, Prince Vasíli Shuísky organized an uprising in Moscow, during which Dmítry was assassinated by the mob. From that time on, one impostor after another contested the Russian Throne.

[8] Eyewitness account of the private life and customs of the 'false' Tsar Dmitry; of his bodyguard, the *streltsy*; of their alleged conspiracy; from *Histoire des Guerres de la Moscovie (1601–1610)* by Isaac Massa de Haarlem.

(Isaac Massa de Haarlem (1587–?) was probably of Italian origin: his family had settled at Haarlem. Still a teenager, he was sent by his parents to Russia to learn Russian and become a leading merchant. He lived there eight years, and both wrote and spoke Russian sufficiently well to be employed as a professional translator and interpreter by the States-General. He lived through the bloody 'Time of Troubles' and left a most vivid and accurate eye-witness account – in particular, of the investiture of Moscow by the First Pretender, Dmitry, and of his atrocious death.)

Every day, here and there, many people were executed. At the same time, God sent visible warnings to Demetrius [Dmitry], but he was blind to them. He paid no attention to the Moscovites, and did not believe the reports he received about how matters stood.

I must now say a few words about his private life.

He sent large sums of money to Poland to settle his debts and to repay everyone what he had borrowed from them. The Poles also arrived in great numbers in Moscow, to sell rich jewels and other precious objects sought after by the Tsar. His desire was stimulated by all that was rare or unusual. Those who ordered such things quickly received their asking price, and could go away satisfied. He built a magnificent palace on the ramparts of the Kremlin from which he could see the whole city. These ramparts are on a high mountain at whose foot flows the Moskova river. The Palace consisted of two adjacent buildings forming an angle: one of them was intended for the future Tsarina [Marina].

Inside the apartments, he hung splendid golden canopies; the walls were dressed with precious cloth-of-gold and embroidered velvet. The nails, the hinges and the other iron-work of the doors were thickly plated with gold. The stoves were masterpieces of art. The windows were draped with crimson cloth and velvet. He also built splendid baths and beautiful towers. Although vast stables already existed within the precincts of the palace, he built a private stable next to his new house. In these new buildings, he put a mass of concealed doors and secret passages, which proves he was following the example of tyrants and that, like them, he lived in perpetual fear.

Throughout his empire, he called for the strongest and fiercest dogs. On Sundays, they would bring cages of wild bears to the rear-court of the palace, and he would take pleasure in setting them against his dogs. Often he even ordered the highest nobles in the land, who in fact are able hunters, into the arena armed with a simple boar-spear to pit themselves against the bears. With my own eyes I saw this chilling scene: several times I saw a man attack an enormous bear which was thrashing about violently, and pierce its throat or its chest with unbelievable skill. Most of these brave men emerge from the fight with wounded hands. But they are often victorious. If their thrust should miss, their life is in the gravest danger, but then hunters, armed with pitch forks, rush at the bear and pierce it with blows. However, at all events, these games are horrible to watch. . . .

Demetrius' two most intimate friends after Massalsky were Pierre Basmanoff, whom he made commander in chief of his armies, and a certain Michel Moltchanoff, who had already attached himself to the Tsar's party in Poland and had always been extremely useful. Moltchanoff was a sycophant and a hypocrite. He was godless and lawless – in short, an unmitigated scoundrel.

These three committed countless misdeeds, and were shameless debauchees. Moltchanoff had the role of procurer. His agents sought out the most beautiful girls. Sometimes using money and sometimes force, he would lead them through secret passages to the Tsar's baths. When Demetrius was satiated, he would pass them on to Basmanoff and Moltchanoff.

If the glance of Demetrius fell on a beautiful nun (and there were a great many in Muscovy), she had no escape from his lust. After his death, about thirty were found to be pregnant by him.

That was his private life. To the world, he appeared a soldier and a hero in all things. Not one of his chancellors or officers failed to experience his anger. More than once he had broken a stick over their loins to teach them courtlier manners and to teach them a lesson. This doubtless did not particularly appeal to them, but they could only wait patiently for better times.

Even among the Streletz [musketeers] there were those who dared say the Tsar was not the true Demetrius. Basmanoff, the leader of this company of 8,000 men, got wind of these rumours which he passed on to the Tsar, warning him to be on his guard and that his life was in great danger. A ruthless and secretive enquiry was held. Seven were picked from the crowd and were taken unawares. No one knew about it. The next day at dawn, all the Streletz were summoned to the rear court-yard where the bear fights usually took place on Sundays. They all assembled here, unarmed, and anxious to know why they had been gathered together. A moment later the Tsar came out of the palace, escorted by his archers and halberdiers, and accompanied by Basmanoff, Mstislafsky, the Nagoys and several Polish noblemen. He stood on the grand staircase of the courtyard and ordered all the doors to be closed. When they saw the Tsar, the Streletz prostrated themselves to the ground, according to their custom, and stared at him bare-headed. Seeing these naked heads touching each other, Demetrius burst out laughing, and shouted, 'God grant that they should all be filled with wisdom!' Then he addressed them with a fine speech. He spoke first of Divine Providence, then of the Holy Scriptures. Then he complained of their obstinacy and their incredulity. 'How long will you seek out discord and its unfortunate consequences?' he said to them. 'Is it not enough for you that the country is rotten to the core? Must it be destroyed to its roots?' Then he reminded them of the Godounoffs' crimes, of their tyranny towards the leading families of the nation, the way they had usurped the Imperial throne. He continued, 'That is the reason why the country has suffered so badly and now that God has delivered me from all the deadly pitfalls which surrounded me, and that he has preserved only me, you are still not satisfied. You are looking for any excuse to commit new treason, and you would already like to be rid of me! What do you have against me? Who among you can prove that I am not the True Demetrius? Let him step forward, and I will allow myself to be struck here before you!

'My mother and all the lords here present are my witnesses. And how would it have been possible for someone to conquer this powerful empire, almost without an army, if he had not been upheld by his just rights? Would God have allowed it? I risked my life, not to raise myself to the supreme rank, but out of pity for you, to deliver you from the deep misery and the terrible slavery in which you would have been plunged by the traitors who oppressed the country. It is with the support of His all-powerful arm that I obtained possession of a throne which was rightfully mine. So why then are you conspiring? Here I am! Tell me without fear and frankly the reasons for your disbelief.'

These words astounded them. Nearly all of them pressed their faces to the ground and swore they were innocent. They begged in tears for the Tsar's mercy, and asked him to tell who had falsely accused them. Then the Tsar ordered Basmanoff to bring out the seven who had been arrested, which was done immediately. 'Here they are,' cried Demetrius, 'those who affirm that you are conspirators and that you are hatching plots against your rightful Tsar and master!'

They immediately threw themselves on the unfortunate seven, and tore them to pieces in such a horrible way that no one would believe the description. Imagine this mass of soldiers with neither arms nor sticks, hurling themselves on the seven victims, and tearing them apart with their bare hands into a thousand pieces, so that their clothes were sodden with blood as though they had been killing cattle. Some of the mob, like hounds pursuing a stag, had torn away lumps of flesh with their teeth. One of them, who had bitten off an ear, carried his ferocity so far as to keep it clenched in his jaws until it was reduced to shreds. Ravenous lions would not have behaved so atrociously with baby lambs as these men did with their own kind. When the execution was over, they shouted, 'Thus perish all the Tsar's enemies and traitors!'

Despite his bloodthirsty instincts, Demetrius could not bear to watch this ghastly business. He withdrew to a room which he paced while it was going on. When it was over, he returned. He delivered another speech to the troops about himself, and repeated that he was their legitimate sovereign. Then he dismissed them. They all prostrated themselves yet again, with their faces to the ground, begging for mercy, and finally they all went home. The remains of the corpses were gathered into a cart and fed to the dogs. The sight of this tumbril openly carrying these human remains through the town made people's hair stand on end. The incident spread terror through Moscow, rumours ceased, and all talk became very guarded. Nevertheless, a few stubborn souls were not worried either by death or by torture. As to the seven unfortunate victims, I do not believe they were guilty as Demetrius convinced his soldiers. His sole aim in sacrificing them was to terrify the masses.

[9] The wedding of Tsar Dmitry to his Polish bride, Marina Mniszek; Boyar Shuysky and the Muscovite mob storm the Kremlin and kill Tsar Dmitry (1606); from *Episode de l'Histoire de Russie: Le Faux Démétrius* by Prosper Mérimée.

On 12 May [1606], Marina made her entry into Moscow. A tremendous crowd had gathered to greet her. The Tsar himself had planned the ceremonial in fine detail, and watched over the preparations for the reception. He was on horseback very simply dressed and *incognito*, as etiquette probably prevented him from confronting his fiancée before she was presented to him in the Kremlin. A splendid tent had been put up on the Moskva bridge. The Tsarina in a coach drawn by eight dappled grey horses, with their tails and manes dyed red, stopped at the entrance to the tent, and got down to receive the congratulations of the great dignitaries. When the speeches were over, she was led to another coach, lined in red velvet with pearl-embroidered cushions and drawn by twelve piebald horses. This was a new present from the Tsar. As soon as she made a move towards it, the chief boyars picked her up respectfully in their arms and placed her in the opulent carriage. Then, to the accompaniment of musical instruments and ringing bells and artillery fire, she was led to the monastery where the Tsarina Marfa lived. She was to remain here until her coronation, and the unbelieving people were told that during her stay she would be instructed in the Orthodox faith by her pious mother-in-law.

If Marina's youth and beauty could sweeten the bitterness of the Muscovites, her procession was enough to rekindle their old national hatreds. German life-guards marched alongside the bride, then came Polish hussars from her suite, or those who had come to pay homage, all armed from head to toe, lance in hand, preceded by their martial music which played national tunes as though they were going into battle. 'They look as though they were entering a conquered city,' muttered the Russians. 'What are those breastplates and lances for? Do you cover yourselves with steel to go to a wedding where you come from?' they asked the foreign merchants long settled in Moscow. It was far worse when the Poles spread out through the city to look for lodgings. All these nobles were expecting to campaign against the tartars, and were carrying their best weapons. Whole arsenals were unloaded from their carts . . .

Demetrius's choice of wife, his preference for Western European customs, particularly the scant attention he paid to religious practice, had already lost him irrevocably to public opinion.

Indeed, every day increased the popular irritation, and the smallest incidents turned into the most serious accusations. Marina, a spoiled child who could not imagine that one should hesitate to satisfy her slightest whim, was very bored in the convent separated from her ladies. She found the rules and customs of a Russian convent unbearable, and she could not reconcile herself to this way of life even for a week. She informed the Tsar that she could not eat Russian cooking, and that she must have her own. Demetrius immediately sent her a Polish butler and cooks, to whom her food-bearers were obliged to give the keys to the pantry and the cellar. The humiliated Russian cooks protested loudly, and not doubting that their ability was in question, announced throughout the city that if the Tsar and his fiancée wished to employ heretic cooks, it was so that they could break the commandments of the Orthodox Church more easily, and eat forbidden meat on days of abstinence. . . .

The marriage and coronation ceremony took place on 18 May 1606 in the Moscow cathedral with magnificent pomp. However, the people were horrified because it was a Friday, an unlucky day, and also the eve of the great feast-day of Saint Nicholas. It was thought scandalous to celebrate a wedding on such a day, and they felt the Tsar had deliberately chosen it to defy public opinion. Besides, the behaviour of the Poles in church was most unseemly, and the Emperor was held responsible for this too. Some leaned against the iconostasis, or sat on the tombs containing venerated relics. They talked aloud, laughed among themselves, and seemed to mock the mysteries celebrated in their presence. On the other hand, the Poles, especially the ambassadors, complained of not being treated with all the regard they were due. They had no seats in the cathedral, and when they made a formal request they were told by the Tsar that no one sat in a Greek church, and that the only reason he himself had a throne on that day was because of the exceptional circumstances of the Tsarina's coronation. Condemned to stand through a long service, Sigismond's envoys became rather malevolent observers of the Russian liturgy with its strange rites, of the traditional etiquette followed by the officiating clergy and the bridal couple, and of the glass of wine from which the spouses sipped three times and which the Tsar finally smashed with his foot. The whole ceremony was the object of criticism and sarcasm. They found the Tsar's haughtiness unbearable. They joked about the two young people who could not take one step in the church without having old men with white beards hold them under the arms like children learning to walk . . .

At last the moment arrived for which Chouisky had been patiently waiting during several months. He saw that revolt was imminent. The foreigners had exasperated the people to a rage, and if he delayed in giving the signal, he would lose the fruits of his long plotting. He secretly gathered in his house several boyars, some merchants and some officers of the Strelitz. Hatred for the Poles had united all classes and professions in this assembly. Chouisky said to them, 'Orthodox Christians, you can see Moscow the Holy City is in the hands of foreigners. The Poles defy and insult us.'

*   *   *

On 26 May, a large number of soldiers from the camp pitched near Moscow entered the city separately. Most of them came from the Novgorod contingent, which had the reputation of being disloyal to the emperor. Demetrius either was not aware of this or did not pay it much attention. He spent the evening and part of the night at a feast, and he only dismissed his guests at daybreak. Before retiring he went out for a breath of air on the palace steps, where he met Afanassi Vlassief, one of the plotters who had been sent to reconnoitre. Surprised to see him at such an hour, the Tsar asked if he had a message from Sigismond's ambassadors, with whom his duties obliged him to live. Vlassief replied evasively, and withdrew to tell his accomplices that the palace was under tight security. The leaders of the plot were gathered at Basil Chouisky's. Some continued to hesitate. Chouisky told them that there was not a minute to lose. The Tsar had discovered their secret, and had already given the order for their deaths. The only way to save their skins was to forestall the tyrant with a bold blow. Seeing them moved by the courage of despair, he gave the prearranged signal.

A troop of boyars and nobles had already assembled on the great square, mounted, wearing chainmail and carrying bows. Leading the most determined among them, Chouisky presented himself at the Saviour's Gate, which was immediately surrendered to him by the guards, who had previously been bought. They entered the Kremlin. When Basil passed in front of the Church of the Ascension, he stopped, dismounted, and prostrated himself before the holy icon of Our Lady of Vladimir, as if to implore her protection at this supreme moment. Then rising with an inspired expression and brandishing a cross above his head, he cried, 'Orthodox Christians, death to the heretic!' A thousand furious voices repeated, 'Death to the heretic!' The great bell was rung, and one after another the three thousand bells of Moscow answered. At the same time, small bands of conspirators ran through the suburbs, shouting, 'To arms, to the Kremlin, they are killing the Tsar!' The excited people ran into the

streets in crowds, asking, 'Who is killing the Tsar?' 'The
Lithuanians,' answered the plotters, and so drew in their
wake a great mob armed with axes and clubs. The people
were convinced that the Poles, whom they detested for their
insolence, were plotting treason. They surged on their
houses, which had already been marked with chalk,
knocked in the doors, and began to massacre the sleeping
residents. The hardiest of the Muscovites, led by the boyars,
went to the Kremlin where the conspirators had a different
war cry. It was declared that the Emperor and the Poles
wanted to assassinate the boyars.

When the alarm bell rang, the Tsar had just returned to
his apartments. At once he sent to ask Demetrius Chouisky,
the duty officer in the palace, what was the cause of the
noise. He replied that a great fire had just broken out. Then
he rushed to join his brother Basil, who was at the head of a
large and well-armed troop. Soon, the tocsin echoed by all
Moscow's churches and mingling with the clamour of the
crowds, warned Demetrius that something more serious
than a fire had set the city in a turmoil. While he dressed
in haste, he sent Basmanof to find out the cause of the
uproar. The outer courtyard was already filling with an
armed mob. As soon as Basmanof appeared on the steps a
thousand menacing voices shouted furiously, 'Give us the
impostor'. He retreated hurriedly into the palace, and ordered the halberdiers to arms. Rushing to the Tsar, he cried,
'Disaster, my lord, the people are threatening to kill you.
Save yourself. As for me, I shall die.' Just then under cover of
the uproar, one of the conspirators entered Demetrius'
room. Coming up to the Tsar, he said, 'Well, wretched
Emperor! Now are you waking up? Come and justify
yourself to the people of Moscow.' Enraged, Basmanof
seized the Tsar's sabre and split the head of the insolent
fellow. Then he rushed to the balcony, which was already
swarming with conspirators. Armed with the sword of one
of his guards, Demetrius followed his loyal general, shouting
to the rebels, 'Scoundrels! I will show you I am not another
Boris!'

They say he killed several with his own hand. Basmanof threw himself among the plotters, sometimes begging, sometimes threatening. He covered the Tsar with his own body and dealt out terrible blows. While he was trying to defend the staircase and its approaches, the boyar Tatischef, for whom he had pleaded to Demetrius a few days earlier, cut him down with his knife, and Basmanof fell at his master's feet. At the same time the guards were forced back by musket fire, and soon had to surrender the staircase. Having no firearms, they pulled Demetrius into the palace and tried to barricade the doors. Then began a series of sieges. Each room from the entrance hall to the inner apartments was defended and taken. The insurgents fired arquebuses through the doors and scattered the bodyguards. A door was broken down with axes, a room was invaded, then the next room was attacked and taken in the same way. Finally, pushed behind their last barrier, the German bodyguards were backed against the Tsar's bath, and obliged to give up their useless halberds. But the Emperor was no longer among them, and no one knew where he was.

Meanwhile, Marina had been awoken by the shots, and was told that the palace had been invaded and the Tsar was either dead or in the power of the rebels. Half-dressed, she ran at random looking for a place to hide. First she tried a cellar, but the stairs were already filled with looters, and she realized that she had chosen a bad spot. Crowded and knocked about by the populace who were pressing at the doors of the storerooms, she nevertheless managed to return to her apartments without being recognized, and mingled with her ladies-in-waiting, who were screaming with terror.

The mutineers appeared. A single Polish chamberlain called Osmulski barred their way with his sabre, and delayed them for a moment. But a single shot knocked him across the threshold he was defending and mortally wounded a Polish lady near the Tsarina. Then, with terrible threats, the maniacs threw themselves into the room which was flooded with blood.* The ladies-in-waiting pressed around the grand mistress of the palace, who alone kept her presence of mind, and hid Marina under her ample robes. 'Hand over the Tsar and Tsarina,' cried the revolutionaries. 'We are not guarding the Tsar,' answered the grand mistress. 'As to the Tsarina, she has been with her father, the Palatin of Sendomir, for the past hour.' Her age protected the grand mistress from these madmen. They contented themselves by heaping her with abuse. The Polish ladies-in-waiting were less fortunate. If one is to believe Baer, the conquerors divided them up as lawful booty, and each boyar took the one he had chosen back to his house. (Baer adds, 'Where during the year she became a mother.') At last a few leaders arrived, and stopped the violence. Marina was then discovered, but protected. They satisfied themselves by seizing her jewels, and putting seals on the chests which had not been ransacked in the first moments of turmoil. She begged earnestly to be taken to her father, but she was too valuable a hostage for the rebel leaders to agree to let her go. They locked her up under a strong guard in one of the rooms of her palace.

As for Demetrius, he became convinced that all was lost when he saw the first gate of the palace forced, and he ran through the Tsarina's room to the apartment furthest removed from the spot the rebels were attacking. It is said that he had a sabre wound in the leg. Nevertheless, he opened a window overlooking the spot where Boris' palace had once stood and which he had had destroyed. The window was over thirty feet above the ground, but there was no one around and he jumped. The leap was unfortunate and he

---

* *Note by Prosper Mérimée:* I will not translate my source's Latin, as he himself did not dare translate the original German. The text reads:
'Volumus nos omnes, unus post alium, stuprum inferre, unus in p . . . alter in v . . . Audivimus polonicas meretrices vestras plurium concubitus bene sustinere posse, nec ipsis unus vir (sic) sufficere.' Et postea nudabant sua equina pudenda (proh! Sodomia) coram toto gynaeceo, dicentes, 'Videte, meretrices, videte nos multo fortiores sumus Polonis vestris. Probate nos.' Sources: Baer, Ustrialov, Petreius.

broke a leg, and the pain was so great that he fainted. He came to a moment later, and his moans attracted a nearby corps of Strelitz guards who recognised him. Moved by compassion, the soldiers picked him up, gave him some water to drink, and sat him on one of the foundation stones of Boris' palace. A little restored, the Tsar was able to speak to the Strelitz who swore to defend him. Indeed, when they heard the first cries of the rebels coming to claim their prey, they responded with their arquebuses, and killed some of the most aggressive. But soon the crowd thickened, drawn by the uproar and the shouts which proclaimed that at last the Tsar had been found. The Strelitz were surrounded and threatened: either they delivered the impostor, or their defenceless wives and children would be massacred in their suburban homes. Then the terrified Strelitz dropped their weapons and abandoned the wounded man.

The mob threw themselves upon him with horrible cries of triumph, and beating him, dragged him to a room of the palace which had already been sacked. Passing in front of his captured bodyguards in the power of his executioners, Demetrius stretched out a hand towards them in a sign of farewell, without saying a word. Enraged, one of his gentlemen, a Livonian called Furstenberg, tried to defend him even though he was unarmed. The rebels ran him through while he only sought to defend his master. If Demetrius was not killed at that moment, it was only because in their hatred his assassins wanted to prolong his suffering. His clothes were ripped off him, and a baker's kaftan put on him. 'Look at the Tsar of all the Russias!' the rebels cried. 'He has put on suitable clothes.' 'Son of a bitch!' said a Russian nobleman, 'tell us from where you came to us.' Demetrius gathered his remaining strength to raise his voice and say, 'Each of you knows that I am your Tsar, the legitimate son of Ivan Vassilievitch. Ask my mother. Or if you want my death, at least allow me the time to be recognized.' Then a merchant called Valouief, cutting through the throng, cried, 'Why talk so long with this heretic dog? Here's how I hear the confession of this Polish flautist,' and he fired his arquebus point-blank into the Tsar's chest, putting an end to his agony.

The whole palace was congested. From outside the besieging mob shouted, 'What does the Polish jester say?' Some answered through the windows, 'He admits he's an impostor.' 'Cut him down, kill him,' shouted thousands of muddled voices, among which one could make out those of the three Chouiski brothers who were on horseback in the palace courtyard, and urging their accomplices to finish off the usurper. Soon a disfigured, slashed corpse with the stomach slit open and the arms chopped by sabres was dragged out on to the steps. It was thrown down the flight where it landed on the body of Basmanof. 'You loved each other living. We will not separate you dead!' cried the murderers in their savage triumph.

[10] The election of Boyar Mikhail Romanov as Tsar in 1613; from *The Kremlin* by Victor Alexandrov.

The cathedral bells of the Kremlin pealed out from morning to evening while the members of the *Sobor* went on with their debating. The discussion was winding up and the Council of Elders was about to vote, when the *Sotnik* Struysky, the leader of the Cossack detachment, suddenly came into the hall of the Kremlin Palace, followed by ten Cossacks armed to the teeth.

'What do you want?' asked Prince Pozharsky.

The *sotnik* read out the motion voted by the Cossacks: 'We desire as our Czar the son of the Tushino sovereign!'

The members of the *Sobor* were obliged to vote on the candidature of the 'thief's' offspring, a child of four.

This outrageous trick played on the *Sobor* was due to Prince Trubetskoy, furious that his candidature had been unsuccessful. It appears that this coarse, undaunted man had said to his friend, the *dyak* Korotkov, 'Those sons of bitches won't have me, a Russian Prince and Cossack *het-*

man. I'll slip in their way the son of a thief and a Polish whore. Then let them get out of that mess!'

Prince Pozharsky, who shared the leadership of the Povolge army with the municipal representative Minin, found a way out of the difficulty by proposing that henceforth no foreigner or son of a non-Russian mother should be elected Czar. After a lengthy prayer in the Uspenie Cathedral, the members adopted the motion. King Sigismund, his son Ladislas and the child of the thief and Marina Mniczek were thus excluded once and for all from the list of candidates for the Russian throne. The *Sobor* had hardly resumed work, when a scuffle broke out between the Cossacks posted at the gates of Moscow and the *Sobor* guard inside the Kremlin. The *sotnik* Struysky, supported by Prince Trubetskoy, insisted that the Cossacks should be admitted to the Kremlin. Once inside the enclosure, the Cossacks lost no time; the same night they kidnapped Prince Galitzin, the most eminent of the candidates, and handed him over to the Poles in Smolensk, who took him to Warsaw. There he found Prince Shuysky, also of the Galitzin line, and the Patriarch Philaret. The following night the Cossacks carried off Prince Mstislavsky but, this time, did not hand him over to the Poles, for it was well known that the prince was *persona grata* at the court of Warsaw. The Cossacks simply made him swear to withdraw his candidature for the throne. The kidnappings continued whenever a prince offered himself as a candidate; the elections were at a standstill.

The Cossacks went to find the Abbot Abraham Palitzin, who had been their friend since the day when, on his advice, they had raised the siege of the Monastery of Triad and Sergius, invested by the Poles.

Abraham Palitzin celebrated a thanksgiving Mass in the Kremlin and appeared before the *Sobor*. 'My brethren', he said, 'you are here to elect a Russian Czar and not to enjoy yourselves. But we cannot accept just anybody for the throne. An elected Czar is not an alderman. A Czar is the father of the nation, and he rules from Moscow. Moscow is the mother of the nation. You can neither select nor elect your father or your mother; they are sent to you by God!'

The *Sobor* responded to this wily speech with thunderous applause: '*Amen*, Abraham! *Amen*! You are right! Tell us now who is he that is sent from God to ascend the throne of Russia's Czar?'

'Who other than Michael Romanov?' exclaimed the cunning Abraham. 'Is he not the nephew of Czar Feodor and the son of Czarina Anastasya? God keep her holy soul in Paradise!* Is he not the grand-nephew of Czar Ivan Vassilevich who sought the presence of God to ask pardon for his sins? God has sent us none other than Michael Romanov. Let us blot out the stain of your foolhardiness in choosing Boris Godunov and Shuysky. Let us elect young Michael Romanov, let us give him our blessing and long may he reign!'

Abraham had hardly finished speaking, when the provincial delegations came through all the Kremlin gates and into the hall where the *Sobor* was in session; and, keeping to the plan previously arranged by Abraham himself, they put forward motions in favour of Michael Romanov. Armed Cossacks followed the delegations. 'Listen to them, my brethren,' went on Abraham; 'heed them, and cast your votes for Czar Michael Romanov'.

At that exact moment, Prince Trubetskoy, the *hetman*, drew his sabre and, leaping on to the dais where Prince Pozharsky was presiding, he shouted†: 'The Cossacks are for Michael Romanov, but they insist that he swear on the Gospel to convene the *Sobor* and govern with the approval of the Russian nation!'

The bells of the Kremlin cathedrals rang out – they had been ringing for days – and on this Friday in Lent, 19 February, 1613, the *Sobor* acclaimed the name of Michael Romanov. Each member had mounted the rostrum to deposit his envelope, (156 members were illiterate and requested Abraham to fill in their voting papers for them).

* Anastasya Romanov, first wife of Ivan the Terrible, was the mother of Feodor.

† As a result of this intervention, Michael Romanov was known as the 'Cossacks' Czar'.

Michael Romanov was unanimously elected Czar of all the Russias.

[11] Routine court business; from *The First Romanovs, 1613–1725* by R. Nisbet Bain.

Let us follow the Tsar to Court and see him transact business, and learn at the same time to know the names and the offices of his chief servants who had the inestimable privilege of 'beholding his bright eyes', to use the semi-oriental Court jargon of the period.

Early every morning the gentry and nobility of old Moscovy were obliged to assemble at Court, the old men coming in carriages or sledges, according to the time of year, the young men on horseback. Everyone dismounted some little distance from the Tsarish Court, and approached the *krasnoe kruil'tso*, or 'red staircase', leading from the great square *na verkh*, or 'upstairs', to the innermost apartments of the Tsar. But only a select few had the right to go so far and so high. The less important *molodine*, or 'young people',* remained at the foot of the staircase awaiting commands from 'upstairs'. Among these are to be noticed some of the five hundred *stolniki*, or chamberlains, the children of fathers in high positions but not of the first rank, whose office at Court it is to carry dishes to the Tsar's table on solemn occasions. They also supplied most of the ordinary envoys to foreign parts, the *voivodes*, or rulers of towns and provinces, and the members of the *prikazes*, or public offices. The *stolniki* were also called *ploshchadniki*, or 'people of the square', in contradistinction to the *komnatniki*, or 'people of the apartments', the children of more illustrious parents who served the Tsar in his private apartments. Along with the *stolniki* on the staircase, we also find many of the two thousand eight hundred *stryapchie*, who were employed on less important missions, and the *d'yaki*

* Young in rank, not necessarily in age.

and *podyachi*, 'scribes' and 'sub-scribes', men of lowly birth but skilled in affairs, and becoming more and more indispensable with the spread of civilization. The *d'yaki* and *podyachi* numbered two thousand at least, and forty of them were constantly in attendance at Court. Flitting continually up and down the staircase are the *zhilt'sui*, or gentlemen-ushers, also employed as couriers. All the 'young people' respectfully make way for the *boyare*, the *okolnichie*, and the *dumnuie d'yaki* who do not stop on the staircase, but gravely ascend it on their way to the Tsar's ante-chamber. They represent the three highest grades of Russian officialdom. The word *boyar* is as old as the Russian language, the dignity existing in the days when the Russian princes were nomadic chieftains, and the boyars their close comrades and trusty counsellors. The *okolnichie** first appeared at a much later date, when a regular Court had become established. They were pre-eminently courtiers, and acted at first as masters of the ceremonies, introducers of ambassadors, and grand heralds. But at a later date they held no particular office, but simply ranked as the second class of the official hierarchy, the boyars being the first. The third grade was held by those who had not yet attained to the *boyartsvo* or boyardom, and yet were members of the Tsar's Council, the *dumnuie dvoryane*, or 'nobles of the Council'. Attached to these three first grades were the four *dumnuie d'yaki*, or clerks of the Council, erroneously identified by many contemporary foreigners with the imperial chancellors elsewhere, because, practically, they conducted the whole business of the Council, and being men of great experience, and relatively learned, were the Tsar's principal advisers, and necessarily enjoyed great influence in a state where the wielders of the sword could not always handle the pen. The *dumnuie d'yaki* first rose to eminence in the reign of Ivan the Terrible, who, constantly suspicious of the nobles, confided more and more in these astute upstarts, and in course of time they came to be regarded as oracles of statecraft. But in the Tsar's ante-chamber also there were

* *I.e.*, those near the Tsar's person.

degrees of privilege and precedence. Thus the *blizhnie boyare*, or 'near boyars', stood a little closer to the door of the *komnata*, or 'bedchamber', than the other boyars, awaiting a favourable opportunity of entry – a privilege denied to the rest, who had to remain outside. But at last the outsiders also received the reward of their patience. The doors of the bedchamber were thrown open and the Tsar entered and sat down in a large armchair in the *peredny ugol*, or 'chief corner', where the lamps burned before the holy ikons, whereupon all present did obeisance to the ground. The Tsar then beckoned to those with whom he would take counsel, any absentees being summoned to his presence forthwith, and severely rebuked for their want of respect. Those whom the Tsar did not honour with his conversation drew discreetly aside while he talked with their more favoured brethren. Then other boyars came forward and prostrated themselves to the ground before the Tsar. These were petitioners begging leave to attend christenings, marriages, or other family feasts at their country-houses. In all such cases the Tsar carefully inquired after the health of the boyar and every member of his family, and gifts were exchanged between them, the Gosudar being regarded not merely as the master, but also as the father of his people. The reception over, the Tsar dined in state with his whole court, and after the usual siesta, the rest of the afternoon was devoted to business, each of the *prikazui*, or public offices, having its allotted day. Business of unusual importance was transacted in a general assembly of all the boyars, called 'The Session of the Great Gosudar and his Boyars', the boyars sitting at a little distance from the Tsar on rows of benches according to rank, first the boyars, then the *okol'ni-chie* and then the *dumnuie dvoryane*, while the *dumnuie d'yaki*, really the most important people there, remained standing unless the Tsar bade them be seated. The Tsar opened the session by asking the opinions of the boyars, but many of them, as a contemporary chronicler quaintly tells us, only 'stroked their beards and answered not a word, inasmuch as the Tsar graciously makes many to be boyars not because of their learning, but because of their high birth, wherefore many boyars are ignorant of letters'. On very urgent occasions, such as the beginning of a war when extraordinary subsidies were required, *sovyetnuie lyudi*, or 'national councils', consisting of representatives of all classes, including the merchants and artificers, were held under the presidency of the Tsar, that they might assess their own burdens and thus have no excuse for subsequent complaint. During the troublous and disastrous seventeenth century, the liberality of these extraordinary popular assemblies had to be appealed to pretty frequently, as we shall see.

All ordinary routine business, on the other hand, was done in the *prikazui*. The difficulty of determining the origin of these, the most salient and characteristic instruments of old Moscovite administration, is due to their very simplicity. From time to time the Gosudar of the day *prikazuival*, or directed, one of his servants to see to this or that affair, gave him a scribe and a sub-scribe to assist him with the necessary clerical work – and a *prikaz*, or 'directory', sprang at once into existence.

[12] Tsar Alexis and the Patriarch Nikon's conflict, 1658 and 1664; from *The First Romanovs, 1613–1725* by R. Nisbet Bain.

On 8/19 July [1658] the feast of Our Lady of Kazan, the Tsar [Alexis Mikhailovitch] contrary to the practice of years, absented himself from divine service in the Uspensky Cathedral. Two days later he sent Prince Yury Romodanovsky to tell the patriarch that he was not to expect him at the still more ancient festival in honour of the translation of the Sacred Coat of the Saviour. 'The Tsar's Highness is wroth with you,' added the prince. 'You write yourself Great Gosudar, and we have only one Great Gosudar, the Tsar. . . . The Tsar's Highness bids me say you are not to write yourself so in future.'

The same day, after the solemn celebration, Nikon bade

the sacristan close the doors of the cathedral, as he would address the congregation. The people crowded round the pulpit to hear the sermon, and a very strange sermon they heard. Nikon informed them, at some length, that he was no longer patriarch, and whosoever henceforth called him by that name was anathema. Then, divesting himself publicly of his patriarchal vestments, he retired into the sacristy, and wrote a letter to the Tsar containing these words: 'I depart because of thy wrath, for the Scripture saith: "Give place to wrath", and again it is written: "If they reject thee in one city go to another, and if they receive thee not, shake the dust from off thy feet as a testimony against them".' Then, enveloped in the hood and mantle of a simple monk, and with a staff in his hand instead of a crozier, Nikon departed, despite an urgent message from the Tsar commanding him not to vacate his office. For three days, however, he lingered at Moscow eagerly awaiting overtures of reconciliation which never came, whereupon he shut himself up in the Voskresensky Monastery, the richest of his foundations which he and his Tsarish friend, in happier days, impressed by its beauty, as they strolled together through its gardens, had called 'The new Jerusalem'.

The consternation at Court was indescribable. More than once Alexius sent friendly boyars to attempt to turn Nikon from his resolution. But Nikon was immovable. Yet he apologized for his hasty departure, which he excused on the plea of ill-health; he sent his blessing to his *locum tenens*, the Metropolitan of Krutisk; and he made tender inquiries respecting the Tsar's bodily and spiritual welfare. His enemies grew alarmed, especially when they perceived that the Tsar was in no hurry to appoint a new patriarch, and, well aware of Alexius' tenderness for his old friend, they did their utmost to widen the breach between them. Their efforts would have been unavailing had not Nikon's mood suddenly changed. As a matter of fact, his abdication had not produced quite the effect he had anticipated. He was treated with indulgence, with respect even; but there was no repetition of the scenes which had occurred at his election. The

Tsar had not begged his pardon. He had not even come to see him. The disappointed prelate grew irritable and in his irritation he said and did things which his best friends could not approve of.

In February, 1660, a synod was held at Moscow to terminate 'the widowhood' of the Moscovite Church, which had now been without a chief pastor for nearly two years. The synod decided not only that a new patriarch should be appointed, but that Nikon had forfeited both his archiepiscopal rank and his priest's orders. Against the second part of this decision, however, the great ecclesiastical expert, Epifany Slavenitsky, protested energetically. He demonstrated that, according to the canons of the orthodox Church, archbishops voluntarily resigning their offices could not, unless guilty of canonical offences, be deprived of their sacerdotal character, or be forbidden to exercise their archiepiscopal functions. Thus the whole inquiry collapsed. The scrupulous Tsar shrank from enforcing the decrees of the synod for fear of committing mortal sin, and Nikon was escorted back to the monastery of the Resurrection.

The boyarin Rodion Stryeshnev, a near relation of the Tsar's, was one of Nikon's bitterest foes who lost no opportunity of ridiculing him. Amongst other things, he called his pet dog the 'patriarch Nikon', and taught the creature to stand on its hind legs and stretch out its front paw as if in the act of blessing. When this witticism was reported to Nikon, he solemnly cursed Stryeshnev for sacrilege, and this was one of the charges subsequently brought against him.

But if Nikon had many foes, his few remaining friends were the most enlightened people in Moscovy, including Rtishchev, Orduin Nashchokin, and Artamon Matvyeev. The sympathy of such men at such a time speaks well for the character and reputation of Nikon. They evidently regarded him as one of themselves, as one of the little band of enlightened reformers of whom Moscovy stood in great need, and they were very anxious to bring about a reconciliation between the Tsar and the patriarch. The means they took to this end was to get a common friend, the boyar Zyuzin, to write to Nikon, advising him to come in secret to Moscow and pay the Tsar a surprise visit. The old affection still subsisting between the two men would then, they hoped do the rest. But again Nikon's masterful temper spoiled everything. He did come to the *Kreml'*, as his friends advised, but he came not as suppliant seeking for forgiveness, but as a conqueror dictating his own terms.

At midnight, on 17/18 December, 1664, a long line of sledges halted before the outer barrier of the city of Moscow. 'Who goes there?' challenged the sentries. 'Prelates from the Savin Monastery,' was the reply. The procession was immediately admitted and made straight for the *kreml'*. At that moment early mass was being celebrated in the Uspensky Cathedral. John, Metropolitan of Rostov, was officiating, and the second *kathizma** had been reached, when a loud knocking was heard outside; the doors of the cathedral opened wide, and a procession of monks entered bearing aloft a cross. Behind the cross, in full canonicals, walked the patriarch Nikon. He at once ascended into the patriarch's place, and the well-known voice, which for six years had not been heard within those walls, exclaimed, 'Cease reading.' He was instantly obeyed, and the presbyters of the monastery of the Resurrection, who had accompanied him, then began singing 'Honour hast Thou, Lord', and 'Thou art worthy'. This done, Nikon ordered a deacon to recite the *Ekteniya*,† and, after doing obeisance to the ikons and relics, he sent the metropolitan John to tell the Gosudar that the patriarch was there. The Tsar, whom they found at mass in the church of St Eudoxia, was amazed at the audacity of this public summons from a prelate in disgrace, who had been forbidden to appear within the walls of Moscow. The whole *kreml'*, dark and silent a moment before, was instantly ablaze with candles and lanterns, and alive with *streltsui* and *zhiltsui* hastening in every

* The name of each of the twenty parts into which the liturgical psalter is divided.

† A prayer to which the choir responds, 'Lord have mercy upon us'.

direction to summon a council of prelates and boyars to the Tsar's staircase. There was as much uproar and confusion as if the Poles and Tatars had suddenly attacked the capital. Half an hour later a deputation of boyars, all more or less hostile to Nikon, headed by his arch-enemy, Rodion Stryeshnev, was sent to the Uspensky Cathedral to order the patriarch to return at once to his monastery. Nikon refused to budge till they had brought back to him an answer to a letter he had written to the Tsar which he now offered to them.* The deputation refused to accept the letter, and roughly insisted on his immediate departure. It was still an hour before dawn when at last Nikon consented to go. On stepping into his sledge, he ostentatiously shook the dust off his feet, and, at the same time, raised his eyes to heaven, where the flaming tail of a huge comet filled the darkened sky. The superstitious *stryeltsui* escort began sweeping up the dust of condemnation shaken off against them by Nikon; but he, pointing to the celestial portent, exclaimed, 'You may sweep and sweep, but God shall sweep you all away with His divine besom before many days be passed.'

[13] The Earl of Carlisle is received by Tsar Alexis as British Ambassador from Charles II, but not without local difficulties; from *A Relation of Three Embassies . . .* by Guy Miège.

(Nothing is known about Guy Miège, apart from the fact that he was a Swiss attendant to the Earl of Carlisle. The Earl, who had been Colonel of Cromwell's Life Guards, was created Baron Dacre, Viscount Howard of Morpeth, and Earl of Carlisle in 1661 by Charles II, and was sent by him as Ambassador Extraordinary to Muscovy, to restore English trade privileges there. He was then to proceed to the Courts of Sweden and Denmark, hence the title of Miège's account.

* This document was full of apocalyptic visions and warnings of which Nikon professed to be the recipient.

The Embassy set out from England for Archangel in 1663, and returned the following year.)

In the mean time there were a great number of *Boyars*, of *Stolnicks*, and other persons of the Court, which came to meet the Ambassador, richly clad in Vests or Tuniques, of cloth of gold and silver, or velvets lined with Sables, with great caps on their heads of black Fox, made in the fashion of a Muff, which they use commonly in their Ceremonies. They were most of them very well mounted upon good horses, with rich trappings and bridles of silver, made like chains, with the linkes very broad and thin, so that whilst their horses were in motion, they made a noise altogether Majestique. There were severall also who had their houffes covered with pretious stones, whose lustre seemed to adde a richer light to the light of the day; and behind them they had their servants carrying covers for their sadles of Leopard skins, cloth of gold, velvet, and scarlet. All the Gentlemen of the *Tzars* chamber were there ready to accompany the Ambassador to his very house.

At length, the Master of the great *Dukes* horse came to present to the Ambassador from the *Tzar* a sledg, & another for my Lord *Morpeth*, with several white horses for the Gentlemen: A while after, came *Pronchissof*, one of the *Tzars* Counsel, and *Gregory Cosmevitz* along with him, who were both deputed to serve his Excellence as *Pristass*, or Masters of the Ceremonies during his residence in *Mosco*. And in this occasion it was we had another ridiculous example of the pride and rusticity of the *Moscovites*, who are so quick and precise in anticipating the Prerogative of Ambassadors. *Pronchissof* being arrived within some small distance of the Ambassadors sledg, gave him to understand that he was sent to receive him from the grand *Duke* his Lord, and that he expected the Ambassador should first come out of his sledg. But his Excellence signified to him by his Interpreter, that his expectations were very ill grounded, that he represented the person of the King his Master, and that in that case all such Kind of respect was due to himself. *Pronchissof* however continued unmovable in his sledg as a Master of Ceremonies, and sent back to the Ambassador that he also was sent from the *Tzar* his Master to represent his person: so that to have seen him, one would have thought he had taken upon him the forme of a statue, to represent the Majesty of his Prince. This answer, how absurd soever it was, caused several smart replies both on one side and the other: till at last the Ambassador to prevent any further delay in his Entrance, condescended to this, That they should both of them come out of their sledges together. But in this *Pronchissof* tooke occasion to deceive his Excellence, and falsify his word, hanging in the aire betwixt the armes of his servants, and but touching the earth with his tiptoes, whilst the Ambassador came out freely. At their meeting, they saluted one another, and *Pronchissof* first delivered his complement, which consisted in declaring his Employment, and acquainting his Excellence, that the *Tzar* had sent him, and his associate *Gregory Cosmovitz* (who was there present also) to take care that all things necessary should be provided during his continuance at *Mosco*. But the greatest part of his complement was the recitation of his Masters Titles, which he enumerated from the first to the last, in a most troublesome and ridiculous maner, as will appeare hereafter. His complement being made, and the Ambassador having answered him with a very good grace, they retired both of them into their sledges, *Pronchissof* returning in the same posture he came, his servants holding him up by his armes, as if they were afraid he should sinke under the burthen of the emploiment, which his Master had given him. . . .

We past thorow the *Tzars* Guards, who were drawn up in rancks on both sides of us reaching to the very bottom of the staires of the Hall, thorow which we were to pass to audience. Near the Castlegate we found another regiment of Guards drawn up also in very good order. A while after we past thorow another Regiment in one of the Courts of the Castle, and in this place we saw a great number of very fair Canon planted on one side and the other with the Canoniers by them, and ready in appearance to fire upon us from all parts. From thence we passed to another Court filled also with Guards, but when we came to the gate of a passage thorow which we were to go, all that were in sladdes or on horseback alighted. Those who were to go up into the Hall of audience were constraind to leave their swords behind them, it being not permitted for any body to pass any further with them by their sides, for the prevention of which ceremony, his Excellence and my Lord *Morpeth* carried none with them. When we had gone some paces this way (which is a way peculiar to Christian Ambassadors, those of Infidel Princes being carried another) there was a *Boyar* came to meet the Ambassador & complemented him from the great *Duke*. From thence we came to a great stone Galerie, where another *Boyar* received his Excellence with another complement. And from thence we came into a Hall thorow which we were to pass in to that of the audience, and here it was we saw the Guards of the *Tzars* body in a most splended Equipage, their Vests of velvet being lined with sables, their caps richly adorned with pearles and precious stones, and their very partesans covered with gold and silver. Neare the door of the Hall of audience, the Ambassador received a third Complement from the *Tzars* own Cousin. After which we opened to the right and left, and the Ambassador entered first into the Hall, after him my Lord *Morpeth*, and then the Gentlemen and the Pages.

And here it was we were like those who coming suddainly out of the dark are dazled with the brightnes of the Sun: the splendor of their jewels seeming to contend for priority with that of the day; so that we were lost as it were in this confusion of glory. The *Tzar* like a sparkling Sun (to speak in the *Russian* dialect) darted forth most sumptuous rays, being most magnificently placed upon his Throne with his Scepter in his hand, and having his Crown on his Head. His Throne was of massy Silver gilt, wrought curiously on the top with several works and Pyramids; and being seven or eight steps higher than the floor, it rendered the person of this Prince transcendently Majestick. His Crown (which he wore upon a Cap lined with black Sables) was covered quite over with precious stones, it terminated towards the top in the form of a Pyramid with a golden cross at the spire. The Scepter glistered also all over with Jewels, his vest was sett with the like from the top to the bottom down the opening before, and his collar was answerable to the same. By his side he had four of the tallest of his Lords standing below his Throne, each of them with his battle-ax upon his shoulder, and with a profound gravity casting their Eys now and then upon their *Tzar*, as inviting us to an admiration of his grandeur. Their habits were no less remarquable than their countenances, being all four of them from the top of their head to the sole of their foot clothed in white vests of Ermine, and having great chaines of Gold, and their Caps of that large sort which they use in their Ceremonies, but whereas others were of black Fox these were of Ermin as well as their Vests, their very Boots also were covered with the same. But that which was farther admirable was the glorious equippage of the *Boyars* present at this audience, who were as so many beams of the Sun elevated in his triumphal Carr, and seemed to have no lustre but to do homage withal to their great Monarch. They were about two hundred cloathed all with vests of cloth of gold, cloth of silver or velvet set with Jewels, all placed in order upon benches covered with tapistry round about by the wall; the floor being raised there three or four steps high and about the bredth of a good walke. At the Entrance into the Hall there was a great number also of his *Goses* which are his Merchants or Factors whom he furnishes with rich robes to appear at such Ceremonies; This was the Splendour we found this great Prince in, with a countenance perfectly majestick; as having not only the advantage of a handsome proportion, but of a lively and vigorous age, for this was but his four and thirtieth year. The Hall notwithstanding answered not very well to this Magnificence, saving in its Vastnes, and that it was covered all the floor over with tapistry. But it was wanting on the walls, which had no other Ornament than a few old pictures; the roof of it was arched, and supported by a great Pillar in the middle.

My Lord Ambassador made a low Reverence to his Majestie assoon as he was entred into the Hall, the Throne being opposite to the Door; then he advanced some paces, and stopping at the Pillar in the midst of the Hall, he made him a second, then being ready to speak, made him a third, and saluted him in the behalf of his Master the King of *England* in these words; The most Serene and most Puissant Prince *Charles* the Second by the Grace of God King of *England*, *Scotland*, *France*, and *Ireland*, Defender of the Faith, &c. To You the most High, most Potent, and most Illustrious Prince Great Lord, Emperour, and Grand Duke *Alexey Michailovitz*, of all the great, and little, and white *Russia* Self-upholder, of *Moscovie*, *Keavie*, *Volodimerie*, *Nofgorod*, Emperour of *Cazan*, Emperor of *Astracan*, Emperour of *Siberia*, Lord of *Pscove*, great Duke of *Lituania*, *Smolensco*, *Twersco*, *Volinsco*, *Podolsko*, *Ughersco*, *Permsco*, *Veatsco*, *Bolgarsco*, & c. Lord and Great Duke of *Nofgorod* in the Lower Countries, of *Chernigo*, *Resansco*, *Polotsco*, *Rostofsco*, *Yeroslafsco*, *Beloozarsco*, *Oudorsco*, *Obdorsco*, *Condinsco*, *Wetepsco*, *Mstisclanco*, and all the Northern parts, Lord of the Country of *Iversco* of the *Tzars* of *Cartalinsco*, and of *Gruzinsco*, and of the Country of *Cabardinsco*, of the Dukes of *Chercaso*, and *Igorsco*, Lord and Monarch of several other Dominions, and Provinces, East, West, and North, of which he is Heir from Father to Son, by me *Charles* Earle of *Carlisle*, Vicomte *Howard* of *Morpeth*, Baron *Dacre* of *Gillesland*, His Majesties Lieutenant in the Counties of *Cumberland* and *Westmorland*, one of his Majesties most honourable Privy Councel, and his Extraordinary Ambassador sendeth greeting, and hath commanded me to deliver these Letters (being his Letters Patents which he held in his hand) to Your Imperial Majestie. Which words being with a loud voice explained by his Interpreter which stood by his Excellencies side, the Ambassador advanced towards the Throne to present the Letter which he immediately delivered into the hands of his Chancellor.

His Excellence returning to his place, the *Tzar* rose up, and the *Boyars* doing the like all of them at the same time, their Vests of Tissue made such a rustling one against another, that we were something amuzed at the suddenness of the noise. Then after a short silence, his Majestic began to speak, and to enquire of the Ambassador concerning the Kings health. . . .

[14] The Tsars before the reign of Peter I; from *On the Corruption of Morals in Russia* by Prince M.M. Shcherbatov.

(Mikhail Mikhailovitch, Prince Shcherbatov (1733–1790) was a historian, writer and public figure. In 1759–60 he wrote a series of articles calling for strong government and using powerful social arguments. At the end of the 1760s he took part in Catherine the Great's law-reforming commission, and published his *Corruption of Morals* in the 1780s.)

Not only the subjects, but even our very monarchs led a very simple life. Their palaces were not large, as is attested by the old buildings that remain. Seven, eight, or at most, ten rooms, were sufficient for the monarch's accommodation. These comprised: a chapel, which was also an audience-chamber, for it was here that the boyars and other dignitaries came and awaited the monarch; a dining-room, which was quite small, for from the Registers of the Nobility, we see that a very small number of boyars was deemed worthy of the honour of being at the monarch's table; while for any grand occasions there was the Granovitaya Palata. I do not know whether the monarchs had an antechamber, but from the layout of the old palaces that I remember, I think they must have done. A bedchamber, and this was not separate from the Czarina's but was always shared in common; beyond the bedchamber were apartments for the Czarina's maidservants (these usually consisted of one room), and for the young children of the Czar, who lived two or three to a room. When they grew up, however, they were given separate apartments; but even these consisted of no more than three rooms, namely, a chapel, bedchamber, and a room beyond the bedchamber.

These very palaces had no great embellishments, for the walls were bare, and the benches were covered with crimson cloth. The magnificence was exquisite when decorations were made around the doors in the form of crude wood-carvings; when the walls and vaults were covered with ikon-paintings, pictures of saints, or simply with floral arab-esques; while if there were a few walnut chairs or arm-chairs upholstered in cloth or imitation-velvet for the Czar and Czarina, then this was the highest level of magnificence.

Beds with awnings were unknown, and they slept without awnings. And even in recent times it was considered a great magnificence when the chapel in the royal palace was upholstered in leather gilt. This chapel stood next to the Red Balustrade. I remember it myself, with its tarnished upholsteries.

The royal table matched this simplicity, for though I cannot say for certain that the monarchs did not eat off silver, yet, since I do not see a proper silver dinner-service in the Masterskaya Palata, I conclude that in those days the monarchs ate off pewter; and that silver dishes, tablestands made in the form of Mount Sinai, and other forms of tableware, were used only on feast days.

Their diet conformed with this pattern. Although the dishes were numerous, yet they all consisted of simple things. Beef, mutton, pork, geese, turkeys, ducks, hens, grouse and sucking-pigs, were sufficient for the grandest table, with the addition of a large number of pastries, not always made of pure wheaten flour. Veal was little con-sumed and milk-fed calves and capons were quite unknown. The greatest luxury was to wrap a leg of roast or ham in gold paper, to add touches of gilt to pies, and so on. Then, they knew nothing of capers, olives or other appetizers, but were content with pickled cucumbers and plums. Finally, it was already considered a luxury to serve a meat brawn with pickled lemons.

The fish fare was even plainer than the meat. There were

very few ponds for the sale of fish, and they did not have the art of conveying live the expensive fish from remote parts, and in any case, the royal court did not depend on purveyors but lived entirely off its own domains. And so in Moscow, where the supply of fish was small, they contented themselves with the fish which they caught in the River Moskva and nearby rivers, and when a real lack was felt at the royal table, then both in Moscow itself and in all the villages belonging to the Crown, ponds were constructed from which fish were caught for the royal table. They also had salted fish which they brought from the towns. In many towns where there is a fishing industry, this was even imposed as a tribute. In Rostov I myself have seen the royal Charters concerning this tribute. In winter they also brought fish from remote parts, frozen and salted for use at the monarch's table.

Their dessert was of equal simplicity. It consisted of raisins, currants, figs, prunes and honey-pastils, as far as dry things were concerned. As for fresh: in summer and autumn there were apples, pears, peas, beans and cucumbers. I do not think they even knew of melons and watermelons except when some of the latter were brought from Astrakhan. Even grapes were still conveyed in syrup, and they had no idea how to convey them fresh; for I remember, it was only in the reign of the Empress Elisabeth Petrovna, through the efforts of Ivan Antonovich Cherkassov, the Cabinet Minister, that they began to be conveyed fresh.

For such a small number of rooms, not much lighting would be needed; but even here, they not only did not use, but considered it a sin to use wax candles, and the rooms were lit by tallow candles, and even these were not set out in tens or hundreds; it was a large room indeed where four candles were set out on candlesticks.

Their drinks consisted of Kvass, Kisly-shchi, beer and various meads; brandy made from ordinary wine, and the following wines: church-wine, that is, ordinary red wine, rhenish – by this name was meant not only Rhine wine but also any ordinary white wine; Romaneya, that is, sweet

Greek wine, and Alicante. These foreign wines were con-
sumed with great economy. The cellars where they were
kept were called frankish, because these wines, and particularly the Greek wines, were first received through the
Franks, while other wines were known to come from
France. They therefore gave them the general name of
Frankish wines.

[15] The riot of the *streltsy*, 1682, and the death of
Ivan Naryshkin; from *Peter the Great, Emperor of
Russia* by Eugene Schuyler.

On 25 May, the Streltsi, armed from head to foot with
swords, halberds and muskets, began to collect at a very
early hour in their churches in the most opposite quarters of
the city, as if waiting for some watchword. Soon a watchword came. About nine o'clock in the morning a man rode
hurriedly through the streets crying out: 'The Naryshkins
have murdered the Tsarevitch Ivan! To the Kremlin! The
Naryshkins wish to kill all the royal family! To arms! Punish
the traitors! Save the Tsar!' A general alarm was at once
sounded. Drums were beaten, bells rung, and the regimental
cannon were brought out. The Streltsi, with their broad
banners embroidered with pictures of the Virgin, advanced
from all sides toward the Kremlin, as if to attack an enemy,
compelling their colonels to lead them on. The peaceable
citizens who met them were astonished at this onset; but to
their inquiries as to its cause the answer returned was: 'We
are going to destroy the traitors and murderers of the family
of the Tsar.' No doubt the majority of them sincerely
believed that the Tsar was really in danger, that the Naryshkins were desirous of mounting the throne, and that they
were patriots going to save their country, and to rescue their
ruler from the traitors and the hated boyars. As they
advanced they cut off the long handles of their spears, so
as to manage them more easily. Meanwhile the boyars were
quietly sitting in the public offices and in the palace, without

the slightest idea of what was passing in the city, or, after finishing the morning's official duties, they were strolling about previous to their midday dinner. Matveief, on coming out upon the staircase leading to the bed-chamber porch, saw Prince Theodore Urusof hastily running toward him, with scarcely breath enough to cry out that the Streltsi had risen, and that all the regiments, fully armed and with beating drums, were advancing towards the Kremlin. Matveief, astonished, immediately returned to the palace with Urusof, to inform the Tsaritsa Natalia. The words were scarcely out of his mouth before three messengers came in, one after another, each with worse news than the preceding. The Streltsi were already in the old town and near the Kremlin walls. Orders were immediately given to close the Kremlin gates and to prepare whatever means of defence there might be, and the Patriarch was hastily sent for. The officer of the guard, however, came with the intelligence that it was impossible to shut the gates, as the Streltsi had already passed them and were now in the Kremlin. All the carriages of the boyars had been driven back to the Ivan place, and the drivers were some wounded and some killed, while the horses were either cut to pieces or removed from the vehicles. No one could get into the Kremlin or out of it, and the frightened boyars took refuge, one after another, in the banqueting-hall of the palace.

The Streltsi surrounded the palace, and stopped before the red staircase. Amid the din, the cries and the uproar it was barely possible to distinguish the words: 'Where's the Tsarévitch Ivan? Give us the Naryshkins and Matveief! Death to the traitors!' A brief council having been held in the banqueting-hall, it was decided to send some boyars out to the Streltsi, to demand of them what they wanted. Prince Tcherkassky, Prince Havansky, Prince Golitsyn and Sheremetief then went out and asked the Streltsi why they had come to the palace in this riotous way. 'We wish to punish the traitors,' was their reply; 'they have killed the Tsarevitch. They will destroy all the royal family. Give up to us the Naryshkins and the other traitors.' When the boyars brought back this answer, the Tsaritsa was advised by her father, Matveief, and others to go out on the red staircase and show to the Streltsi both the Tsar Peter and the Tsarevitch Ivan. Trembling with terror, she took by the hands her son and her step-son, and – accompanied by the Patriarch, the boyars, and the other officials – went out upon the red staircase. 'Here is the Tsar, Peter Alexeievitch; here is the Tsarevitch, Ivan Alexeievitch,' the boyars cried out in loud voices, as they came out with the Tsaritsa and pointed the children out to the Streltsi. 'By God's mercy they are safe and well. There are no traitors in the royal palace. Be quiet; you have been deceived.' The Streltsi placed ladders against the rails, and some of them climbed up to the platform where the Tsar's family stood, in order the more closely to examine them. Peter stood still and looked at them, face to face, without blanching or showing the least sign of fear. On coming to the Tsarevitch Ivan, the Streltsi asked him if he really were Ivan Alexeievitch. 'Yes,' answered the youth, in an almost inaudible voice. Again the question was repeated. 'Are you really he?' 'Yes, I am he,' was the reply. The Patriarch then wished to descend the staircase and talk with the rioters; but the cry came up from below, 'We have no need of your advice; we know what to do,' and many men forced their way up past him. The Tsaritsa, seeing their rudeness and fearing the consequences, took the children back into the palace.

Matveief, who had formerly been a favourite commander of the Streltsi, went down outside of the wicket and spoke to them in a confident yet propitiatory tone, reminding them of their former faithful services, especially during the time of the Kolomenskoe riots,* and of their good reputation which they were now destroying by their proceedings, and explaining to them that they were anxious without reason by believing false reports. He told them that there was no cause

---

* There were very serious riots during the reign of Alexis, in 1662, originating in the misery and discontent produced by the debasement of the currency. The rioters marched out from Moscow to the country-house of the Tsar at Kolomenskoe.

for their alarm about the royal family, which, as they had just seen with their own eyes, was in perfect safety. He advised them to beg pardon for the disturbance which they had made, which had been caused by their excessive loyalty, and he would persuade the Tsar to overlook it and restore them to favour. These sensible, good-natured words wrought a deep impression. The men in the front grew quiet; and it was evident that they had begun to reflect. Further off were still heard voices in discussion and conversation, as though a better feeling were taking possession of the multitude. It gradually became calmer.

Matveief hastened back into the palace to allay the fears of the Tsaritsa, when, unfortunately, Prince Michael Dolgoruky, the second in command of the Department of the Streltsi, came out and, relying on the words of Matveief, and thinking that all irritation was over, wished to put himself forward and to show his powers of command. In his rudest and roughest tones he ordered the Streltsi to go home immediately, and to attend to their own business. All the good impression which Matveief's words had produced was immediately dispelled. The opponents of the Naryshkins, who had been rendered silent by the changed disposition of the multitude, again began to raise their voices; and some of the Streltsi, who were more drunken or riotous than the rest, seized Dolgoruky by his long gown, threw him down from the platform into the square, asking the crowd at the same time whether such was their will, while the men below caught him on their spears, exclaiming 'Yes, yes,' and cut him to pieces.

This first act of bloodshed was the signal for more. Lowering their spears, the Streltsi rushed into the rooms of the palace, which some had already succeeded in entering from another side, in order to seize upon Matveief, who was in the ante-room of the banqueting-hall, with the Tsaritsa and her son. The Streltsi moved toward him; the Tsaritsa wished to protect him with her own person, but in vain. Prince Tcherkassky tried to get him away, and had his coat torn off in the struggle. At last, in spite of the Tsaritsa, the Streltsi pulled Matveief away, dragged him to the red staircase, and with exultant cries, threw him down into the square, where he was instantly cut to pieces by those below.

The Streltsi then burst again into the palace, and went through all the rooms, seeking for those they called traitors. The boyars hid themselves where they could. The Patriarch was scarcely able to escape into the Cathedral of the Assumption, while the Tsaritsa Natalia and her son took refuge in the banqueting-hall . . .

The Streltsi ran through all the inner rooms of the palace, looked into the store-rooms, under the beds, into the chapels, thrust their spears under the altars, and left no place without a visit. From a distance they saw Theodore Soltykof going into one of the chapels. Someone cried out: 'There goes Ivan Naryshkin,' and the unlucky man was so frightened that he could not pronounce a single word, or even tell his name. He was at once killed, and his body thrown below. When it was ascertained who it was, and that he was not a Naryshkin, the Streltsi sent the body to old Soltykof, and excused themselves by saying that his son had been killed by mistake. 'God's will be done,' said the old man, who had even the presence of mind to give the messengers something to eat and drink. After they had left the house, in trying to console his weeping daughter-in-law, he quoted a Russian proverb to the effect that 'their turn will come next.' A servant who had overheard this, and who had a grudge against his master, immediately rushed out, and told the Streltsi that his master had threatened them. They returned and murdered him on the spot.

In the Church of the Resurrection the Streltsi met one of the court dwarfs, named Homyak. 'Tell me where the Naryshkins, the Tsaritsa's brothers, are hid?' they asked. He pointed to the altar, and they pulled out Athanasius Naryshkin, dragged him by the hair to the chancel steps, and there cut him to pieces. His younger brothers, his father, and his other relatives, as well as Matveief's son, whose description of these events we chiefly follow, took refuge in the apartments of the little Princess Natalia, Peter's sister, which apparently were not searched . . .

Early the next day, the 26th, the Streltsi came again, fully armed, and, with beating drums advancing to the gilded lattice near the apartment of the Tsar, demanded with loud cries the surrender of Ivan Naryshkin, the Councillor Kirilof, and the two doctors, Daniel the Jew and Jan Gutmensch. The princesses endeavoured to save the lives of these people, but they were obliged to surrender Kirilof and Doctor Gutmensch, although they succeeded in concealing the wife of Doctor Daniel Von Gaden in the room of the young Tsaritsa Martha, the widow of Theodore. The others were killed.

The Streltsi then went to the residence of the Patriarch and threatened with spears and halberds not only the servants but the Patriarch himself, demanding the surrender of the traitors concealed there; looked through the cellars and outhouses; turned topsy-turvy boxes and beds, and not finding anyone, again came to the Patriarch and repeated their demands. The Patriarch, who had put on his robes, replied that there were no traitors in his house, but that he himself was ready to die . . .

On the third day, 27 May, the Streltsi again came to the Kremlin, and to the beating of drums stationed themselves about the palace, while some of them climbed straight up to the balcony and insisted on the surrender of Ivan Naryshkin. They threatened all the servitors of the palace with death if they did not find him, and declared they would not leave the Kremlin until they had possession of him. They even threatened the life of the Tsaritsa Natalia and of the other members of the Tsar's family. At last it became evident that nothing could be done, and the Princess Sophia went to Natalia and said: 'There is no way of getting out of it; to save the lives of all of us you must give up your brother.' Natalia, after useless protests, then brought out Ivan Naryshkin and conducted him into the Church of the Saviour beyond the Wicket. Here he received the Holy Communion and prepared himself for death. Sophia handed him an image of the Virgin and said, 'Perhaps when the Streltsi see this holy picture they will let him go.' All in the palace were so terrified that it seemed to them that Ivan Naryshkin was lingering too long. Even the old Prince Jacob Odoiefsky, a kindly but timorous old man, went up to the Tsaritsa and said: 'How long, O lady, you are keeping your brother. For you must give him up. Go on quickly, Ivan Kirilovitch, and don't let us all be killed for your sake.' The Tsaritsa led him as far as the Golden Wicket, where the Streltsi stood. They immediately seized on him and begun to indulge in all sorts of abuse and insult before her eyes. He was dragged by the feet down the staircase through the square to the Constantine torture-room. Though most fearfully tortured, Naryshkin set his teeth and uttered not a word. Here was also brought Dr Daniel Von Gaden, who was caught in the dress of a beggar, wearing bark sandals, and with a wallet over his shoulders. He had escaped from the town and had passed two days in the woods, but had become so famished that he had returned to the German quarter to get some food from an acquaintance, when he was recognized and arrested. Von Gaden, in the midst of his tortures, begged for three days more, in which he promised to name those who deserved death more than he. His words were written down, while others cried out: 'What is the use of listening to him? Tear up the paper,' and dragged him, together with Naryshkin, from the torture-room to the Red Place. They were both lifted up on the points of spears; afterward their heads and feet were cut off, and their bodies chopped into small pieces and trampled into the mud. With these two deaths the murders came to an end. The Streltsi went from the Red Place to the palace of the Kremlin and cried: 'We are now content. Let your Tsarish Majesty do with the other traitors as may seem good. We are ready to lay down our heads for the Tsar, for the Tsaritsa, for the Tsarevitch and the Tsarevnas.

That very day permission was granted for the burial of the bodies, many of which had been lying in the Red Place since the first day of the riot; and the faithful black servant of old Matveief went out with a sheet and collected the mutilated remains of his master, and carried them on pillows to the parish church of St Nicholas, where they were buried.

[16] The revolt of the *streltsy* in 1698 in Peter the Great's absence – loyal troops put down the rebellion; Peter returns from Vienna to punish the *streltsy* himself: from *Diary of an Austrian Secretary of Legation at the Court of Czar Peter the Great*, by Johann George Korb.

When they saw that some were stretched lifeless, courage and fierceness at once deserted the terror-stricken *streltsy*, who broke into disorder. Those that retained any presence of mind endeavoured by the fire of their own artillery to check and silence that of the Tsar; but all in vain; for Colonel de Grage had anticipated that design, and directing the fire of his pieces upon the artillery of the seditious mob, whenever they would go to their guns, vomited such a perfect hurricane upon them that many fell, numbers fled away, and none remained daring enough to return to fire them. Still Colonel de Grage did not cease to thunder from the heights into the ranks of the flying. The *streltsy* saw safety nowhere; arms could not protect them; nothing was more appalling to them than the ceaseless flash and roar of the artillery showering its deadly bolts upon them from the German right. And the same men who, but an hour before, had spat upon proferred pardon, offered in consequence to surrender – so short is the interval that separates victors from vanquished. Supplicant, they fell prostrate, and begged that the artillery might cease its cruel ravages, offering to do promptly whatever they were ordered. The suppliants were directed to lay down their arms, to quit their ranks, and obey in everything that would be enjoined to them . . .

When the ferocious arrogance with which they were swollen had been made to subside completely, in the manner we have just narrated, and all the accomplices of mutiny had been cast into chains, General Shein instituted an inquiry, by way of torture, touching the causes, the objects, the instigators, the chiefs, and the accomplices of this perilous and impious machination. For there was a very serious suspicion that more exalted people were at the head of it. Every one of them freely confessed himself deserving of death; but to detail the particulars of the nefarious plot, to lay bare the objects of it, to betray their accomplices, was what no person could persuade any of them to do. The rack was consequently got in readiness by the executioner, as the only means left to elicit the truth. The torture that was applied was of unexampled inhumanity. Scourged most savagely with the cat, if that had not the effect of breaking their stubborn silence, fire was applied to their backs, all gory and streaming, in order that, by slowly roasting the skin and tender flesh, the sharp pangs might penetrate through the very marrow of their bones, to the utmost power of painful sensation. These tortures were applied alternately, over and over again. Horrid tragedies to witness and to hear. In the open field above thirty of these more than funeral pyres blazed at the same time, and thereat were these most wretched creatures under examination roasted amidst their horrible howlings. At another side resounded the merciless strokes of the cat, while this most savage butchery of men was being done in this very pleasant neighbourhood . . .

[The news of the *streltsy* rebellion reached Peter in Vienna]; he took the quick post, as his ambassador suggested, and in four weeks' time, he had got over about three hundred [German] miles without accident and arrived [in Moscow] on the 4th of September [1698], a monarch for the well-disposed but an avenger for the wicked. His first anxiety after his arrival was about the rebellion. In what it consisted? What the insurgents meant? Who had dared to instigate such a crime? And as nobody could answer accurately upon all points, and some pleaded their own ignorance, others the obstinacy of the *streltsy*, he began to have suspicions of everybody's loyalty, and began to cogitate about a fresh investigation. The rebels that were kept in custody, in various places in the environs, were all brought in by four regiments of the guards to a fresh investigation and fresh tortures. Prison, tribunal, and rack, for those that were brought in, was in Preobrazhenskoe [the village where Peter spent his youth]. No day, holy or profane, were the inquisitors idle; every day was deemed fit and lawful for torturing. As many as there were accused there were knouts, and every inquisitor was a butcher. Prince Feodor Iurevich Romadonovskii showed himself by so much more fitted for his inquiry, as he surpassed the rest in cruelty. The very Grand Duke himself [Peter], in consequence of the distrust he had conceived of his subjects, performed the office of inquisitor. He put the interrogatories, he examined the criminals, he urged those that were not confessing, he ordered such *streltsy* as were more pertinaciously silent to be subjected to more cruel tortures; those that had already confessed about many things were questioned about more; those who were bereft of strength and reason, and almost of their senses, by excess of torment, were handed over to the skill of the doctors, who were compelled to restore them to strength, in order that they might be broken down by fresh excruciations. The whole month of October [1698] was spent in butchering the backs of the culprits with knout and with flames; no day were those that were left alive exempt from scourging or scorching, or else they were broken upon the wheel, or driven to the gibbet, or slain with the axe – the penalties which were inflicted upon them as soon as their confessions had sufficiently revealed the heads of the rebellion . . .

Vaska Girin, the insurgent ringleader, after undergoing four times the exquisite tortures, confessing nothing, was condemned to be hanged. But on the very day appointed for his execution, there was led out of prison, with the rebel *streltsy*, to the question, a certain youth of twenty years of age, on being confronted with whom, he, of his own accord, broke his stubborn silence, and revealed the counsels of the traitors, with all the circumstances. Now that youth of twenty had fallen in by chance with these rebels near the borders of Smolensk, and being forced to wait on the principal instigators of the mutiny, they took no notice of his listening, nor was his presence forbidden even when they used to deliberate about the success of their nefarious enterprise. When he was dragged along with the rebels before the tribunal, he, in order to prove his innocence the more easily, cast himself at the judge's feet, and with the most ardent sighs implored not to be subjected to the torture – that he would confess all that he knew with the most exact truth. Vaska Girin, who was condemned to the halter, was not hanged before having made his judicial confession; for he was one of the prime rebels, and an excellent witness of what he very truly detailed . . .

[Sophia] was interrogated by the Tsar himself, touching these attempts, and it is still uncertain what she answered. But this much is certain – that in this act the Tsar's Majesty wept for his own lot and Sophia's. Some will have it the Tsar was on the point of sentencing her to death, and used this argument: 'Mary of Scotland was led forth from prison to the block, by command of her sister Elizabeth, Queen of England – a warning to me to exercise my power over Sophia.' Still once more the brother pardoned a sister's crime, and, instead of penalty, enjoined that she should be banished to a greater distance, in some monastery [the Novo Dyevichi] . . .

[17] The great bell of the Kremlin; and the fire of 1737; from *Le Kremlin de Moscou, Esquisses et Tableaux* by M.P. Fabricius.

The renowned bell known as the 'Queen of Bells' was cast during the reign of Anna Ivanovna. It is one of the sights of the Kremlin. It must have weighed 14,000 'pouds' [8.54 tons]. It was cast by the ironmaster Ivan Matorin, who had had casting foundries made with all the necessary equipment opposite Ivan the Great's Belfry. But Matorin was not able to finish this job in which the Empress showed a keen interest. He died after the first attempt at casting, and his son was left to complete the undertaking. The job was successfully finished in November 1736, in the presence of Benjamin, Archbishop of Kolomna. The 'Queen of Bells' was cast, but it proved impossible to hoist her into the belfry.

Under Anna Ivanova, the appalling fire of 29 May 1737 devastated the Kremlin and Moscow. It started in Alexander Miloslavski's house in the Avenue of St John the Baptist. A powerful wind helped to spread the fire, and before long it reached the palace of Tsarina Catherine Ivanovna at Borovitski Bridge. From there, the flames invaded the Kremlin and reached the stables, the counting-houses, the chanceries, the 'Facetted' Palace and the Arsenal. During Vespers, the roofs of the churches of Assumption, the Annunciation, and the Archangels were consumed by flames, and the interior filled with smoke. Then the fire took on enormous proportions. The flames spread from the Monastery of the Epiphany to the Armoury on one side, and on the other from the Monasteries of the Miracles and the Ascension to the Synod, to the Chancery of the Treasury, and to the palace of Prince Troubetskoy at St Nicholas' Gate. Several bells fell from the belfry of Ivan the Great and a burning beam broke the rim of the 'Queen of Bells' in its fall . . .

The closeness of the Kremlin buildings, many of which were wooden, helped the fire to spread. To the west side, the salt store, which once had been the residence of Tsarina Martha Matvievna, was destroyed. Further to the left, the fire burnt up the *Podvorie* of the Trinity and the house of the Synod; to the right, the War Office and the clothing commissary. The buildings behind the upper *Terems* were burnt, as well as all the buildings between the Church of the Nativity and the food depot. The roofs of the houses near the *Spasski* Tower (of the Saviour), the Library, and the bronze and iron doors were destroyed. Only the upper and lower gardens along the river banks, with their six pavilions, the palace greenhouse, the kitchen garden and the orangeries remained unscathed.

The Church of the Annunciation at Nikitski and that of Constantine and Helen were totally burnt, as were the religious houses there.

The roof of the guard-house or prison, another prison adjoining behind the torture chamber, five barracks, yet another guard-house, a check-point, a chapel, a military post, and a barracks where those under arrest were held, were prey to the flames. More than 300 prisoners were transferred to the granary at Kalouga Gate.

To sum up, all the wooden Kremlin houses were reduced to ashes, and the stone buildings were severely damaged. Even the Kremlin towers and the walls suffered. The covered passage-ways, the bridges, and the roofs which covered them, were damaged in many places. The same fire also destroyed a mass of buildings at Kitai-Gorod and at Bieli-Gorod. Several years later, during the reign of Elizabeth, the Kremlin still bore visible signs of this hideous catastrophe. By an *Ukaz* of 22 June 1737, Anna Ivanovna ordered the churches which had been burnt to be rebuilt at the Crown's expense.

[18] Catherine the Great's betrothal while still a German princess, 1743; from *The Memoirs of Catherine the Great, 1743–4* edited by Dominique Maroger.

In the evening we went incognito to the Kremlin, an ancient castle which served as a residence of the Tsars. I was given a room at the top, so high that one could hardly see the people who walked at the foot of the wall.

The Grand Duke had shown some interest in me during my illness and continued to do so after I recovered. While he seemed to like me, I cannot say that I either liked or disliked him. I was taught to obey and it was my mother's business to see about my marriage, but to tell the truth I believe that the Crown of Russia attracted me more than his person. He was sixteen, quite good-looking before the pox, but small and infantile, talking of nothing but soldiers and toys. I listened politely and often yawned, but did not interrupt him and as he thought that he had to speak to me and referred only to the things which amused him, he enjoyed talking to me for long periods of time. Many people took this for affection, especially those who desired our marriage, but in fact we never used the language of tenderness. It was not for me to begin, for modesty and pride would have prevented me from doing so even if I had had any tender feelings for him; as for him, he had never even thought of it, which did not greatly incline me in his favour. Young girls may be as well brought up as you could wish, but they like sweet nonsense, especially from those from whom they can hear it without blushing.

The next day, St. Peter's Day, when my betrothal was to be celebrated, the Empress's portrait framed in diamonds was brought to me early in the morning, and shortly afterwards the portrait of the Grand Duke, also encircled with diamonds. Soon after, he came to take me to the Empress who, wearing her crown and Imperial mantle, proceeded on her way under a canopy of massive silver, carried by eight major-generals and followed by the Grand Duke and myself. After me came my mother, the Princess of Homburg, and the other ladies according to their rank. (From the moment of my conversion it was ordained that I should precede my mother, though I was not yet betrothed.) We descended the famous flight of stairs called Krassnoe Kriltso,* crossed the square and walked to the cathedral, the Guards regiments lining the road. The clergy received us according to custom. The Empress took the Grand Duke and myself by the hand and led us to a platform carpeted with velvet in the centre of the church where Archbishop Ambrose of Novgorod betrothed us, after which the Empress exchanged our rings – the one the Duke gave me cost twelve thousand roubles and the one I gave him fourteen thousand. Guns were fired after the service. At midday the Empress lunched with the Grand Duke and myself on the throne in the hall named Granovitaia Palata.†

* Palace and churches inside the enclosure of the Kremlin.
† Hall with facets. The walls are cut like diamonds or facets similar to the interior of a pomegranate.

[19] The Empress Elisabeth's transvestite balls, 1744; from *The Memoirs of Catherine the Great, 1743-4*, edited by Dominique Maroger.

The Court balls never numbered more than one hundred and fifty or two hundred people; those that were public numbered eight hundred.

In 1744 in Moscow, as I have already related, the Empress had a fancy to have all men appear at the Court balls dressed as women and the women as men, without masks; it was like a Court day metamorphosed. The men wore whaleboned petticoats, the women the Court costume of men. The men disliked these reversals of their sex and were in the worst possible humour, because they felt hideous in their disguises. The women looked like scrubby little boys, while the more aged had thick short legs which were anything but attractive. The only woman who looked really well and completely a man was the Empress herself. As she was tall and powerful, male attire suited her. She had the handsomest leg I have ever seen on any man and her feet were admirably proportioned. She dressed to perfection and everything she did had the same special grace whether she dressed as a man or as a woman. One felt inclined to look at her and turn away with regret because nothing could replace her.

At one of those balls, I watched her dance a minuet; after it was over she came up to me. I took the liberty of telling her that it was lucky for all women that she was not a man, for even a mere portrait made of her in that attire could turn the head of any woman. This compliment was expressed in full sincerity and she accepted it with grace, replying in the same tone and in the sweetest manner, that had she been a man, it would have been to me that she would have given the apple.

I bent down to kiss her hand for so unexpected a compliment; she kissed me and the rest of the company tried to discover what had taken place between the Empress and myself. I did not conceal it from Mme Choglokov, who whispered it to two or three others, so that it passed all round the room and within a quarter of an hour everybody knew about it.

[20] The coronation of Tsar Paul I in the Kremlin, 1797; from *La Cour et le Règne de Paul Ier* by Comte Feodor Golovkin.

(Count Feodor Golovkin (1766–1823) was sent to Berlin to study in 1778. He was an ADC to I.P. Saltykov in the Swedish Campaign, and then became Ambassador to Naples in 1794 for one year. In 1800 he was disgraced by Paul I. After Alexander I came to power, he left Russia for Paris. He was Master of Ceremonies at Court again in 1812.)

April 1: In the morning the Emperor brought the colours of the guards to the Kremlin, and came to live in this ancient palace.

April 2: Washing of the feet; preparation of the holy oils.

April 3: Rehearsal of the coronation ceremonies. The Emperor attended. This rehearsal was not the least piquant of the scenes we witnessed until exhausted by heat. The Emperor behaved like a child, delighted with the pleasures prepared for him, and with the docility you would expect of a child. It took a strong dose of fear or of caution not to allow anything more than surprise to show on one's face. In the afternoon he wanted a second rehearsal in the throne for the instruction of the Empress. When he told her to come and sit beside him on the dais, the Princess, either through ignorance or calculated modesty, took the side steps. But he said to her, 'Madam, that is not how one ascends a throne. Go back down and come up the front steps.' There was not a moment for simple and natural acts. From morning till night one was always in the presence, and as Moscow is enormous and all the members of the court lived very far from the Kremlin, no one had the physical time to absent himself. I know that, for myself, during the three days before the coronation I only had a few hours at night to rest, and the innumerable changes of clothes were performed in the corridors of the convent, or in the countless recesses of this ancient dwelling of the Tsars.

April 4: Their Imperial Majesties attended a Mass at the Tchoudov convent.

April 5: Easter and Coronation Day. Towards 8 o'clock the procession set out. The distance between the palace and the cathedral is so short, that to stretch it a little it went around the great belfry. The Emperor was in uniform and booted. The Empress wore cloth of silver embroidered with silver, and was bare-headed. The Emperor was attended by the two Grand Dukes, and the Empress by the Grand Chancellor and Marshal Count Saltikov.

The ceremony was long, and followed by a hundred others which the Emperor and the grand master of ceremonies invented according to their whim. After the coronation there was a dinner below the dais, during which we were ordered to curtsey like women, as one used to in France crossing the floor of the *Parlement* room. The dishes were brought by colonels accompanied by two horse-guards who presented arms when they were placed on the table. After dinner we had the ceremonial distribution of honours. These were truly princely. Count Bezborodko and the Princes Kourakin were given millions . . .

Annoyed that the ceremonies had come to an end, the Emperor invented such an indecent one that I was on the verge of requesting an audience to have it put off. It consisted in taking apart piece by piece the honours of the Empire before taking them back in a procession to the treasury. Their Majesties appeared in full order of coronation and seated themselves upon the throne. The grand officers removed successively the crowns, the sceptre, the orb, the necklaces of the order, the mantles. They were left there so denuded that in a rush of emotion, which I could not describe today, I found my eyes full of tears.

They had brought back great panniers for the ladies and taken away all the seats in the Kremlin apartment, and the Court was so overwhelmed by fatigue that one saw the great of the land, men and women, leaning against the walls with barely the strength to speak. On the last day I could not resist making a joke in the audience chamber. While we were waiting for Their Majesties to come out, I slid along the walls thus draped with people, bowing deeply and saying as

I did so, 'I flatter myself that I will not be seeing you again very soon.' If any one had dared to laugh in this court, it would have produced great guffaws, especially when Field-Marshal Repnin's wife said aloud with an icy expression, 'Just see how little one can trust court gossip. We had been assured that Count Golovkin was forbidden to make witticisms under His Majesty's reign.'

One thing one did not dare discuss during those days, but which could have profound results and gave cause for deep thought, was that the Emperor in his capacity as head of the church wanted to say Mass. Not daring to risk such a startling innovation in the heart of the capital, he decided to say the first in Kazan, where he was ready to go. Magnificent vestments were made. He felt sure he would establish himself as confessor to his family and ministers, but the Synod saved him from this absurdity with admirable presence of mind. At the Emperor's first mention of his plan, without showing the least surprise (and it was great) they told him that the canon of the Greek Church forbade the celebration of the Holy Mysteries by a priest who had remarried. As this had not occurred to him, and either he did not dare to or did not choose to alter the law of the priesthood, he had to give up the project. He contented himself by appearing at his devotions in a short crimson velvet dalmatic, all embroidered with pearls, which turned him into one of the most curious sights one could see, with his uniform, his boots, his long wig, his great three-cornered hat, and his puny figure. Having heard of this plan to officiate, and finding myself one morning in the Kremlin alone with Metropolitan Platon, I said to him, 'Your Excellency must be delighted, we have on the throne a highly religious prince.'

'Alas!'

'How is that, My Lord? Don't you believe in it?'

'How can I not believe it? But unfortunately his religion instead of being here,' putting his hand on his heart, 'is here,' putting his hand on his forehead.

Without denying the truth of this observation, it must be said in praise of Paul I that he had a great propensity for religion.

[21] The invasion by the French under Napoleon, 1812; from *Russian Heroic Poetry* by N. Kershaw.

It happened in the land of France,
Our dog of an enemy, King Napoleon, appeared.
He collected an army from various lands,
He loaded his galleys with various goods,
And these various goods were lead and powder;
And he wrote a dispatch to the Tsar Alexander;
'I beg you, Tsar Alexander, I beg you, do not be angry,
Prepare for me a lodging in the Kremlin of Moscow,
Prepare your royal palace for me, the French king'
The Tsar Alexander sat down in his chair to think it over,
The expression of his royal countenance changed;
Before him stood a general – Prince Kutuzov himself:
'Fear not, fear not, Tsar Alexander, do not be dismayed!
We will welcome him half-way, that dog of a foe.
We will prepare him delicacies of bombs and bullets,
As an entrée we will present him with deadly grapeshot,
So that his warriors will march home again under their
    banners'.
Then our Tsar Alexander rejoiced greatly,
The Tsar Alexander cried out and proclaimed in a loud voice:
'Exert yourselves to the utmost, you warrior Cossacks,
And I will richly reward your horsemen,
I will confer high rank upon your officers;
I will discharge you, my children, to the glorious silent Don'.

[22] The burning of the Kremlin, 15–16 September 1812; from *Memoirs of General de Caulaincourt, Duke of Vicenza, 1812–13* edited by Jean Hanoteau.

(Armand Augustin Louis de Caulaincourt (1773–1827) was a French diplomat, Grand Equerry to Napoleon from 1804 (and at his side during many of his battles), and later Napoleon's Foreign Minister. He had been to Russia in 1801–2, and had impressed Tsar Alexander I. From 1807–

11 he was France's Ambassador in Russia, working for peace – though in 1811 Napoleon upbraided him and accused him of being 'Russian'. He alone accompanied Napoleon in his sleigh on the retreat from Moscow to Paris. Alexander I saved him from proscription in 1815.)

At eight o'clock in the evening flames broke out in one of the suburbs. Assistance was sent, without more attention being paid to the matter, for it was still attributed to the carelessness of the troops.

The Emperor [Napoleon] retired early; everyone was fatigued and as anxious to rest as he was. At half-past ten my valet, an energetic fellow who had been in my service during my embassy to Petersburg, woke me up with the news that for three-quarters of an hour the city had been in flames. I had only to open my eyes to realize that this was so, for the fire was spreading with such fierceness that it was light enough to read in the middle of my room. I sprang from bed and sent to wake the Grand Marshal (Duroc) while I dressed. As the fire was spreading in the quarters farthest away from the Kremlin, we decided to send word to the Governor of the city, to put the Guard under arms, and to let the Emperor sleep a little longer, as he had been extremely tired during the past few days. I mounted my horse hurriedly to go and see what was happening and gather what assistance I could muster, and to make sure that the men connected with my own department, scattered throughout the city as they were, were running no hazards. A stiff wind was blowing from the north, from the direction of the two points of conflagration that we could see, and was driving the flames towards the centre, which made the blaze extraordinarily powerful. About half-past twelve [16 September] a third fire broke out a little to the west, and shortly afterwards a fourth, in another quarter, in each case in the direction of the wind, which had veered slightly towards the west. About four o'clock in the morning the conflagration was so widespread that we judged it necessary to wake the Emperor, who at once sent more officers to find out what was actually happening and discover whence these fires could be starting.

The troops were under arms; the few remaining inhabitants were flying from their houses and gathering in the churches; there was nothing to be heard but lamentation. Search had been made for the fire-engines since the previous day, but some of them had been taken away and the rest put out of action. From different houses officers and soldiers brought *boutechnicks* (street constables) and *moujiks* (peasants) who had been taken in the act of firing inflammable material into houses for the purpose of burning them down. The Poles reported that they had already caught some incendiaries and shot them, and they added, moreover, that from these men and from other inhabitants they had extracted the information that orders had been given by the governor of the city and the police that the whole city should be burned during the night . . .

The Emperor [Napoleon] was deeply concerned. At first he attributed the fire to disorders among the troops and the state in which the inhabitants had abandoned their dwellings. He could not persuade himself, as he said at Ghjat, that the Russians would deliberately burn their houses to prevent our sleeping in them. At the same time he made serious reflections on the possible consequences of these events for the army with regard to the resources of which they would deprive us. He could not believe that it was the result of a firm resolution and a great voluntary sacrifice. But the successive reports left no further doubt, and he renewed his orders to take every possible measure to stop the disaster and discover those who were carrying out these cruel measures.

Towards half-past nine he left the courtyard of the Kremlin on foot, just when two more incendiaries caught in the act were being brought in. They were in police uniform. Interrogated in the presence of the Emperor they repeated their declarations: that they had received the order from their commanding officer to burn everything, that houses had been designated for this end, that in the different quarters everything had been prepared for burning in accordance with orders from the Governor Rostopchin, as they had heard. The police officers had spread their men in small detachments in various quarters, and the order to put their instructions into action had been given in the evening of the previous day and confirmed by one of their officers on the following morning. They were reluctant to give the name of this officer, but at last one of them ended by declaring that the man concerned was a minor non-commissioned officer. They could not, or would not, indicate where he was at the moment, nor where he was to be found. Their replies were translated to the Emperor in the presence of his suite. Many other depositions confirmed unmistakably what they said. All the incendiaries were kept under observation, some were brought to judgment and eight or ten executed.

The conflagration invariably spread from the extremities of the district where it originated. It had already reached the houses around the Kremlin. The wind, which had veered slightly to the west, fanned the flames to a terrifying extent and carried enormous sparks to a distance, where they fell like a fiery deluge hundreds of yards away, setting fire to more houses and preventing the most intrepid from remaining in the neighbourhood. The air was so hot, and the pinewood sparks were so numerous, that the beams supporting the iron plates which formed the roof of the arsenal all caught fire. The roof of the Kremlin kitchen was only saved by the men placed there with brooms and buckets to gather up the glowing fragments and moisten the beams.* Only by super-human efforts was the fire in the Arsenal†

---

* 'Only a divine inspiration could save us. This it was which led a company of Grenadiers posted in this spot (the Lubianka) to seize buckets and pour water on the roofs of such houses as were most exposed to danger; and this with such promptness that they averted the attacks of the flames. This proved the salvation of the entire district, which was the only one left intact.' (Letter from the Abbé Surugue, curé de Saint-Louis at Moscow, quoted by Fain, *Manuscrit de 1812*, II, 87.)

† 'By noon the fire had enveloped the Palace stables and one tower contiguous to the Arsenal; sparks even fell in the courtyard of the Arsenal, on a pile of tow that had been used in the Russian ammunition wagons. The wagons of our own artillery were standing there. The danger was immense, and the Emperor was informed. He went to the spot.' (Fain, *Manuscrit de 1812*, II, 91.)

extinguished. The Emperor was there himself; his presence inspired the Guard* to every exertion.

I hastened to the Court stables, where some of the Emperor's horses were stabled and the coronation coaches of the Tsar were kept. The utmost zeal, and, I may add, the greatest courage on the part of the coachmen and grooms, were necessary to save the place; they clambered on to the roof, and knocked off the fallen cinders, whilst others worked two fire-engines which I had had put in order during the night, as they had been totally dismantled. I may say without exaggeration that we were working beneath a vault of fire. With these men's help I was able to save the beautiful Galitzin Palace and the two adjoining houses, which were already in flames. The Emperor's men were ably assisted by Prince Galitzin's servants, who displayed the utmost devotion to their master. Everyone did his best to further the measures we took to check this devouring torrent of flame, but the air was charged with fire; we breathed nothing but smoke, and the stoutest lungs felt the strain after a time. The bridge to the south of the Kremlin was so heated by the fire and the sparks falling on it that it kept bursting into flames, although the Guard, and the Sappers in particular, made it a point of honour to preserve it. I stayed with some generals of the Guard and aides-de-camp of the Emperor, and we were forced to lend a hand and stay in the midst of this deluge of fire in order to spur on these half-roasted men. It was impossible to stay more than a moment in one spot; the fur on the Grenadiers' caps was singed.

The fire made such progress that the whole of the northern and the greater part of the western quarter, by which we had entered, were burned, together with the splendid playhouse and all the larger buildings. One breathed in a sea of fire, and the westerly wind continued to blow. The flames spread continuously; it was impossible to predict where or

* 'The gunners and soldiers of the Guard, apprehensive at seeing Napoleon expose himself to such great danger, only added to it by their eagerness; General Lariboisière begged the Emperor to go away, pointing out to him that his presence was making the gunners lose their heads.' (Fain, *Manuscrit de* 1812, II, 91.)

when they would stop, as there was no means of staying them. The conflagration passed beyond the Kremlin; it seemed that the river would surely save all the district lying to the east.

About four o'clock in the afternoon, while the fire was still raging, the Emperor began to think that this great catastrophe might be connected with some movement of the enemy,* though the frequent reports from the King of Naples assured His Majesty that the Russians were pushing forward their retreat along the Kasan road. Napoleon therefore gave orders to leave the city, and forbade anything to be left within its walls. Headquarters were established at the Petrowskoie Palace, on the Petersburg road, a country mansion where the Tsars were accustomed to take up residence before making their solemn entry into Moscow for their coronation. It was impossible to proceed thither by the direct road on account of the fire and the wind; one had to cross the western part of the town as best one could, through ruins, cinders, flames even, if one wanted to reach the outskirts.† Night had already fallen when we got there, and we spent the following day in the Palace.

* According to Gourgaud (*Napoléon et la Grande Armée*, 278), Napoleon's decision was taken after Berthier had made this remark: 'Sire, if the enemy attacks the army corps outside Moscow, Your Majesty has no means of communicating with them.'

† Denniée (*Itinéraire*, 95) thus describes the Emperor's departure: 'The Emperor gave orders for the departure. He slowly came down the stairs of the tower of Ivan (whence he had watched the fire) followed by the Prince of Neuchatel and other of his officers. Leaning on the arm of the Duke of Vicenza, he crossed a little wooden bridge which led to the Quay of the Moskowa. There he found his horses.' Ségur (*Histoire de Napoléon*, II, 52) says that: 'After some gropings a small gate was found which opened on to the Moskowa' and he continues with a dramatic recital of the dangers to which Napoleon was exposed on the way. Gourgaud (*Napoléon et la Grande Armée*, 278) contradicts Ségur's account and says that: 'The Emperor left by one of the great doors of the Kremlin, accompanied by his officers, in the same manner as he had arrived, and did not go out across the rocks. He descended on to the Moskowa quay, where he mounted his horse. One of the policemen of Moscow walked in front of him, serving as guide. For some time they followed the river and entered the districts where the wooden buildings had been completely destroyed.' According to the *Itinéraire des Archives de Caulaincourt*: 'The 16th September. At half-past five in the evening the Emperor left the palace of the Kremlin on foot by the gate on the river-side, mounted *Tauris* at the stone bridge, cont'd/

[23] The coronation of Nicholas I, 1826; from
Original Letters from Russia, 1825–1828, edited by
Charlotte Disbrowe.

(Lady Disbrowe was the wife of Edward Cromwell Disbrowe, a successful British diplomat. In 1825 he was appointed British Minister Plenipotentiary to the Russian
Court, in the absence of the Ambassador. He arrived in
St Petersburg in April, and was followed in June by Mrs
Disbrowe and her father and brother John. They remained
in Russia until 1828. Charlotte, their eldest daughter, published her parents' letters from Russia in a private edition in
1878, and incorporated them in a new volume in 1903.)

At half-past seven this morning the Corps Diplomatique
assembled in the ancient Palace of the Tsars, in a low hall
whose walls were covered with gilding and saints at full
length.

Monday. The above showed my good intentions, not a
line farther could I proceed, what with the chattering around
me and the fatigue I could not overcome . . . But no more
egotism, let us talk only of yesterday's glorious spectacle, it
was at once a magnificent and interesting sight, splendour
and feeling combined, a rare occurrence. The procession
began to enter the Cathedral of the Assumption about half-
past eight o'clock, the Empress mother opened it and took
her seat upon a small throne entirely covered with turquoise,
and under a canopy to the right of the Emperor's. It must
have been a trying moment for her, this is the third time she
has performed in a coronation. The procession was composed of the several Imperial establishments, deputations
from the provinces and of the merchants, the general officers, etc., etc., and clergy. The Emperor was attended by his
two brothers, the Grand Dukes Constantine and Michel,
and the Emperor and Empress were seated on great chairs

† *cont'd*   took the road for Mojaisk in the midst of the fire, re-crossed
the river at a league from the city in order to reach the Palace of
Petrowskoie. Arrived at half-past seven. To bed.'

yclept thrones, under a canopy, the Great Officers of State arranged on either side of them, the Grand Dukes close to the thrones, the Corps Diplomatique stood on the left on raised benches by the wall of the building, the ladies of the Court were on the opposite side; the thrones of course faced the High Altar, where stood the Priests magnificently habited. The ceremony began by music, which was quite divine, the Archimandrite or Archbishop then approached the Emperor and read him a long exhortation in very good Slavonic or Russe, I know not which, H. I. M. then took another book and also read aloud, this I conclude were his promises to be good, his brothers and other dignitaries then invested him with the Imperial Mantle. Here began Constantine's fine part, placing his younger brother in his own stead, voluntarily resigning to him that Imperial sway to which he himself had so just a right, performing the duties of a subject in a manner that showed he was one of his own free will, and apparently happy in so doing. It was very fine indeed, and is I believe an unparalleled trait in history. In appearance he is greatly inferior to the Emperor, being short, thick, and *sans trancher le mot*, remarkably ugly, with a most disagreeble expression of countenance, quite a caricature of the Emperor Alexander; but his want of beauty does not militate against his noble conduct, for which we must give him full credit. When the mantle was arranged the priest presented the crown to the Emperor, who took it and placed it on his own head, he then bent over the Bible and the Archbishop prayed over him. The Empress mother now approached and embraced her son; this was quite affecting, for Imperial dignity and grandeur seemed forgotten, and it looked like the happy union of a domestic circle, the Grand Dukes and the Little Hereditary Prince followed, and the Emperor seemed quite overcome with emotion. The young Empress now approached and knelt before the Emperor, who removed the crown from his own head and placed it upon hers for a few seconds, he then resumed it and put a smaller one on her head, which four Ladies of Honour advanced to fasten on, she was next invested with an

Imperial *Mantle*, the Emperor then raised and embraced her, and she received the felicitations of the Empress mother and the Grand Dukes, they both descended to the altar and received the Sacrament, after which the Archbishop delivered an extemporary discourse, prayers and psalms were sung. The whole lasted about three hours and a half; it had been curtailed on the Empress's account, otherwise it would have been much longer. It was delightful to see the Emperor's solicitude about the Empress, he looked round to see how she was every five minutes, and insisted upon her sitting down almost the whole time. She looked fatigued, but seemed to bear it very well altogether, she wore nothing on her head but her pretty little crown, and her hair was arranged in a profusion of curls and long ringlets hanging to her shoulders . . .

It is impossible to describe the spectacle that presented itself on the exterior of the Cathedral, the immense crowds of people that were assembled and arranged on raised benches to a great height. It was quite beautiful, even the sky seemed to be crowded with spectators, for some of the scaffolding was raised to the steeples. Only the two first classes were admitted into the Cathedral, and therefore this crowd on the exterior was remarkably elegant, being chiefly composed of the nobility of the other classes. The Cathedral I believe I have already described, it looked very handsome when lighted up, but its chief ornament is the gilding; neither the paintings nor the architecture are fine, and it is extremely small. Everything was so well arranged yesterday that it was neither too crowded nor too warm . . .

In the evening the Kremlin and public buildings were most beautifully illuminated, the steeples and towers of the churches, the gateways and walls seemed as if they were made of light, the outlines of the architecture and forms were so well traced out. I never saw anything to equal it either in extent or execution; it was all done in the style of the illumination of the capital, everything in yellow lamps but the great Ivan Veliky Tower, which was lighted to the cross in dark colours.

[24] The end of Pushkin's exile in 1826; Nicholas I pardons him; from *Pushkin* by Ernest J. Simmons.

> No, I don't flatter when in free
> Praise of the tsar I use my art.
>
> *Stanzas*

Still in his dirty travelling clothes, Pushkin entered the Kremlin and was closeted with the Tsar of all the Russias, a man only three years older than himself. There have been many accounts of this famous interview, which lasted over an hour, but the true story was never told in detail by either of the principals. In the excitement of the occasion Pushkin forgot much that took place. Some shreds of the conversation have been handed down as reported by the poet and the tsar, and hence have gained a certain authenticity. The room was cold, and Pushkin stood with his back to the stove, warming his feet while he spoke to the emperor, a breach of etiquette which seemed to annoy Nicholas. The tsar is credited with saying:

'You hate me because I have crushed the party to which you belonged. But, believe me, I also love Russia, I am no enemy to the Russian people; I desire its freedom, but first it must be strengthened.'

Nicholas asked him if he were not a friend of many of the conspirators who had been sent to Siberia.

'It is true, Sire,' Pushkin answered. 'I loved and esteemed many of them, and I continue to nourish the same feeling for them.'

Then Nicholas inquired: 'What would you have done if you had been in Petersburg on the fourteenth of December?'

'I should have been in the ranks of the rebels,' Pushkin frankly answered.

This well-known reply, which neither the tsar nor the poet ever denied, ought to set at rest any doubt concerning Pushkin's real sympathy for the cause of the Decembrists. According to Baron Korf, Nicholas also said:

'To my question of whether or not he would change his

form of thought and give me his word to think and act otherwise, he replied with many compliments about the 14th of December, but he hesitated for some time to make a direct answer, and only after a long silence did he extend his hand with the promise to behave differently.'

Upon being questioned about his writing, Pushkin complained of difficulties with the censor, and the tsar said: 'You will send me everything you write; from now on I will be your censor.'

Nicholas finally informed Pushkin that he was free, free to go wherever he wished in the empire, with the exception of Petersburg. A special permission was required to visit this city. At the conclusion of the interview the tsar is reported to have led the poet into an adjoining room filled with courtiers. 'Gentlemen,' he said, 'here is the new Pushkin for you; let us forget about the old Pushkin.' The poet left the palace with tears in his eyes.

Pushkin's exile was over. He hurried to uncle Vasili's house to break the joyful news. From all accounts he conducted himself well in this audience. As a private citizen he had preserved his dignity before his sovereign and had said nothing of which he was ever ashamed. Apparently Nicholas himself had been much impressed. That evening at a ball given by the French ambassador, he remarked to one of his generals concerning Pushkin: 'Do you know, today I talked for a long time with the most intelligent man in Russia.'

The happy outcome of the interview had not been anticipated in the least by Pushkin. A curious fact indicates that he had been prepared for the worst. Either on the road to Moscow, or shortly before this, he had composed four incomplete verses which may have been intended as a concluding quatrain to *The Prophet*. One tradition maintains that he lost them on the palace stairs and found them upon leaving the Kremlin. Later he destroyed the manuscript. The story goes that if the tsar had decided to punish him further, Pushkin had planned to hand him the following verses as a last gesture of farewell:

Arise, arise, O Russian prophet,
And in thy vestments now dishonored,
Around thy humbled neck a halter,
To the tsar . . . appear!

[25] The Kremlin as seen by a British naval captain; from *Narrative of a Visit to the Courts of Russia and Sweden in the Years 1830 and 1831* by Captain C. Colville Frankland, RN.

(Charles Colville Frankland (1797–1876) entered the navy in 1813, was made captain in 1841 and retired as admiral in 1875. He published a book of his travels to Constantinople in 1829, and this narrative of his visit to Russia and Sweden in 1832.)

After dinner I visited all the churches of the Kremlin, beginning with the Cathedral of the Assumption, (Ouspenskoï.) This is a very curious and interesting church, of I know not what style of architecture, but partaking of the Norman, Saxon, Byzantine, and Lombard. Its interior is decorated with very curious old frescoes, which are valuable, not for their intrinsic merit, but inasmuch as they show what was the state of the art of painting in 1475, or rather in 1514, when the church was decorated by the Tsar Vassili Ivanovitch. This cathedral boasts of a Virgin ('but well I wot the only virgin there,') painted by St Luke, (the sweet physician,) – the said St Luke could have hardly had time to paint all the pictures, bad as they are, attributed to him, and to write his Gospel into the bargain. This black ill-looking idol is decorated with a superb solitaire, valued at 80,000 roubles: the frame containing her ladyship's portrait is estimated at 200,000 more. Money badly spent, thought I.

There are so many holy pictures of Saints, Martyrs, & c. here, miraculous as well as ludicrous, that I cannot attempt to name them. This church contains the tombs of the Patriarchs, and abundance of highly venerated relics. *C'est un triste sort que celui d'un Saint*; he is not permitted to rest quietly in his tomb, but is exposed to the gazings, and mouthings, and mumblings of *devóts* of all ages, classes and sexes, from the rising up of the sun until the going down of the same. The Iconostase, or Holy of Holies, is resplendent with gold and silver, and magnificence. It contains inestimable riches, consisting of ornaments belonging to the Patriarchate and priesthood, and to the divine service; besides which, are various valuable presents made to the church, and abundance of relics, by Tzars and nobles. The silver lamps alone in this cathedral are said to weigh 8 poods. The Iconostase contains 50 poods more silver.

2nd. The Cathedral of the Annunciation, founded in 1397, rebuilt in 1489, finished by Aleviso in 1507, repaired by Peter the Great, and brushed up by Catharine II in 1770; it is also ornamented with curious frescoes, among which are the heads of heathen philosophers. The Iconostase dazzles the eyes with gilded silver. This church contains a great variety of musty and disgusting relics set in silver frames, which the deluded and absured people were kissing with great veneration. Independently of these spiritual riches, the temporal of the church amount to 2 poods, 5 pounds, 2 zolotniks of gold, and 34 poods of silver.

3rd. The Cathedral of the Archangel Michael, founded in 1333, in commemoration of a famine, contains the tombs of the Grand Princes and Tzars up to Peter I ranged in battle-array all round its interior. Here are likewise the relics of St Michael of Tchernigoff, and of St Dimitri of Ouglich.

4th. The Church of the Saviour in the Woods is a curious old specimen of Muscovite architecture. It contains the relics of St Stephen of Perme. It was founded in 1330.

5th. The Monastery and Church of Tchoudoff, founded in 1365. Here the Grand-Duke Vassili Vassiliévitch shut up the metropolitan Isidore, who was upon the point of making common cause with the Western Church, by acknowledging the supremacy of the Pope. Here are a few relics of saints, &c. and a great many Persian banners captured by Yermoloff and Paskewitch.

6th. The Church of the Nunnery of Vossnassenié. Here I saw all the nuns, and d–d ugly they were.* They looked like travestied men. Nothing can be more unbecoming than their high black cap, shaped like the helmet of the infantry of the feudal times; and their long, slovenly, black and dirty gown, or rather coat.

[26] The Kremlin as seen by the Marquis de Custine; from *The Empire of the Czar* . . . by the Marquis de Custine.

(Astolphe, Marquis de Custine (1790–1857) served as a young man as an aide to Talleyrand at the Congress of Vienna. His father and grandfather were both guillotined in the French Revolution. Though conventionally married, his tastes were homosexual, and a major scandal in 1824, when he was beaten up in an unsavoury robbery, always affected his reputation, so that he was excluded from smart French society. He turned as consolation to travel, literature and religion. Widowed in 1823, he found a charming (male) companion to share his life, and was a friend of Chopin, Balzac and other Romantic stars. Heine cuttingly called him a '*demi-homme de lettres*', which does not do justice

* The morals of the cloister are said to be dreadfully depraved; I hear of things so grossly licentious, that I can with difficulty attach credit to them. I must here observe, that the nuns in Russia are not confined to the convent, excepting at night, so that they have abundance of opportunity for depravity. The young Russ seigneurs of my acquaintance assure me, that the convents are complete bagnios, and that the favours of any particular nun may be had for asking. I am more especially informed of a convent in the neighbourhood of the famous Pilgrimage of Troitza. To this convent a post-house and inn is attached; *les bonnes religieuses* think it, no doubt, quite right to do nothing by halves, and that they should contribute their utmost efforts to the consolation, bodily as well as spiritual, of the weary pilgrims. I have a great mind to make the pilgrimage on purpose to verify the fact. If, however, the sisterhood be as ill-favoured as that of the Vossnassenié, I may as well remain at Moscow. Shall I be believed in England if I even prove the truth of these stories?

The conventual regulations and vocations in Russia, totally differ from those in Papal Europe.

to his famous (and in Russia notorious) book, *Russie en 1839.*)

The fear of a man possessing absolute power is the most dreadful thing upon earth; and with all the imagery of this fear visible in the Kremlin, it is still impossible to approach the fabric without a shudder.

Towers of every form, round, square, and with pointed roofs, belfries, donjons, turrets, spires, sentryboxes upon minarets, steeples of every height, style and colour, palaces, domes, watch-towers, walls embattlemented and pierced with loopholes, ramparts, fortifications of every species, whimsical inventions, incomprehensible devices, chiosks by the side of cathedrals – every thing announces violation and disorder, every thing betrays the continual *surveillance* necessary to the security of the singular beings who were condemned to live in this supernatural world. Yet these innumerable monuments of pride, caprice, voluptuousness, glory, and piety, notwithstanding their apparent variety, express one single idea which reigns here everywhere – such is the allegory figured by this satanic monument, as extraordinary in architecture as the visions of St John are in poetry. It is a habitation which would suit some of the personages of the Apocalypse.

In vain is each turret distinguished by its peculiar character and its particular use; all have the same signification, – terror armed.

Some resemble the caps of priests, others the mouth of a dragon, others swords, their points in the air, others the forms and even the colours of various exotic fruits; some again represent a head-dress of the czars, pointed, and adorned with jewels like that of the Doge of Venice; others are simple crowns: and all this multitude of towers of glazed tiles, of metallic cupolas, of enamelled, gilded, azured, and silvered domes, shine in the sun like the colossal stalactites of the salt-mines in the neighbourhood of Cracow. These enormous pillars, these towers and turrets of every shape, pointed, pyramidical, and circular, but always in some manner suggesting the idea of the human form, seem to

reign over the city and the land. To see them from afar
shining in the sky, one might fancy them an assembly of
potentates, richly robed and decorated with the insignia of
their dignity, a meeting of ancestral beings, a council of
kings, each seated upon his tomb; spectres hovering over the
pinnacles of a palace. To inhabit a place like the Kremlin is
not to reside, it is to defend one's self. Oppression creates
revolt, revolt obliges precautions, precautions increase dangers, and this long series of actions and reactions engenders
a monster; that monster is despotism, which has built itself a
house at Moscow. The giants of the antediluvian world,
were they to return to earth to visit their degenerate successors, might still find a suitable habitation in the Kremlin.

Every thing has a symbolical sense, whether purposely or
not, in its architecture; but the real, the abiding, that appears
after you have divested yourself of your first emotions in the
contemplation of these barbaric splendours, is, after all,
only a congregation of dungeons pompously surnamed
palaces and cathedrals. The Russians may do their best,
but they can never come out of the prison.

The very climate is an accomplice of tyranny. The cold of
the country does not permit the construction of vast
churches, where the faithful would be frozen at prayer: here
the soul is not lifted to heaven by the glories of religious
architecture; in this zone man can only build to his God
gloomy donjons. The sombre cathedrals of the Kremlin,
with their narrow vaults and thick walls, resemble caves;
they are painted prisons, just as the palaces are gilded gaols.

[27] The Treasury; from *The Empire of the Czar*
. . . by the Marquis de Custine.

At last I summoned courage to face the Corinthian columns
of the Treasury; so braving with closed eyes those dragons
of bad taste, I entered the glorious arsenal, where are
ranged, as in a cabinet of curiosities, the most interesting
historical relics of Russia.

What a collection of armour, of vases, and of national jewels! What profusion of crowns and of thrones, all gathered into the same place! The manner in which they are arranged adds to the effect. It is impossible not to admire the good taste as well as the political wisdom which has presided over the disposition of so many insignia and trophies. The display may be a little boastful, but patriotic pride is the most legitimate of any. We forgive a passion which aids us in fulfilling our duties. There is here a profound idea, of which the things are but symbols.

The crowns are placed on cushions raised upon pedestals, and the thrones, ranged along the wall, are reared in separate alcoves. There is wanting only in this evocation of the past, the presence of the men for whom all these things were made. Their absence is equivalent to a sermon on the vanity of human life. The Kremlin without its Czars is like a theatre without lights or actors.

The most respect-worthy, if not the most imposing of the crowns, is that of Monomachus; it was brought from Byzantium to Kiew in 1116. Another crown is also said to have belonged to Monomachus, though many consider it yet more ancient than the reign of that prince. In this royal constellation of diadems, are crowns also of the kingdoms of Kazan, Astrachan, and Georgia. The view of these satellites of royalty, maintaining a respectful distance from the star that governs all – the imperial crown – is singularly imposing. Everything is emblematic in Russia: it is a poetical land – poetical as sorrow! What are more eloquent than the tears that fall internally and gather upon the heart? The crown of Siberia is found among the rest. It is an imaginary insignia of Russian manufacture, deposited as though to point out a grand historical fact, accomplished by commercial adventures and soldiers under the reign of Ivan IV, an epoch from whence dates, not exactly the discovery, but the conquest of Siberia. All these crowns are covered with the most enormous and the most costly jewels in the world. The bowels of this land of desolation have been opened to furnish a food for the pride of that despotism of which it is the asylum!

The throne and crown of Poland help to enrich the superb imperial and royal galaxy. So many jewels, enclosed in a small space, blazed in my eyes like the train of a peacock. What sanguinary vanity! I muttered to myself, at each new marvel before which my guides forced me to stop.

The crowns of Peter I, of Catherine I, and of Elizabeth, particularly struck me: – what gold! – what diamonds! – and what dust!! Imperial orbs, thrones, and sceptres – all brought together to attest the grandeur of things, the noth-ingness of men!

Vases chased in the style of Benvenuto Cellini, cups enriched with jewels, arms and armour, precious stuffs, rich embroideries, costly crystal ware of all lands and all ages, abound in this wonderful collection, of which a real curioso would not complete the inventory in a week. Besides the thrones of all the Russian princes of every age, I was shown the caparisons of their horses, their dress, their furniture; and these various things perfectly dazzled my eyes. The palace in the Arabian Nights is the only picture I can suggest that will give an idea of this marvellous, if not enchanted abode. But here, the interest of history adds to the effect of the magnificence. How many curious events are pictur-esquely registered and attested by the venerable relics! From the finely-worked helmet of Saint Alexander Newski to the litter which carried Charles XII at Pultawa, each object recalls an interesting recollection, or a singular fact. The Treasury is the true album of the giants of the Kremlin . . .

If I were ever to see the throne of Russia majestically replaced upon its true basis, in the centre of the empire, at Moscow; if St Petersburg, its stuccoes and gilt work, left to crumble in the marsh whereon it is reared, were to become only what it should have always been, a simple naval port, built of granite, a magnificent entrepôt of commerce be-tween Russia and the West, as, on the other side, Kazan and Nijni serve as steps between Russia and the East; I should say that the Slavonian nation, triumphing by a just pride over the vanity of its leaders, sees at length its proper course, and deserves to attain the object of its ambition. Constantinople waits for it; there arts and riches will naturally flow, in recompense of the efforts of a people, called to be so much the more great and glorious as they have been long obscure and resigned.

The Emperor Nicholas, notwithstanding his practical sense and his profound sagacity, has not discerned the best means of accomplishing such an end. He comes now and then to promenade in the Kremlin; but this is not sufficient. He ought to have recognized the necessity of permanently fixing himself there: if he has recognized it, he has not had the energy to make such a sacrifice, – this is his error. Under Alexander, the Russians burnt Moscow to save the Empire: under Nicholas, God burnt the palace of Petersburg to advance the destinies of Russia; but Nicholas does not answer to the call of Providence. Russia still waits!

[28] The Kremlin as seen by the Earl of Mayo; from *St Petersburg and Moscow, A Visit to the Court of the Czar* by Richard Southwell Bourke, 6th Earl of Mayo.

(Richard Southwell Bourke (1822–1872) was educated at Trinity College, Dublin, and his tour of Russia took place in 1845. In the late 1840s he entered politics, eventually becoming Viceroy and Governor General of India. He was assassinated while on a visit to a convict prison, and was mourned by the Establishment as a great statesman.)

The interior of the Kremlin, therefore, differs in nothing, save a little irregularity, from the new streets of the restored town. But the finishing stroke to this incongruity of style, so ill-befitting the sacred ground whereon these modern innovations stand, is the new palace, now rising on the site of the ancient habitation of the Czars. It is an enormous pile, without the smallest pretensions to architectural beauty, and looks more like a Manchester cotton factory than the Imperial residence of the sacred Kremlin.

How the Russian committee of taste could have induced themselves to set up an eye-sore of such gigantic proportions on so holy a spot, can only be conceived by those who have mused upon the edifices of Trafalgar Square. They might have left the old palace as it was: but if an Imperial residence was wanting in Moscow, and it was necessary that it should stand on this place, with the talent for imitation that the Russians are known to possess, why not have copied the Alhambra in the courts of the Kremlin?

In the interior of this renowned fortress, therefore, thanks to the outrageous taste of the Russian architects of latter years, we found nothing to impress our minds with reverence or awe, save the memories of the past; but they fortunately could not remove by brick and plaster imitations of Grecian porticoes and antique façades, the glorious and unequalled view from the terrace.

[29] The *entrée joyeuse* into the Kremlin of Tsar Alexander II after his coronation; from *Letters from Russia* by Field-Marshal Count Helmuth von Moltke.

(Helmuth Carl Berhard, Count von Moltke (1800–1891) was a Prussian field-marshal, for thirty years Chief of Staff of the Prussian army, and the greatest strategist of the second half of the nineteenth century. He was the victor of Koniggratz in 1866, and of the Franco-Prussian war. A taciturn linguist, 'silent in seven languages', he was also a writer, publishing (among other things) essays on Belgium, Holland and Poland, and a translation of Gibbon's *Decline and Fall*. He visited Moscow for the coronation of Alexander II, accompanying Prince Frederick William.)

As we approached the Kremlin, the guns thundered from every tower, and the great '*John*' expressed his joy by ringing all the *Kolokols*, which hang around him. Then the great Wetschewoi boomed which had once called the warlike population to arms, in the time of the great Republic of Novgorod, when the Muscovite grand-dukes threatened their freedom, and then there was a booming, and a tinkling, and a humming of all the bells, large and small, far and near, with which Ivan keeps high festival.

Only one bell remains dumb, as in joy or sorrow it has been dumb since the first day of its existence. It stands on a layer of granite, at the foot of the great tower, a house of brass with walls two feet thick. A piece which came out in the casting lies there before it, and leaves a free entrance through which the twenty or thirty men can pass whom this ruined bell can comfortably accommodate.

Before the outer gate of the Kremlin, in a beautiful little chapel, is the image of the Iberian *Boshja matter'*, which is so much venerated that hardly the busiest tradesman passes it by without entering for a moment and crossing himself.

Here the Emperor descended from his horse, and went in to pay his devotions. The whole suite, however, rode through the gate, and marched in front of the wall of the Kremlin on to the great open space, Krasnoj Ploschtschad. The Czar quickly rejoined us, and we all went through the *Redeemer's* door, the sacred *spass woroto*, into the inner court.

Through this door no Russian, and indeed no stranger, passes without uncovering – the highest personage and the lowest alike testify their respect for this miraculous picture of the Saviour. In time past, when the Tartars attacked the Kremlin, such a mist came forth from the picture, that they were unable to find the entrance; and when the French wished to destroy the gate with the arsenal, the tower was cracked all the way down to the crystal plate of the picture, which remained unhurt, and held the whole wall together.

On the other side of the door we dismounted, very well pleased to get out of the crowd of loose horses and stand quietly on the red carpet to await the arrival of the Empresses and the grand duchesses. First came the Empress' mother, and then the reigning Empress in a dress of gold brocade and ermine. The *manteaux* of the grand duchesses were of velvet or lace with gold and pearls. All the ladies of the court wore the national costume, which you know is of scarlet velvet.

Their Majesties now went in solemn procession to Uspenski Sabor, the Church of the Redemption, the veritable cathedral before which the superior clergy awaited the Emperor. This church, in which the coronation takes place, and in which the Patriarchs are buried, is like all Russian churches, extremely rich, but narrow and dark. The great thick pillars take up half the space; the windows are small and deep; the cupolas high and narrow like towers. All the walls and pillars are gilded from top to bottom, and on this gold ground the peculiar, long drawn, often quite distorted, pictures of the saints are painted. Frightful mosaic pictures look down from the cupola above, amongst others one of an old man with a gray beard, which can be no one else but God the Father Himself. I pass over the enormous treasures of gold, silver, and jewels, with which the pictures of the saints are covered, and only notice the book of the gospels of Natalie Narischkin, which was presented by the mother of Peter the Great. The binding is of gold, and is worth a million of roubles. The book has to be carried by two priests, because it is too heavy for one.

The Emperor performed his devotions before the principal images of the saints. He knelt down quite close to me, crossed himself, and kissed the relics. The Empress followed with her long train carried by two pages, and did the same.

The Court of the Redeemer is shut off by a beautiful trellis, and is, except a part of the old palace of the Czars, entirely surrounded by churches, which contain the most sacred relics of Russia. A shorter procession led their Majesties and their whole retinue into Archangelski Sabor, the Church of the Archangel Michael, which contains the graves of all the Czars till the first Emperor, then into Blagowestschenki, or the Church of the Annunciation, which is narrower, more peculiar, and more gorgeous than all the others. It is a perfect little jewel-box. The cross and cupola are of pure gold, and the pavement is inlaid with jasper, agate, and cornelian, from Siberia.

Everywhere the Emperor was received with the wonderful Russian church-melodies, and now that he had given glory to God, the whole splendid procession passed down the open steps, Krasnoi Kryltzo, which were covered with scarlet cloth, to the old Palace of the Czars, which directly communicates with the magnificent rooms of the new palace built by the Emperor Alexander. Then we went through the enormous St George's Hall, whose walls bear the names of all the knights of St George, to St Andrew's Hall, which is like the nave of an old Gothic cathedral, and St Nicolas' Hall, at the end of which is the throne itself. In the midst of the imperial escutcheons are to be seen the family arms of the Romanow and the Duke of Holstein, the two cross-beams of Oldenburg, the lion of Norway, the nettle leaf of Holstein, the lion of Schleswig, and others. And so at last we came once more to the Imperial residence, whose *comfortable* magnificence we had already seen, and at six o'clock, all the ceremonies being concluded, we hastened home to our well-earned dinner in Princess Trubetzkois' house.

[30] A banquet for the Prince of Wales given by the Governor-General of Moscow; from *A Month in Russia during the Marriage of the Czarevitch* [Alexander Alexandrovitch] by Edward Dicey.

(Edward James Stephen Dicey (1832–1911) was an author and journalist, and as leader writer of the *Daily Telegraph* he wrote accounts of visits to America, Russia, Italy, the Holy Land, and Egypt. He was editor of the *Observer* 1867–70, and was called to the bar in 1875. He greatly influenced public opinion by his knowledge, humour, judgement and vivid style.)

Not the least interesting of the many sights of Moscow was that of the guns captured from the *Grande Armée* in 1812, which are all arranged in the courtyard of the Kremlin. 365 French, 189 Austrian, 123 Prussian, 70 Italian, 34 Bavarian,

40 Neapolitan, 22 Dutch, and 5 Polish guns, make up the long muster-roll of 848 guns.

After the stock sights had been seen, the Prince [of Wales] went through the bazaars, where he made some purchases, and looked in at the great Moskovski Traktir, the tea-mart restaurant of Moscow. All day long the Royal party was followed by a mob of idlers, who never seemed to grow tired of staring at the Prince. Even the sealskin pea-jacket which his Royal Highness wore was an object of never-failing curiosity on the part of the bystanders. The short winter day was soon over, and it was dark before the royal sight-seers got back to the Kremlin. At seven the Princes, with their suites, were to dine with Prince Dolgorouki, the Governor-General of Moscow. The Russians may be bar-barians; but if so, barbarians understand hospitality far better than civilized nations. Everybody who was in any way connected with the Royal party had lodgings provided for him in the Kremlin; and the authorities went out of their way to show civility to any Englishman who happened to be passing through Moscow on the occasion of the Prince's visit. The expense incurred in entertaining the Royal visitors must have been considerable. On the Prince's arrival at the Kremlin, the halls were lighted up with 9,000 wax candles to receive him as he passed along, and everything was con-ducted on the same scale of lavish liberality.

Anything more gorgeous of its kind than the Governor's banquet it has never been my lot to witness. On arriving at the palace, I was shown up a broad flight of stairs, decked out with flowers blazing with light and colour. Footmen, clad in rich red liveries, stood upon every step, bowing their powdered heads as the guests came following each other. At the doorway stood Prince Dolgorouki, shaking hands with each new comer, and addressing to each a few civil words in French. A long suite of rooms, lighted with endless chande-liers, hung with yellow damask, were thrown open to the guests, who strolled up and down them at their leisure. The square in front of the palace was illuminated with the electric light; and from between the window curtains you could look out on the great snow-covered space, and on the strange masses of fur-clad spectators, flitting to and fro from out the deep shadows into the dazzling spots of light. Soon after seven there was a stir in the rooms, and the Royal visitors made their entrance, being received in the same manner as the ordinary guests. Then servants entered the room, bearing trays loaded with liqueur bottles. For those who were ready to accommodate themselves to Muscovite customs, there were also plates of caviar, smoked herrings, and cheese. Then the band struck up 'God save the Queen', the folding doors were thrown open, and the company entered the banqueting hall. At the cross table facing the doorway, the royal guests took their seats, the Prince of Wales sitting on the right hand of Prince Dolgorouki; the side tables were reserved for persons not belonging to the staff of the Princes who seated themselves wherever they thought fit. In all there were about a hundred persons present. In the galleries looking over the hall there were numbers of ladies, but at the tables there were none. The *menu* of the dinner – precisely as I received it – was as follows:

DINER DU 4–16 NOVEMBRE, 1866. – Potages: Chasseur à l'Anglaise; consommé aux légumes. Hors-d'oeuvre: Petits vol-au-vent à la Marinière; Petites bouchées à la Reine. Relevés: Esturgeons à la Russe; Faisans à la Vallière. Entrées: Poulets à la Villeroi; Crême de gélinottes aux truffes. Punch. Rôt: Cailles, perdreaux, chapons; Salade aux concombres frais. Entremets: Asperges en branches et petits pois à la Parisienne; pain de fruits à la Béarnaise; glaces à la Napolitaine.

Looking on the question after the fumes of the wines and viands have passed away, I can truly say that never, even at a private house, do I remember to have had a better dinner. Where everything was good, it is invidious to select articles for praise. But the 'crême de gélinottes aux truffes' (gélinotte is a sort of Russian partridge) was one of those dishes you think of after they have been eaten and digested; and

asparagus in the month of November, as fine and as large as
you would get it in London in June, is a thing to reflect upon.
Every moment the servants behind your chair kept placing
fresh filled glasses before you. I counted thirteen different
sorts of wines, not to mention liqueurs. All were good; the
Château d'Iquem and the red Burgundy perhaps the best.
The champagne, like all Russian champagne I have yet
drunk, was too sweet for English taste; that, however, is
a matter of detail. But excellent as the dinner was, the
splendour of the appointments struck me even more for-
cibly. Massive gold forks and spoons, which one would
have liked to carry away as a *souvenir*, were laid before
every plate; against the white marble walls, footmen stood
erect and motionless, in their gorgeous liveries, not for use,
but ornament. Flowers were strewed about everywhere; the
immense silver *épergnes* were a sight to gaze at. During the
whole of the repast the band played with a precision I have
not yet heard in Russia. A friend of mine, who has had
considerable experience in the details of civic banquets,
estimated the cost of the entertainment at some fourteen
hundred pounds; and, comparing the prices of Moscow and
London, I should think the estimate was below the mark . . .

Then there was a move to another room, where a company of Tyrolese singers gave their national entertainment.
We have most of us seen the self-same persons perform the
same songs and dances in our own country, and all I need
say is, that the yodel was as loud and the waltzing as perfect
as usual. But the next entertainment provided for the Royal
visitors was one not to be matched, I think, west of the
Vistula. In a saloon at the end of the suite of rooms we found
seated a company of some forty gipsies. The faces were the
same as those which Londoners know so well at Ascot and
Epsom; but instead of being dressed in rags and tatters, these
gipsy men and women were clad in rich silks and gorgeous
colours, which contrasted strangely with their dark olive
skin and tawny hands . . .

The women, in a circle, gazed upon the scene with their
large, dark, lascivious eyes, as if they possessed a sort of magic

power to attract those who looked upon them. The men stood behind, tambourine in hand, still, and to all outward look, utterly unconcerned. Then the Governor gave the signal, and the entertainment began. It is impossible to describe it in words. A long, low, guttural cry from the mouths of all the women seemed to open the ball; sometimes wailing, sometimes piercing in shrillness, but always fitted to a strange weird harmony, the sound of many voices rose and fell. Then one or two of the handsomest and youngest took up the dialogue in a sad sing-song tone; and then, before you exactly knew when song changed to motion, the women were whirling round in a wild fantastic measure. The strange feature was that their feet hardly seemed to move. The arms were thrown forwards and up and down again, the head rocked to and fro, the body quivered, the shoulders shook, and with every pulsation of the frame the chorus of seated women shrieked in unison. Somehow the feet moved, but you could scarcely trace their motion. If you fancy a woman walking in her sleep, half fastened to one spot with terror, half maddened with a fever of passion which sets in motion every muscle of her frame, you will form some idea of that gipsy dance which began with a cry and ended with a scream.

[31] The coronation of Nicholas II, 1896; from *The Life and Tragedy of Alexandra Feodorovna, Empress of Russia* by Baroness Sophie Buxhoeveden.

At the Coronation the whole old-world pomp of the Russian Court was displayed. It was a glorious pageant for the whole country, apart from the importance it had in the eyes of those who saw in the religious rites the real consecration of their sovereign. Everything was done to foster this feeling in the people who came to Moscow for the celebrations from every part of the vast Russian Empire. The Emperor granted amnesties to prisoners, and bounties to all classes of his subjects: fines were remitted, and facilities given for payment of taxes . . .

The next day, heralds in mediaeval dress read out the proclamation announcing to 'the good people of Our first capital' that the coronation was fixed for the 26th of May and was to be held in the old Cathedral of the Assumption, 'Ouspensky Sobor'. This was a fitting setting for so impressive a ceremony. Though the Cathedral had suffered much at the time of the French invasion in 1812, when Napoleon's troops had stabled their horses there, its ancient splendour had long since been restored. All its walls and pillars were covered with fifteenth-century frescoes, depicting the Saints and scenes from the Old and New Testaments. This brilliant background enhanced the beauty of the uniforms and robes. The jewels worn were wonderful, the Grand Duchess Serge's famous emeralds and the old Grand Duchess Constantine's sapphires, every flawless stone of which was about two inches across, attracted the attention of all. The 'Ikonostase' (altar screen) glittered with gold and silver, and in it were enshrined some very old and venerated ikons. The ceremony began early in the morning and lasted for several hours. The Emperor and Empress came on foot to the Cathedral in a state procession from the Kremlin. First came the Dowager-Empress alone, pale and serious-looking, with sad eyes, that reminded the onlookers that her own coronation had been not many years before. After her, each walking under a separate canopy, came Nicholas II and the Empress Alexandra Feodorovna, attended by numerous court officials in splendid uniforms. In contrast to the Dowager-Empress, who was blazing with diamonds and wearing an Imperial crown, the young Empress had no jewels except a string of pearls round her neck. She wore a Russian court dress of silver tissue, her hair in two long 'love-locks', and no ornaments on her head where the Imperial crown was to rest. She looked lovely. At first she was a little flushed and nervous, but regained her self-possession as the ceremony proceeded. The Emperor wore the uniform of the Preobrajensky regiment, the oldest regiment in Russia. He had at first expressed the wish to wear the robes of the old Tsars and their old 'Monomach' crown, as the newer 'Imperial' crown was very heavy (9 lb) and he had suffered from acute headaches ever since he had been wounded in the head by a Japanese fanatic at Otsou. Iron etiquette proclaimed the change impossible, and the Emperor was condemned to suffer considerable pain from the heavy crown.

The whole long five-hours' ceremony was a time of intense emotion to the Empress Alexandra. She was not tired at all, she told her sisters, everything was so beautiful. It seemed to her to be a kind of mystic marriage to Russia. She became one with Russia, sealed for ever a Russian in heart and soul, and so she remained from that day and all her life. The long Mass, the robing of the Emperor, his investiture with the Imperial insignia, she saw as in a dream. It is easy to imagine how ardent were her prayers as she knelt with every other person, while the Metropolitan read the prayer for the Emperor, and how her heart went out to his when he knelt, this time all alone, the others standing, and prayed for Russia and his people. Then Their Majesties alone received the Holy Communion, and the Metropolitan anointed the Emperor with the holy oils. On this one day, the only time in his life, the Russian Emperor enters the sanctuary and receives the Blessed Sacrament like a priest. When Nicholas II went up the altar steps the chain of the order of St Andrew fell to the ground – a bad omen to superstitious eyes. But the Empress was not troubled by this. She only saw the sunbeam that fell at that moment on his head, and felt it to be a kind of halo. The Emperor crowned himself, the Metropolitan handing him the crown. Then the Empress left her place and knelt before him. The Emperor took off his crown and touched her forehead with it. Then he took a smaller crown and with the utmost gentleness put it on her head. Her ladies fixed it on. The Emperor kissed her, took her hand as she rose, and both went to their places on their thrones. The church ceremony ended with the Empress Marie and all the Princes present doing homage to their crowned and anointed ruler. When his mother approached, pale with emotion, the Emperor's embrace seemed to everyone to be, not that of sovereign to subject, but of a dutiful son to his mother.

The whole procession left the Cathedral on foot and returned to the Kremlin. This time the Emperor and Empress Alexandra Feodorovna headed it in full regalia. Bells rang in all the '40 times 40' Moscow churches, cannon thundered, and the countless multitudes in the streets shouted themselves hoarse. The Imperial couple turned at the top of the celebrated 'red staircase', and bowed low to the crowd three times. This symbolized their greeting to the country. In the palace they passed the representatives of their Mahommedan subjects, whose religion did not allow them to enter a Christian church. These were, certainly, the most picturesque of all the guests; the splendour of their dress alone would take pages to describe. In a room by themselves stood a group of people in ordinary clothes. The foreign Princes inquired who these were, and were told that they were all descendants of people who had saved the lives of Russian sovereigns at different times. There were descendants of Ivan Soussanine, who had, by sacrificing his own life, saved the first Romanoff from the hands of the Poles, others who had saved Alexander II from assassination. Their presence spoke of the constancy of Imperial gratitude, but was a suggestive reminder.

[32] Easter ceremonies, 1906; from *What I Saw in Russia, 1905–1906* by Maurice Baring.

(Maurice Baring (1874–1945), fifth son of Edward Baring, 1st Lord Revelstoke, was a poet and man of letters whose genius for languages led him first to the Diplomatic Corps. In 1904 he resigned from the Foreign Office and went abroad as a war correspondent in Manchuria for the *Morning Post*. After the war he remained as special correspondent in St Petersburg, where he learnt Russian and developed an abiding sympathy for the Russian people. His *Landmarks in Russian Literature*, published in

1910, showed for the first time his remarkable gifts as a translator and literary critic.)

Certainly Russia is different from all other countries, and by saying it is the most Western of Oriental nations you get no nearer an explanation of its characteristics than by saying it is the most Oriental of Western nations. You live here, walk about, talk, and forget that you are in a place which is quite unique until some small sight or episode or phrase brings home the fact to you, and you say 'This is Russia', as Vernon Lee in her book on *The Spirit of Rome* exclaims, 'This is Rome', when driving towards Monte Maggiore she hears the sound of the harmonium and the school-children's hymn issuing out of a piece of broken ruin covered with fennel. Such a moment has just occurred to me tonight, when driving home through the empty streets at 11 pm. I passed a church as the clock struck, and I heard a voice speaking loud quite close to me. I turned round, and saw a policeman standing on the pavement, having faced about towards the church. He was saying his prayers in a loud sing-song; his whole body was swaying as he repeatedly crossed himself; in his arms he carried a twig of budding willow, which is the symbol of the palm-branches of to-day's festival. These branches yesterday and today have been sold and carried about all over Russia. Palm Sunday here is called the Feast of the Willow-branches. When I saw this policeman saying his prayers, I experienced that peculiar twinge of recognition which made me think: 'This is Russia.'

Moscow, *15 April, 1906*

I have spent Easter in various cities – in Rome, Florence, Athens, and Hildesheim – and although in each of these places the feast has its own peculiar aspect, yet by far the most impressive and the most interesting celebration of the Easter Festival I have ever witnessed is that of Moscow. This is not to be wondered at, for Easter, as is well known, is the most important feast of the year in Russia, the season of festivity and holiday-making in a greater degree than Christmas or New Year's Day. Secondly, Easter, which is kept with equal solemnity all over Russia, is especially interesting in Moscow, because Moscow is the stronghold of old traditions, and the city of churches. Even more than Cologne, it is

> 'Die Stadt die viele hundert
> Kapellen und Kirchen hat.'

There is a church almost in every street, and the Kremlin is a citadel of cathedrals. During Holy Week, towards the end of which the evidences of the fasting season grow more and more obvious by the closing of restaurants and the impossibility of buying any wine and spirits, there are, of course, services every day. During the first three days of Holy Week there is a curious ceremony to be seen every two years in the Kremlin. That is the preparation of the chrism or holy oil. While it is slowly stirred and churned in great cauldrons, filling the room with hot fragrance, a deacon reads the Gospel without ceasing (he is relieved at intervals by others), and this lasts day and night for three days. On Maundy Thursday it is removed in silver vessels to the Cathedral. The supply has to last the whole of Russia for two years. I went to the morning service in the Cathedral of the Assumption on Maundy Thursday. 'It's long, but it's very, very beautiful.' The church is crowded to suffocation. Everybody is standing up, as there would be no room to kneel. The church is lit with countless small wax tapers. The priests are clothed in white and silver. The singing of the noble plain chant without any accompaniment ebbs and flows in perfectly disciplined cadences; the bass voices are unequalled in the world. Every class of the population is represented in the church. There are no seats, no pews, no precedence or privilege. There is a smell of incense and a still stronger smell of poor people, without which, some one said, a church is not a church. On Good Friday there is the service of the Holy Shroud, and besides this a later service in which the Gospel is read out in fourteen different languages, and finally a service beginning at one o'clock in the morning and ending at four, which commemorates the Burial of Our Lord. How the priests endure the strain of these many and exceedingly long services is a thing to be wondered at; for the fast, which is strictly kept during all this period, precludes butter, eggs, and milk, in addition to all the more solid forms of nourishment, and the services are about six times as long as those of the Catholic or other Churches.

The most solemn service of the year takes place at midnight on Saturday. From eight until ten o'clock the town, which during the day had been crowded with people buying provisions and presents and Easter eggs, seems to be asleep and dead. At about ten people begin to stream towards the Kremlin. At eleven o'clock there is already a dense crowd, many of the people holding lighted tapers, waiting outside in the square, between the Cathedral of the Assumption and the tower of Ivan Veliki. A little before twelve the cathedrals and palaces on the Kremlin are all lighted up with ribbons of various coloured lights. Twelve o'clock strikes, and then the bell of Ivan Veliki begins to boom: a beautiful full-voiced, immense volume of sound – a sound which Clara Schumann said was the most beautiful she had ever heard. It is answered by other bells, and a little later all the bells of all the churches in Moscow are ringing together. Then from the Cathedral comes the procession: the singers first in crimson and gold; the bearers of the gilt banners; then the Metropolitan, also in stiff vestments of crimson and gold, and after him the officials in their uniforms. They walk round the Cathedral to look for the Body of Our Lord, and return to the Cathedral to tell the news that He is risen. The guns go off, rockets are fired, and illuminations are seen across the river, lighting up the distant cupola of the great Church of the Saviour with a cloud of fire.

The crowd begins to disperse and to pour into the various churches. I went to the Manège – an enormous riding school, in which the Ekaterinoslav Regiment has its church. Half the building looked like a fair. Long tables, twinkling with hundreds of wax tapers, were loaded with the three articles of food which are eaten at Easter – a huge cake called *kulich*; a kind of sweet cream made of curds and eggs, cream and sugar, called *Paskha* (Easter); and Easter eggs, dipped and dyed in many colours. They are there waiting to be blessed. The church itself was a tiny little recess on one side of the building. There the priests were officiating, and down below in the centre of the building the whole regiment was drawn up. There are two services – Matins, which begins at midnight, and which lasts about half an hour; and Mass, which follows immediately after it, lasting till about three in the morning. At the end of Matins, when 'Christ is risen' is sung, the priest kisses the congregation three times, and then the congregation kiss each other, one person saying 'Christ is risen', and the other answering 'He is risen indeed'. The colonel kisses the sergeant; the sergeant kisses all the men one after another.

[33] Holy Week in the Kremlin before the First World War; from *The Fourth Seal* by Sir Samuel Hoare.

(Sir Samuel John Gurney Hoare, 2nd Baronet and Viscount Templewood (1880–1959), was a classical scholar and MP for Chelsea from 1910–1944. During the 1914–18 War, he was a General Staff Officer, and served in the Military Mission to Russia, being mentioned in despatches, and given a CMG in 1917. During his subsequent distinguished political and diplomatic career between the Wars, he held more high offices than anyone except Churchill.)

No one, who did not see the Kremlin Cathedrals before the revolution, can realize the intimacy, the mystery and the splendour of these ceremonies. The small churches, their walls covered with frescoes of Byzantine figures on a background of gold, their screens, a blaze of precious stones and metals, the only lights, the candles before the Ikons and in the hands of the faithful, the only music, the bass of the deacon, the baritone of the bishop, and the concerted harmonies of the Imperial choir, produced as complete a picture of Holy Russia as could well be imagined. Amidst these impressive surroundings it was impossible not to be deeply moved by the fervour of the standing people, and the haunting sighing of the Slavonic language. Sometimes, the services would last far into the night. Yet, such was their dramatic hold, such their wealth of picturesque detail, that we cheerfully stood, hour after hour, and returned to them again after a hurried rest. Day by day, we followed the ordered sequence that commemorated the tragedy of Holy Week. Day by day, we came to feel something of the suppressed excitement that brought Moscow, and indeed the whole of Russia, into a veritable paroxysm of joy on Easter Day.

We began the week by visiting the long refectory in which the Holy Chrysm is boiled for the use of the Orthodox Church. There, in a dimly lit hall, we saw the great silver cauldron stirred by the monks in their black Basilian habits, we heard the reading of the psalms that continued day and night without intermission, and we smelt the curious scents of the many herbs and spices of which the Chrysm is composed. On Maundy Thursday, when the mixing and boiling were complete, the Chrysm was taken from the College of the Holy Synod and blessed by a Bishop in the Cathedral of the Assumption . . .

'April 22nd. Sunday. Last night's service at the Cathedral of the Assumption was very impressive, but very long. It did not begin until 1 and was not over until 4.45. Again, we stood in the choir. The Cathedral, as usual, was packed and, except for the lamps on the shrines, at first, completely dark. Then, as the service went on, everyone lit candles. No one except Johnny and I had books, and how the people packed as close as can be imagined are able to stand for four or five hours on end I cannot imagine. The service took the form of a funeral service round the catafalque – in this case, a pall. There were any number of clergy in black and silver and two fanning the pall with the big golden fans called *Ripidi*. There were innumerable Psalms, Troparia, litanies, and, amongst other things, the whole of the 119th Psalm, interleaved with a Troparion for each verse said in a kind of dramatic duet by two priests. Towards the end of the service the clergy with the pall and lighted candles processed round the Cathedral. It was impossible for us to get through the crowd, otherwise we should have joined in the procession. The service was very dramatic, culminating in a bishop reading the Gospel about guarding the tomb fast.

'By this time it was quite light and as we came away all the bells of Moscow were ringing – as they all do during the processions round the churches. You should have heard the voices of the readers – they are amazing, and the way they keep it up for hours on end!

'Today I was surprisingly little tired. However, I stopped in bed until 11. Then after luncheon we went off to the Cathedral of the Assumption for the end of the Liturgy. This was splendid, as we came in for the Nebuchadnezzar and the Image lesson, the *Benedicite* sung to a wonderful chant, and the sudden changing of all the vestments from black to white . . .'

The irritations of daily life, the plots of politicians, the futilities of the Government, the scandals in high places had been purged from my mind by the solemnities of Holy Week, and by the religious fervour of the men and women, soldiers and civilians, whom I had seen standing and kneeling before the sacred places of Russia.

One scene in particular remained vividly in my mind's eye. We had been to the ceremony of Easter Matins in the Cathedral of the Assumption. Of all the services that I had attended, it alone had depressed me by its atmosphere of ceremonial conformity. The congregation had been overwhelmingly official, Generals and bureaucrats in uniforms and decorations with their wives in stiff and ugly dresses. They had come to conform with the practice that puts Easter Matins into the same category as a levée or a parade. It was with a feeling of relief that Birkbeck and I, remembering the congregations of the simple and devout that had filled the church throughout Holy Week, pushed our way through the crowd and entered the Palace of the Kremlin. The Governor and his wife, Prince and Princess Odoevsky-Maslov, had bidden us attend the Matins and Liturgy in their private chapel, and stay with them for the supper that celebrated the coming of Easter.

A very old footman in the Imperial livery guided us through a labyrinth of little rooms into a small and ancient chapel. The old Prince and Princess were kneeling, he, in the white uniform of the Gardes à Cheval with the cross of St Vladimir round his neck, and the Star of the White Eagle on his tunic, she, in a white dress, such as might have been fashionable thirty years before, whilst four priests in gold vestments were finishing Easter Matins and beginning the Liturgy. In another corner was a group of servants, footmen and maids, most of them as old as the man who had guided us, acting as choir and singing the difficult chants with evident devotion and a traditional skill. The chapel was the most ancient in the Kremlin; the service, the culmination of the Russian winter and the Orthodox fast; the men and women taking part, the truest and most loyal representatives of the Russia that was passing away. Here, at least, was single-hearted devotion in a moment of doubt; here, at least, was unquestioning loyalty to the Orthodox Church and to the Tsar as God's vicegerent.

The supper that followed the Liturgy gave me a scarcely less striking scene from the Russia of the past, the Prince and Princess, the four priests, Birkbeck and myself, bidding each other Easter wishes, eating the Easter sweet cheese, all of us tired by the strain of Holy Week, the priests with the bright eyes and drawn faces that come after protracted fasting, all of us rejoicing at the great festival like children at Christmas.

[34] The declaration of war on Germany in August 1914; from *An Ambassador's Memoirs, 1914–1917* by Maurice Paléologue.

(Maurice Georges Paléologue (1854–1944) was a French diplomat and writer, who was appointed Deputy Director of the French Foreign Office in 1909. In 1914 he was sent to Russia as French Ambassador, and he remained there, consolidating the Franco-Russian alliance, until 1917. Later he became Secretary General of the Ministry of Foreign Affairs, and was elected to the French Academy in 1928.)

Tuesday 18 August 1914

When I arrived at Moscow this morning I went with Buchanan about half-past ten to the great Kremlin Palace. We were ushered into the St George's hall, where the high dignitaries of the empire, the ministers, delegates of the nobility, middle classes, merchant community, charitable organizations, etc., were already assembled in a dense and silent throng.

On the stroke of eleven o'clock the Tsar, the Tsaritsa and the imperial family made their ceremonial entry. The grand dukes had all gone to the front and besides the sovereigns there were only the four young grand duchesses, the Tsar's daughters, the Tsarevitch Alexis, who hurt his leg yesterday and had to be carried in the arms of a Cossack, and the Grand Duchess Elizabeth Feodorovna, the Tsaritsa's sister, abbess of the Convent of Martha-and-Mary of Pity.*

The imperial party stopped in the centre of the hall. In a full, firm voice the Tsar addressed the nobility and people of Moscow. He proclaimed that, as the traditions of his ancestors decreed, he had come to seek the moral support he needed in prayer at the relics in the Kremlin. He declared that a heroic national impulse was sweeping over all Russia, without distinction of race or nationality, and concluded:

'From this place, the very heart of Russia, I send my soul's greeting to my valiant troops and my noble allies. God is with us!'

A continuous burst of cheering was his answer.

As the imperial group moved on the Grand Master of the

---

* Widow of the Grand Duke Serge-Alexandrovitch, who was assassinated at Moscow on 27 February 1905. She herself was murdered by the Bolsheviks on 17 July 1918.

Ceremonies invited Buchanan and myself to follow the royal family, immediately after the grand duchesses.

Through the St Vladimir room and the Sacred Gallery we reached the Red Staircase, the lower flight of which leads by a bridge with a purple awning to the *Ouspensky Sobor*, the Cathedral of the Assumption.

The moment the Tsar appeared a storm of cheering broke out from the whole Kremlin where an enormous crowd, bareheaded and struggling, thronged the pavements. At the same time all the bells of the Ivan Veliky chimed in chorus, and the Great Bell of the Ascension, cast from the metal saved from the ruins in 1812, sent a thunderous boom above the din. Around us Holy Moscow, with her sky-blue domes, copper spires and gilded bulbs, sparkled in the sun like a fantastic mirage.

The hurricane of popular enthusiasm almost dominated the din of the bells.

Count Benckendorff, Grand Marshal of the Court, came up to me and said:

'Here's the revolution Berlin promised us!'

In so saying he was probably interpreting everyone's thoughts. The Tsar's face was radiant. In the Tsaritsa's was joyous ecstasy. Buchanan whispered:

'This is a sublime moment to have lived to see! . . . Think of all the historic future being made here and now!'

'Yes, and I'm thinking, too, of the historic past which is seeing its fulfilment here. It was from this very spot on which we now stand that Napoleon surveyed Moscow in flames. It was by that very road down there that the Grand Army began its immortal retreat!'

We were now at the steps of the cathedral. The Metropolitan of Moscow, surrounded by his clergy, presented to their Majesties the cross of Tsar Michael Feodorovitch, the first of the Romanovs, and the holy water.

We entered the *Ouspensky Sobor*. This edifice is square, surmounted by a gigantic dome supported by four massive pillars, and all its walls are covered with frescoes on a gilded background. The iconostasis, a lofty screen, is one mass of precious stones. The dim light falling from the cupola and the flickering glow of the candles kept the nave in a ruddy semi-darkness.

The Tsar and Tsaritsa stood in front of the right ambo at the foot of the column against which the throne of the Patriarchs is set.

In the left ambo the court choir, in XVIth century silver and light blue costume, chanted the beautiful anthems of the orthodox rite, perhaps the finest anthems in sacred music.

At the end of the nave opposite the iconastasis the three Metropolitans of Russia and twelve archbishops stood in line. In the aisles on their left was a group of one hundred and ten bishops, archimandrites and abbots. A fabulous, indescribable wealth of diamonds, sapphires, rubies and amethysts sparkled on the brocade of their mitres and chasubles. At times the church glowed with a supernatural light.

Buchanan and I were on the Tsar's left, in front of the court.

Towards the end of the long service the Metropolitan brought their Majesties a crucifix containing a portion of the true cross which they reverently kissed. Then through a cloud of incense the imperial family walked round the cathedral to kneel at the world-famed relics and the tombs of the patriarchs.

During this procession I was admiring the bearing and attitudes of the Grand Duchess Elizabeth, particularly when she bowed or knelt. Although she is approaching fifty she has kept her slim figure and all her old grace. Under her loose white woollen hood she was as elegant and attractive as in the old days before her widowhood, when she still inspired profane passions. To kiss the figure of the Virgin of Vladimir which is set in the iconostasis she had to place her knee on a rather high marble seat. The Tsaritsa and the young grand duchesses who preceded her had had to make two attempts – and clumsy attempts – before reaching the celebrated ikon. She managed it in one supple, easy and queenly movement.

The service was now over. The procession was reformed and the clergy took their place at its head. One last chant, soaring in triumph, filled the nave. The door opened.

All the glories of Moscow suddenly came into view in a blaze of sunshine. As the procession passed out I reflected that the court of Byzantium, at the time of Constantine Porphyrogenetes, Nicephorus Phocas or Andronicus Paleologue, can alone have seen so amazing a display of sacerdotal pomp.

At the end of the covered-in passage the imperial carriages were waiting. Before entering them the royal family stood for a time facing the frantic cheers of the crowd. The Tsar said to Buchanan and myself:

'Come nearer to me, *Messieurs les Ambassadeurs*. These cheers are as much for you as for me.'

Amid the torrent of acclamations we three discussed the war which had just begun. The Tsar congratulated me on the wonderful ardour of the French troops and reiterated the assurance of his absolute faith in final victory. The Tsaritsa tried to give me a few kind words. I helped her out:

'What a comforting sight for your Majesty! How splendid it is to see all these people swept by patriotic exaltation and fervour for their rulers!'

Her answer was almost inaudible but her strained smile and the strange spell of her wrapt gaze, magnetic and inspired, revealed her inward intoxication.

The Grand Duchess Elizabeth joined in our conversation. Her face in the frame of her long white woollen veil was alive with spirituality. Her delicate features and white skin, the deep, far-away look in her eyes, the low, soft tone of her voice and the luminous glow round her brows all betrayed a being in close and constant contact with the ineffable and the divine.

As Their Majesties returned to the palace Buchanan and I left the Kremlin amidst an ovation which accompanied us to our hotel . . .

I spent the afternoon seeing Moscow, lingering particularly over the places hallowed by memories of 1812. They stood out in sharp relief by contrast with the present moment.

At the Kremlin the ghost of Napoleon seems to rise up at every step. From the Red Staircase the Emperor watched the progress of the fire during the baneful night of 16 September. It was there that he took counsel of Murat, Eugène, Berthier and Ney in the midst of the leaping flames and under a blinding shower of cinders. It was there that he had that clear and pitiless vision of his pending ruin: 'All this,' he said repeatedly, 'is the herald of great disasters!' It was by this road that he hastily went down to the Moskowa accompanied by a few officers and men of his guard. It was there that he entered the winding streets of the burning city. 'We walked,' says Ségur, 'upon an earth of fire, under a sky of fire, between two walls of fire.' Alas! does not the present war promise us a second edition of this Dantesque scene? And how many copies to the edition?

North of the Kremlin and between the Church of St Basil and the Iberian Gate lies the Red Square, of glorious and tragic memory. If I had to give a list of those spots in which the visions and sentiments of the past have most vividly passed before my eyes I should include the Roman Campagna, the Acropolis at Athens, the Eyub cemetery at Stambul, the Alhambra in Granada, the Tartar city of Pekin, the Hradschin in Prague and the Kremlin of Moscow. This curious conglomeration of palaces, towers, churches, monasteries, chapels, barracks, arsenals and bastions, this incoherent jumble of sacred and secular buildings, this complex of functions as fortress, sanctuary, seraglio, harem, necropolis and prison, this blend of advanced civilization and archaic barbarism, this violent contrast of the crudest materialism and the most lofty spirituality – are they not the whole history of Russia, the whole epic of the Russian nation, the whole inward drama of the Russian soul?

[35] Lenin finds a new flat in the Kremlin; from *Lenin and the Bolsheviks* by Adam B. Ulam.

Few people in Russia in the spring of 1918 had the time and disposition to ponder the significance of the capital being shifted to Moscow. Two centuries before, Peter the Great left the ancient city that reminded him of the semi-Asiatic past and customs of the country and transferred the seat of government to the newly built capital which was to be Russia's window on Europe, both the symbol and the tangible proof of the new European ways he tried so despotically to impose on his subjects. Now a group of revolutionaries was fleeing back to the depths of Russia, to the old capital of the Grand Dukes and Tsars of Muscovy. Few would have seen in it an augury of how important Russian communism would become, how this movement conceived in the international spirit would in due time come to revere the awesome figures who also ruled Russia from the Kremlin: Ivan the Great and Ivan the Terrible, 'the gatherers of the Russian lands', who would bequeath the task to the son of a Georgian cobbler. Equally astounded in 1918 would be one told that this movement, heavily staffed at its highest positions by Jews, Poles, and Latvians, would become in its personnel and even more in its spirit fiercely nationalistic, that just as the patriarchs of the Orthodox Church used to thunder against foreign ways so from Communist Moscow, from the heirs of Marx and Lenin, would issue edicts and anathemas against the 'rootless cosmopolites', the 'innovators', the 'imitators of the rotten West'.

But no historic reflections could be afforded that spring, for the people had to pay full attention to the needs and miseries of the hour: a catastrophic defeat, the Civil War just beginning in the South, hunger and disorganization that were bound to grow worse with the loss by Russia of her most fertile and some of the most industrialized regions. The manner of the transfer of the capital was in itself significant. The government literally stole away from Petrograd. There had been fears that the Railwaymen's Union, still not fully friendly to the Bolsheviks, would block the move, or that the Germans by dispatching a few battalions would capture the fleeing commissars bag and baggage. Only from a nearby station was the Moscow soviet notified about the imminent arrival of the government of the Russian Federated Republic headed by Vladimir Ilyich Ulyanov-Lenin. No guard of honour awaited him upon his arrival. As a matter of fact there were no official greeters at all. Another commentary on those times: the arrivals were appalled to discover that the Moscow Bolsheviks had just set up a 'government' of their own, the Moscow Council of the People's Commissars, headed by a Left Communist, historian M. Pokrovsky. Lenin was soon to put an end to 'that idiocy', as he called it.

The government (the right one) immediately faced the prosaic task of finding offices and living space. After a few days in a hotel the Chairman of the Council of the Commissars moved into the Kremlin. The huge walled enclosure, the ancient seat of the Tsars, was to become a rabbit warren of the Bolsheviks' apartments and agencies. The Kremlin was in a deplorable shape: wartime neglect and the recent fighting in Moscow had left once magnificent living quarters filthy and barely fit for occupation. But there was no alternative: even with the confiscation of the residences of the rich, space was at a premium. As a seat of government and residence of its leaders the Kremlin had another advantage in those tumultuous days: it was, in a manner of speaking, a fortress. Tomorrow, any day, the reaction, the Anarchists, or the Left Socialist Revolutionaries might raise a revolt, and as in the old times the new Tsars would have to fight from behind its walls until help came.

There was as a matter of fact a veritable battle of Moscow waged among various commissariats and agencies for the most desirable residences. Stalin's personal assistant recalls how his boss, dissatisfied with the house assigned for the Commissariat of Nationalities, occupied on his own a building assigned to the State Economic Council. Accompanied by his henchmen, the future dictator tore off the sign the Council had affixed and moved into this former residence of a rich merchant. His assistant hired some Lettish sharpshooters at two roubles a day (they were allegedly the elite guard of the Bolsheviks and one wonders how they reconciled their regular military duties with this 'private' employment) to guard his conquest against the economists. But the latter managed to dislodge them, a sign that the Soviet administration was settling down to more conventional ways.

Lenin's own apartment was modest enough. He and Krupskaya occupied five rooms, his one bedroom being in those hard times the legal norm for a state functionary. To the end of his days Lenin would resist the ideas of a more commodious apartment or of extensive repairs to the one he occupied. (They had to be done stealthily, while he was vacationing.) Nor would he accept valuable rugs and furniture from the Kremlin's store-room. At a time when some Bolshevik bigwigs were beginning to enjoy the tangible rewards of power Lenin insisted upon the simple unpretentious comfort reminiscent of the conditions under which he had lived in migration. With constant food-shortages admirers would insist upon sending him special packages, which he received with embarrassment, often ordering that they be distributed to hospitals or children. Thus the new ruler of Russia lived in the old residence of her Tsars, protected by a guard of Lettish sharpshooters and watched over by the *Cheka*, the Bolshevik political police, headed by a Pole.

BEYOND
THE KREMLIN

The Red Square

[36] The Red Square (an alternative translation of *'Krasnaya' Ploshchad* also means 'beautiful' square) is used as a place of execution – the *Lobnoye Mesto*; from *Peter the Great* by K. Waliszewski.

That blood-stained spot, the *Lobnoié miesto*, has a character of its own, and a strange history, well worth knowing, which explains (I dare not say, it justifies) both the sanguinary scenes in which Peter insisted on playing so active a part, and that part itself, inexcusable as it appears. The origin of the name is quite uncertain. Some authorities derive it from the Latin word *lobium*, 'a high or raised place'; others ascribe it to the Russian word *lob* – 'head' – the place where the heads of criminals are placed. There is a legend, too, that Adam's head was buried on the spot, and here my readers will begin to perceive the strange and whimsical mixture of ideas and feelings, with which popular tradition has invested this ghastly enclosure. A place of execution indeed, but a holy spot as well! It stood, like the *Lithostrote* at Jerusalem, before one of the six principal gates leading into the Kreml, and had a religious and national significance of its own. Here the relics and holy images brought to Moscow were first deposited; here, even yet, on solemn occasions, religious ceremonies were performed; here it was, that the Patriarch gave his blessing to the Faithful; and here too, the most important Ukases were promulgated, and changes of ruler announced to the people. Here, in 1550, Ivan the Terrible came to confess his crimes, and publicly ask pardon of his subjects. Here too the mock Dimitri proclaimed his accession, and here, a few weeks later, his corpse was exposed to the mob, with a mask on the face, and a musical instrument in the dead hand.

Thus the executioner's tools, and his victims' corpses, and all the hideous paraphernalia of criminal punishment, did not here produce the impression which would elsewhere have made them objects of horror and repugnance. For they were associated with the most august incidents in the public life, and when Peter appeared on the scaffold, axe in hand, he neither derogated from his high dignity, nor made himself odious in the eyes of his subjects. All he did was to carry out his functions as their supreme judge. Any man, at that period, might turn executioner, if the occasion arose. When the work was heavy, supplementary assistance in the bloody business was sought for in the open streets, and the supply never failed. Peter, without ceasing to be Tsar, could still be the Tsar's headsman, just as he had been his drummer and his sailor. He turned his hand to the executioner's duty, just as he had previously turned it to the rigging of his ships. No one was shocked by his action nor blamed him for it. He was much more likely to be praised!

[37] The execution of Stenka Razin; from *La Vie Quotidienne à Moscou au XVIIe Siècle* by Princess Zinaïda Shakhovskoye.

On 4 June 1670, the Cossacks of Tcherkaski on the Don delivered to Moscow the man who had set the country alight. Stenka Razin was handed over to the Tsar's justice.

Razin, too, was a Don Cossack, 'very tall and well built, whose features were regular and proud and grave'. He represented perfectly that type of 'free man' who chose to live dangerously; life would be short but good. A law unto himself, he felt boxed in in any community or organization: he hated discipline: he only served those he would choose, quite prepared to betray them if such was his mood. Razin's adventure is the tale of a brigand who became the head of a vast popular revolt.

And it is the unbridled march of Razin towards the Moscow throne which history chronicles as a feverish illusion gorged on the blood of men. His fleet was comprised of two mysterious boats luxuriously set up; he swore that in one, black-lined, lived the disgraced patriarch, the famous Nikon; in the other, this time lined in red, was the Tsarevitch Alexis. It did not matter that Nikon should still be in his monastery, and the Tsarevitch in his tomb.

In the seventeenth century, no truly popular revolt could succeed if it did not appear sponsored by Church and Monarch to deceive the masses. All conquerors know that defeat in the end will follow the victories. The wheel turns. Those boyars and nobles Razin had promised to exterminate were not the only ones anxious to kill him off.

The seed of doubt was sown. Defections followed; as well as the Zaporojets Cossacks, those of the Don were mostly loyal to the government. It was easy for them to discover the mutineers. The Tcherkaski Cossacks forced Razin out of his much shrunken camp near this town.

Razin's lieutenants were hung instantly. The Ataman and his chained brother Frolka started on their last journey, knowing full well what to expect. The cart taking them to the capital bumped along the dusty roads of the Russian summer, carrying them to an ignominious death. After torture, Stenka Razin climbed the Moscow scaffold. On 6 June 1671, the crowds were even more packed than when, in Astrakan, they had cheered him admiringly in its streets as head of the popular revolt. Now no admiration or even pity could be seen in the eyes of those following his last gestures amongst the living. The game was over, the mirage had evaporated. The man whose head would roll off on to the scaffold, with its thick hair and full beard, was no more the hero Ataman Stefan Timofeievitch, but only Stenka Razin, excommunicated by the Church.

Jacob Reitenfels, nephew of the leading Court doctor of Alexis Mikhailovitch, wrote in his description of Muscovy to the Duke of Tuscany:

> This traitor was brought to town and tied by chains to the scaffold which was in fact an elevated cart similar to a triumphal chariot so that all could see him. Frolka, his brother, equally in chains, followed on foot the travelling scaffold. Behind the cart, marched in pell-mell order soldiers and other prisoners. The streets teemed with spectators, some coming out of their houses to watch the extraordinary spectacle, others moved to indignation or even pity.
>
> In prison, Stenka Razin had been flogged with the knout, tortured by fire, undergone the water torture, and other more extraordinary horrors. All his body was a living sore, so that the knout fell on raw bones. He was stubbornly brave, never uttered a cry or a whimper and only reproached his brother (tortured as appallingly) for 'his lack of courage'.
>
> The final drama came. Stenka listened to his sentence, which was very long. 'Robber, blasphemer, Don Cossack, Stenka Razin! You have forgotten to fear God, and your Great Sovereign; you are a traitor to your oath, leaving your home on the Volga where you committed abominations and crimes. This document states and repeats that after having been pardoned by the Tsar a first time, Razin abjured again, forgetting the Tsar's charitable grace.

After having heard the death sentence pronounced by the judge in a loud voice, Razin made the sign of the cross and lay down on the scaffold. A hatchet severed his legs and arms, followed by his head.

The English author of *The Revolt of Stenka Razin*, a

sailor from the *Queen Esther*, also described this execution, impressed by the courage of this wretched bandit:

> He did not seem to be moved; he never said a word but bowed low to the ground. When the executioner was ready, he made the sign of the cross several times, then greeted the crowd three times, turning himself round and each time saying, 'Pardon'. He was stretched between two beams, his right hand was cut at the elbow and the left foot at the knee, then off came the head, but this was all done so quickly that Stenka did not utter a murmur.

Witnesses differ a little in the description of the tortures, but all are at one in admiring Razin's courage.

The Secretary of the Dutch Embassy, Koets, was also a witness; after having had a hearty lunch, he went off to contemplate the head and four quarters of the victim, impaled on pikes.

[38] The fair on the Red Square – Palm Sunday, 1906; from *What I Saw in Russia, 1905–1906* by Maurice Baring.

It is Palm Sunday, and the customary fair is being held on the Red Place in front of the Kremlin, and as it has been a lovely day the crowd of strollers was immense. This fair is one of the most amusing sights to be seen in Russia. Two lines of booths occupy the space which stretches opposite the walls of the Kremlin. At the booths you can buy almost anything: birds, tortoises, goldfish, grass snakes, linoleum, carpets, toys, knives, musical instruments, books, music, cakes, lace, ikons, Easter eggs, carved woodwork, etc. There are besides these a number of semi-official stalls where kwass is sold to drink, and a great quantity of itinerant vendors sell balloons, things that squeak, penny whistles, trumpets and chenille monkeys. The trade in goldfish was brisk (people often buying one goldfish in a small tumbler), but that in a special kind of whetstone which cut glass and

sharpened knives and cost twenty kopecks was briskest of
all. The crowd round this stall, at which the vendor gave a
continual exhibition of the practical excellence of his wares
by cutting up bits of glass, was dense, and he sold any
quantity of them. At the bookstall the selection was varied in
the extreme. I bought two cheap copies of *Paradise Lost* in
Russian with wonderful illustrations; but there were also
back numbers of *Punch* to be got, some fragments of the
Cornhill Magazine, and the Irish State Papers from 1584 to
1588. One man was selling silvered Caucasian whips which,
he said, had just missed being silver. One man sold little
sailors made of chenille, which, he said, represented the crew
of the *Potemkin* without the captain. There was one fasci-
nating booth called an American bazaar, where everything
cost five kopecks, and where you could buy almost anything.

The Iverian Mother of God's Chapel (now destroyed)

[39] The Chapel of the Iverian Mother of God, home of Moscow's most popular and miraculous icon, built in 1669; from *Russia: 1842* by J.G. Kohl.

(Johann Georg Kohl (1808–1878) was a German scholar who became a tutor, but was obsessed by travel from his childhood. He published his first book in 1833, but it was after he had returned to Germany from St Petersburg in 1838 that he discovered his true vocation as a travel writer. '*Veni, vidi, scripsi*' became his motto about a host of countries, including Ireland, Scotland and Hungary, as well as Russia.)

This celebrated nestling-place of the 'Iberian Mother' consists of one undivided area. She herself, however, is in a kind of sanctuary hollowed out at the further end. The immediate space in front is adorned with many pictures of saints, and filled with silver candlesticks, and other glittering ware. She sits in the half-darked background, in the midst of gold and pearls. Like all Russian saints, she has a dark-brown, almost black complexion. Round her head she has a net made of real pearls. On one shoulder a large jewel is fastened, shedding brightness around, as if a butterfly had settled there. Such another butterfly rests on her brow, above which glitters a brilliant crown. In one corner of the picture, on a silver plate, is inscribed, ἡ μητηρ Θεοῦ Τῶν Ἰβερων. Around the picture are gold brocaded hangings, to which angels' heads, painted on porcelain with silver wings, are sewn: the whole is lighted up by thirteen silver lamps. Beside the picture there are a number of drawers containing wax tapers, and books having reference to her history. Her hand and the foot of the child are covered with dirt from the abundant kissing; it sits like a crust in little raised points, so that long since it has not been hand and foot that have been kissed, but the concrete breath of pious lips. The doors of the chapel stand open the whole day, and all are admitted who in sorrow, and heavy laden; and this includes here, as everywhere else, a considerable number. I often beheld with astonishment the multitudes that streamed in, testifying the inordinate power which this picture exercises over their minds. None ever pass, however pressing their business, without bowing and crossing themselves. The greater part enter, kneel devoutly down before 'the Mother', and pray with fervent sighs. Here come the peasants early in the morning before going to market: they lay aside their burdens, pray a while, and then go their way. Hither comes the merchant on the eve of a new speculation, to ask the assistance of the angels hovering round 'the Mother'. Hither come the healthy and the sick, the wealthy, and those who would become so; the arriving and the departing traveller, the fortunate and the unfortunate, the noble and the beggar. All pray, thank, supplicate, sigh, laud, and pour out their hearts before 'the Mother'. There is really something touching in seeing the most sumptuously-clad ladies, glittering with jewels, leave their splendid equipages and gallant attendants, and prostrate themselves in the dust with the beggars. On a holiday I once counted two hundred passing pilgrims, kneeling down before 'the Iberian Mother'; and thought with astonishment of the importance of this little spot of ground. Since Alexis, the Czars have never failed to visit it frequently. The present emperor never omits to do so, when he comes to Moscow. It is said that he has come more than once in the middle of the night, and wakened the monks, in order that he might perform his devotions.

The picture is also, if desired, carried to the houses of sick persons. For this purpose, a carriage with four horses is kept constantly ready, in which it is transported with pomp; not the real picture, but a copy that hangs in the fore-chapel; – at least so said the attendants at the chapel; but others contradicted it, and said that the copy remained behind for passing worshippers, and the original was carried to the sick. The visit costs five rubles, and a voluntary present is usually made to the monks.

I had almost forgotten to mention the principal thing; namely, that there is a very little scratch in the right cheek, that distils blood. This wound was inflicted, nobody knows when or how, by Turks or Circassians, and exactly this it is by which the miraculous powers of the picture were proved; for scarcely had the steel pierced the canvass, than the blood trickled from the painted cheek. In every copy the painter has represented this wound, with a few delicate drops of blood. As I was speaking of this and other miracles to a monk, he made, to my imprudent question, whether miracles were now daily wrought by it, the really prudent reply, 'Why, yes, if it be God's pleasure, and when there is faith; for it is written in the Bible, that faith alone blesses.'

St Basil's Cathedral

[40] The Cathedral of St Basil; from *The Empire of the Czar . . .* by the Marquis de Custine.

I shall never forget the chilly shudder which came over me at the first sight of the cradle of the modern Russian empire: the Kremlin alone is worth the journey to Moscow.

At the gate of this fortress, but beyond its precincts – at least, according to my feldjäger, for I have not yet been able to visit it – rises the church of St Basil, *Vassili Blagennoï*; it is also known under the name of the Cathedral of the Protection of the Holy Virgin. In the Greek church they are lavish of the title of cathedral; every city possesses several. That of Vassili is certainly the most singular, if it is not the most beautiful edifice in Russia. I have as yet only seen it at a distance. Thus viewed, it appears as an immense cluster of little turrets forming a bush, or rather giving the idea of some kind of tropical fruit all bristled over with excrescences, or a crystallization of a thousand rays: the scales of a golden fish, the enamelled skin of a serpent, the changeful hues of the lizard, the glossy rose and azure of the pigeon's neck, would all, as regards colour, serve as comparisons: above, rise minarets of a brownish red. The effect of the whole dazzles the eye, and fascinates the imagination. Surely, the land in which such a building is called a house of prayer is not Europe; it must be India, Persia, or China! – and the men who go to worship God in this box of confectionary work, can they be Christians? Such was the exclamation that escaped me at the first view of the church of Vassili. That building must indeed possess an extraordinary style of architecture to have drawn my attention, as it did, from the Kremlin, at the moment when the mighty castle for the first time met my eyes.

[41] The Cathedral of St Basil; from *Russian Pictures* by Thomas Mitchell.

We were at once struck by the eccentric appearance of the Cathedral of St Basil the Beatified. It justifies the description of it given by Théophile Gautier:

> It is without doubt the most original monument in the world: it recalls nothing that one has ever seen, and belongs to no known style. One would imagine it to be a gigantic madresore, a crystallized colossus, a stalactite grotto turned upside down; a thing which has neither prototype nor similitude. It might be taken for a Hindoo, Chinese, or Thibetan pagoda. In looking at this impossible church, one is tempted to ask if it is not a whimsical will-o'-the-wisp, an edifice formed of clouds fantastically coloured by the sun, which the movement of the air will presently cause to change in form, or vanish into nothingness.

Ivan the Terrible, after conquering Kazan, built on this site (anciently a cemetery in which was buried Basil, 'a prophet and miracle-worker, idiotic for Christ's sake'), with the treasure he had taken from the Tartars, a wooden church dedicated to the Intercession of the Holy Virgin. It was rebuilt in stone AD 1555, in commemoration of the additional acquisition of Astrakhan . . .

It was pillaged and defiled by the Poles early in the seventeenth century, and in 1626 a fire which broke out in the dome of one of its chapels spread over the whole of Moscow. Again in 1668, the great fire that devastated the Kitaigorod destroyed all the cupolas of Basil the Beatified. In 1737 another great conflagration destroyed the church, with its domes and eighteen chapels and all the vessels and treasures within it. Restored seven years later, and again thoroughly renovated in 1784, in strict accordance with ancient drawings, Napoleon, in 1812, found it in its present form, and ordered 'that Mosque' to be destroyed.

Fortunately for later visitors not of iconoclastic temperament, his orders, in the confusion and danger of the French occupation of Moscow, were not carried out, although the edifice suffered to the extent of being robbed and used as a stable . . .

In one of the lower chapels, Basil, the tutelary saint, reposes in a costly shrine little in harmony with the equally venerated emblems of his austerity, in the form of heavy iron chains and crosses which he wore for penance. Another chapel is famed for the relics and the penitential weights of cast iron of 'Ivan the Idiot', who acquired also the epithet of 'Big-cap', from the heavy iron head-piece on which he was wont to carry buckets of water as an exercise of charity; this *curio* disappeared in 1812. The Protestant reader must bear in mind that idiocy is a form of mendicancy very common in Russia and the innate compassionate feelings of the people are much moved by it. Another common, perhaps more painful appeal to charity, consists in the exhibition of sores resulting from accidents by fire, and it is not unusual even to see beggars going about barefooted in winter.

The Church of the Trinity

[42] The Church of the Trinity on Nikitnikov Pereulok; from *Moscow, An Architectural History* by Kathleen Berton.

Side by side with the pyramid-style churches the cube churches, the true descendants of Byzantine architecture, were developing into the most extravagant and colourful buildings ever to be built in Russia, surpassed only by St Basil's. These many sectional asymmetrical, highly decorated and vividly coloured churches with differing roof levels gave a total effect of immense gaiety and even today lend colour and variety to Moscow's peeling, drab streets. Their particular characteristics are the elaborate exterior sculpture and brick-work around the windows (*nalichniki*) with the upper part over the windows sometimes shaped like a *kokoshnik* gable, sometimes in semicircles and triangles and other more complicated forms. The walls around the window and doors are often decorated with engaged columns of brightly coloured bricks. The tops of each storey of

wall were decorated with entablatures and pierced parapets
so that the upper part of every section stands out in outline
giving a bold delineation to the next level . . .

The most characteristic example of this wild disregard for
absolute uniformity and love of rich adornment is the Troitsa
v Nikitnikakh, the Church of the Trinity on Nikitnikov
Pereulok off Ipatievsky Pereulok in Kitaigorod near Ulitsa
Razina. It is known locally as the Church of the Georgian
Virgin from an icon that once hung there. Completely
submerged by tall buildings and the narrowness of the lane,
it is a shock to come across the vividly red and white
conglomeration of pyramid-towered porch, full-blown cupolas, richly sculptured window decorations and oddly
protruding sections all joined together to form a gay and
striking building, its size more like that of a cathedral than of
a simple parish church. In fact it was the private chapel of a
very important citizen, Nikitnikov, a wealthy merchant and
leading member of the most influential guild, the *gost*, of
which the Tsar was also a member. This was the guild of
about thirty most favoured merchants, entrepreneurs who
had unlimited rights of importation and were exempted from
payment of custom dues. They also enjoyed the freedom of
unlimited travel within Russia and abroad, an important
concession at a time when serfs were unable even to leave
their landlords and the artisans and small traders of the
various settlements in Moscow were forbidden to move even
to another part of the city. As the leading member of the *gost*
guild Nikitnikov helped shape the Tsar's economic policies
by acting as a sort of senior financial adviser. In spite of his
wealth and power Nikitnikov, not being of boyarial descent,
was barred from making his home inside the Kremlin walls.
So in 1635–53 he built a palace and magnificent church here,
in Kitaigorod, not far from the Kremlin. The palace disappeared long ago and the church is crowded by modern
buildings mushrooming higher and higher on every side. Yet
when it was built it dominated this part of Kitaigorod, rising
majestically above the little single-storey wooden houses and
palaces and could be seen from a long way off.

The surrender and evacuation of the Kremlin by the Poles in 1612.
Muscovites bitterly resented their occupation of Moscow during the
'Troubled Times', 1598–1612. Watercolour by Lissner.

Ivan the Terrible shows his treasures to the English Ambassador;
painting by A. Litovtchenko.

Above: Dmitry, the 'false' Tsar, and his Polish bride, Marina Mniszek; from the collection of the Grand Duke Sergey Alexandrovitch.

The riot of the *streltsy*, 1682. In the top half of this eighteenth-century illustration to Krekshin's *History of Peter the Great* is the child Peter; in the lower half Artamon Matveief is impaled.

The great bell of Moscow whose rim was broken before it could be hoist and rung; nineteenth-century engraving by André Durand.

Peter the Great's mass torture and execution of the rebellious *streltsy*, 1698.

The great fire of 1812, by an unknown artist.

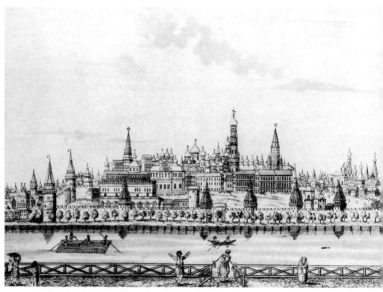

The Kremlin seen across the River Moskva: an eighteenth-century view.

The Chapel of the Iverian Mother of God (now destroyed) at the
entrance to the Red Square; by an unknown artist, 1850.

Gilliardi's Moscow University; watercolour by K.F. Yuon.

The Moscow Theatre burns to the ground, 1853. Rebuilt in 1855,
it is now the Bolshoi Theatre.

The palace at Kolomenskoye, built by Tsar Alexis Mikhailovitch in 1666; by G. Quarenghi.

Soliciting custom in the Gostinny Dvor.

Below: Moscow's water-carts by the Sukharev Tower; nineteenth-century painting by Ap. M. Vasnetsov.

Like the Putnikakh Church it has a basic nucleus surrounded by a number of additional chambers, chapels, porch, staircase and passageway and a secret room for storing valuables. The deep soft red of the exterior walls contrasts with the white sculpture of the window decorations, the cornices and fine *kokoshniki* and the drums of the cupolas. The high, wide sub-basement or undercroft was an important part of a wealthy merchant's private church in which he would place his most valuable goods, safe under the protection of the altar from greedy thieves. The interior frescoes and iconostasis are still magnificent. The severe dark faces are by the hand of Simon Ushakov, considered to be the last of the great icon painters in Russia during the revival in icon painting after the hiatus of the Time of Troubles.

The Novo Dyevichy Convent

[43] Peter the Great hangs *streltsy* in front of his sister Sophia's convent cell; from *Diary of an Austrian Secretary of Legation* . . . by Johann Georg Korb.

Seventh Execution, 27 October 1698

Today was assigned for the punishment of the *popes*, that is to say, of those who by carrying images to induce the serfs to side with the *streltsy*, had invoked the aid of God with the holy rites of his altars for the happy success of this impious plot . . .

The Tsar's Majesty looked on from his carriage while the *popes* were hurried to execution. To the populace, who stood around in great numbers, he spoke a few words touching the perfidy of the *popes*, adding the threat, 'Henceforth let no one dare to ask any *pope* to pray for such an intention.' A little while before the execution of the *popes*, two rebels, brothers, having had their thighs and other members broken in front of the Castle of the Kremlin, were set alive upon the wheel; twenty others on whom the axe had done its office lay lifeless around these wheels. The two that were bound upon the wheel beheld their third brother among the dead. Nobody will easily believe how lamentable were their cries and howls, unless he has well weighed their excruciations and the greatness of their tortures. I saw their broken thighs tied to the wheel with ropes strained as tightly as possible, so that in all that deluge of torture I do believe none can have exceeded that of the utter impossibility of the least movement. Their miserable cries had struck the Tsar as he was being driven past. He went up to the wheels, and first promised speedy death, and afterward proffered them a free pardon, if they would confess sincerely. But when upon the very wheel he found them more obstinate than ever, and that they would give no other answer than that they would confess nothing, and that their penalty was nearly paid in full, the Tsar left them to the agonies of death, and hastened on to the Monastery of the Nuns, in front of which monastery there were thirty gibbets erected in a quadrangular shape, from which there hung two hundred and thirty *streltsy*. The three principal ringleaders, who presented a petition to Sophia, touching the administration of the realm, were hanged close to the windows of that princess, presenting, as it were, the petitions that were placed in their hands, so near that Sophia might with ease touch them. Perhaps this was in order to load Sophia with that remorse in every way, which I believe drove her to take the religious habit, in order to pass to a better life.

St Dmitry Donskoy

[44] Mass at St Dmitry Donskoy; from *Letters from Russia* by Field-Marshal Count Helmuth von Moltke.

Sunday 31 August 1855.

We drove to the convent of St Dimitri Donskoj, a complete fortress with battlemented walls and towers. The church is very beautiful, high, and unusually light; the Ikonostasis, which is covered with gold and pictures up to a hundred feet high, is of exceeding splendour. We heard mass, and had enough of the constant repetition of '*gospodi pomilui*' as the priest raised the bread high above his head and carried it through the Emperor's door; he shut this behind him and was seen through the golden lattice in a cloud of incense, the sparkling jewels of his tiara flashing here and there as he moved. Then there was a tinkling and some mysterious movements, after which the voices of the singers were heard as they began one of those wonderful melodies which in Russia alone can be heard in such perfection! Who could have expected to hear in this place such voices and such execution? We remained motionless till the singing ceased, the doors opened, and the priests displayed the miracle to the kneeling multitude.

The English Club

---

[45] Dinner with Pushkin in 1830; from *Narrative of a Visit to the Courts of Russia and Sweden in the Years 1830 and 1831* by Captain C. Colville Frankland RN.

At three o'clock I drove to the English Club, (so called because hardly any Englishman belongs to it). Here I was inscribed by M. Pouschkin, with whom I dined. It is a splendid establishment, upon a very large scale, and is clean, and cool, and comfortable. I was introduced to Count Potemkin, Prince Wladimir Gallitzin, and young Count Alexis Bobrinski (a descendant of Catharine II). Cards and billiards seemed to bear away the palm from the gastronomic science. I never sat so short a time at dinner anywhere. The Russians are dreadful gamblers. No English newspapers are taken in the English Club; nor any of our Reviews. I found an article in La Revue Britannique, upon the strength and composition of the Russ army, mutilated by the Censure. The library consists of almost exclusively old

French works. There is a very spacious and agreeable garden in the rear of the club-house, where the gentlemen amused themselves in bowling at nine-pins, and with the national game of the Swaicka (a stupid school-boy sort of play, consisting of driving an iron pin into a brass ring laid upon the ground).

My friend M. Pouschkin abandoned me here to my fate, and escaped, as I suspect, quietly to join his pretty bride – (he was quite right). However, I was left rather in an awkward predicament by his sudden desertion, for I had to pay my own bill, in order to do which I was obliged to have recourse to Prince Wladimir Gallitzin's kind offices to serve me as interpreter. All poets, I suppose, have a right to eccentricity and distraction.

Moscow University

[46] Moscow University, 1843; from *My Past and Thoughts* by Alexander Herzen.

(Alexander Ivanovitch Herzen (1812–1870) was a Moscow-born Russian author, the illegitimate son of a rich noble-man. At the age of 22 he was arrested for 'dangerous liberalism' and three years later was exiled to Viatka, where he worked as a clerk in the Civil Service. In 1840 he returned to Moscow, and took a prominent part in the 'debate' between Westerners and Slavophiles. He was arrested again, and exiled to Novgorod. He left Russia in 1847, never to return, moving for the rest of his life between Paris, London, and Geneva, and dying in Paris.)

'Granovsky's lectures,' Chaadayev said to me as we came away from the third or fourth, out of a lecture-hall packed to overflowing with ladies and all the aristocratic society of Moscow, 'are of historical significance.' I entirely agreed with him. Granovsky turned the lecture-hall into a drawing-room, a place for meeting, for social intercourse of the *beau monde*. To do this he did not deck our history in laces and silks; quite the contrary: his language was severe, extremely grave, full of force, daring, and poetry, which vigorously jolted his hearers and woke them up. He escaped the consequences of his boldness, not from any compromise he made but from the mildness of expression which was natural to him, from the absence of sentences *á la française*, which put huge dots on tiny i's, like the moral after a fable. As he laid the events of history before his audience, grouping them artistically, he spoke *in them* so that the thought, unuttered but perfectly clear, was the more readily assimilated by his hearers that it seemed to be their own thought.

The conclusion of his first course of lectures was a regular ovation, a thing unheard of at Moscow University. When at the end, deeply moved, he thanked the audience, everyone leapt up in a kind of intoxication, ladies waved their handkerchiefs, others rushed to the platform, pressed his hands and asked for his portrait. I myself saw young people with flushed cheeks shouting through their tears: 'Bravo! Bravo!' There was no possibility of getting out. Granovsky stood as white as a sheet, with his arms folded and his head a little bent; he wanted to say a few words more but could not. The applause, the shouting, the fury of approbation doubled, the students ranged themselves on each side of the stairs and left the visitors to make a noise in the lecture-room. Granovsky made his way, exhausted, to the council-room; a few minutes later he was seen leaving it, and again there was endless clapping; he turned, begging for mercy with a gesture and, ready to drop with emotion, went into the office. There I flung myself on his neck and we wept in silence . . .

Tears as happy flowed down my cheeks when the hero Ciceruacchio,* in the Coliseum illuminated by the last rays

---

* Ciceruacchio, a popular leader (his real name was Angelo Brunetti) in Rome, who had great influence from 1847 onwards, supporting the reforms of Pius IX, and was active in bringing about the proclamation of a republic in February 1849. He was captured and shot with his sons in the following July.

of the setting sun, dedicated his youthful son to the Roman people, who had risen in armed insurrection, a few months before they both fell shot without trial by the military executioners of the urchin* who wore a crown!

Yes, those were precious tears; the first, born of my faith in Russia, the second, of my faith in the Revolution!

Where is that Revolution? Where is Granovsky? Gone together with the boy with the black curls, the broad-shouldered *popolano*, and the others who were so near and dear to us. My faith in Russia is still left. Surely it will not be my lot to lose that too?

And why did blind chance carry off Granovsky, so noble and so active, that deeply suffering spirit, on the very threshold of a new age for Russia, as yet obscure, but different, at all events? Why did not chance let him breathe that fresh air of which we have had a breath and which does not smell so strongly of the torture-chamber and the barracks?

[47] Chekhov at Moscow University; from *Chekhov, A Life* by David Magarshack.

Moscow with its cobbled, humpbacked streets, its rich mansions and wooden hovels, its drab churches which filled the air with the sound of bells, its fire-stations with their tall towers on which two look-out men were constantly watching for the first signs of smoke, its theatres and amusement places, its markets and shops, its horse-trams and cabs, its cheap pubs and magnificent restaurants, its hotels and lodging houses, its daily and periodical press, its civil servants, students, writers, actors, artists, wealthy business-men, shopkeepers, shop assistants, errand boys, factory workers, water carriers, house-porters, beggars and prostitutes – that was the human scene, rich in character and incident, which provided Chekhov with his material for the

* The Emperor of Austria, Franz Joseph, who ascended the throne in December 1848, at the age of eighteen.

hundreds of stories and articles he was to begin writing even before he had time to familiarize himself with it. Moscow had fascinated him during his first visit in 1877, and it fascinated him even more two years later when he plunged into its life with the zest and enthusiasm of a nineteen-year-old student who believed in seeing and experiencing everything for himself. But Moscow also gave him his first shock that removed the romantic spell the city had cast upon him and made him see it in its true light. It was his visit to the university to fill up the necessary forms for his admission to the medical faculty that brought him down to earth. 'Anton', Michael records, 'did not know Moscow very well and it was I who took him to the university. We entered a small dirty room with a low ceiling, full of tobacco smoke and crowded with young people. Anton apparently expected something grand from a university, and the place in which he found himself produced a far from pleasant impression on him.' Recalling his first impression of Moscow university ten years later, Chekhov wrote in *A Boring Story*: 'And there are the gloomy, battered gates of the university; the bored caretaker in his sheepskin coat, a broom, heaps of snow . . . On an inexperienced boy who has just arrived from the provinces and who imagines that a temple of learning is a real temple such gates cannot produce a healthy impression. Indeed, the dilapidated condition of the university buildings, the gloomy corridors, grimy walls, bad light, and the depressing stairs, coat-stands and benches have undoubtedly played an important role in the history of Russian pessimism.'

The Sparrow Hills

[48] A 'sacred' vow on the Sparrow Hills; from *My Past and Thoughts* by Alexander Herzen.

The Sparrow Hills, at the foot of which Karl Ivanovich had been so nearly drowned, soon became our 'sacred hills'.

One day after dinner my father proposed to drive out into the country. Ogarëv was with us and my father invited him and Sonnenberg to go too . . .

At Luzhniki we crossed the river Moskva in a boat at the very spot where the Cossack had pulled Karl Ivanovich out of the water. My father walked, bent and morose as always; beside him Karl Ivanovich tripped along, entertaining him with gossip and scandal. We went on in front of them, and getting far ahead ran up to the Sparrow Hills at the spot where the first stone of Vitberg's temple was laid.

Flushed and breathless, we stood there mopping our faces. The sun was setting, the cupolas glittered, beneath the hill the city extended farther than the eye could reach; a fresh breeze blew on our faces, we stood leaning against each other and, suddenly embracing, vowed in sight of all Moscow to sacrifice our lives to the struggle we had chosen.

This scene may strike others as very affected and theatrical, and yet twenty-six years afterwards I am moved to tears as I recall it; there was a sacred sincerity in it, and our whole life has proved this . . .

We did not know all the strength of the foe with whom we were entering into battle, but we took up the fight. That strength broke much in us, but it was not that strength that shattered us, and we did not surrender to it in spite of all its blows. The wounds received from it were honourable. Jacob's strained thigh was the sign that he had wrestled in the night with God.

From that day the Sparrow Hills became a place of worship for us and once or twice a year we went there, and always by ourselves. There, five years later, Ogarëv asked me timidly and shyly whether I believed in his poetic talent, and wrote to me afterwards (1833) from his country house: 'I have come away and feel sad, as sad as I have never been before. And it's all the Sparrow Hills. For a long time I hid my enthusiasm in myself; shyness or something else, I don't myself know what, prevented me from uttering it; but on the Sparrow Hills that enthusiasm was not burdened with solitude: you shared it with me and those moments have been unforgettable; like memories of past happiness they have followed me on my way, while round me I saw nothing but forest; it was all so blue, dark blue, and in my soul was darkness, darkness.

'Write then,' he concluded, 'how in this place' (that is, on the Sparrow Hills) 'the story of our lives, yours and mine, began to unfold.'

The Sukharev Tower
(now destroyed)

[49] Moscow's water-supply; from *Russia: 1842* by J.G. Kohl.

Very few houses in Moscow possess wells; nearly all the water used is drawn from the few stone basins in the streets. The manner in which the people draw the water is extraordinarily rude and simple. They drive the carts on which the barrels are placed close to the basin, bale out the water in little pails to which long poles are fastened, and from the pails, without any medium of spout or funnel, into the square bung-hole of the cask. Their aim is certainly remarkably good, and the greater part of the water goes into the barrel, but enough runs over, notwithstanding, to make a constant swamp in the summer, and a very inconvenient hill of ice in the winter. This waste is the more unpardonable, because the water is brought, with much labour and great cost, by the canal of *Sukhareva Bashnia*.

This *Suchareva Bashnia* – that is, the tower of Sukhareff – was originally a building erected by Peter the Great for the administration of the Strelitz, and was named after a certain Sukhareff, who, though himself a Strelitz, did the emperor good service during the revolt of those Russian pretorian bands. It is a lofty square tower in the Garden-street, standing in the centre of a long building, and serves, as before said, as a reservoir for the city. The water from which the tower is supplied rises seventeen versts from Moscow, is brought by an aqueduct to within three versts, and there raised by a steam-engine erected by the Emperor Nicholas, and impelled into the basin of the tower, whence it is carried to the different basins in the city. The water pours into the basin of the tower from a silver vessel, placed on one side, which sends out constantly fifty streams, each an inch in diameter. The Russian eagle, likewise of silver, expands his wings over these fifty fountains; and on the wall above all, the picture of a saint is suspended, under whose auspices all this labour is carried on. Such a guardian is placed over every spring used by man in Russia.

Moscow Theatres

[50] Moscow's first theatre – the Petrovsky; from *The Russians at Home. Unpolitical sketches* by Sutherland Edwards.

In the year 1763, it was provided that a fourth part of the receipts of the Moscow actors should be given to the Foundling Hospital. In 1766 ballet performances were introduced by an Italian. The Moscow company had now regularly established itself in Count Vorontstoff's house, which was, in fact, the Moscow theatre, when, in 1780, while 'Demetrius the Impostor' – a piece founded on events in the national history – was being performed, the building caught fire, and was burnt to the ground.

The drama, then, was houseless in Moscow. But it was no longer destined to lodge with rich noblemen. It was at length to have a home of its own, and, strangely enough, it received its habitation from an Englishman. However, although comparatively but few Englishmen have mixed themselves up with the public life of Russia (and we hear of none entering the odious civil service, of which the Germans are so fond), many have signalized themselves in independent capacities, and also in the army and navy. Thus, General Patrick Gordon defeated the rebellious Strelitzes during Peter the Great's absence from Russia. Admirals Greig and Elphinstone destroyed the Turkish fleet in one of the few general actions ever fought by the Russian navy. One of Catherine the Great's most distinguished naval commanders was Captain Sutherland; and her physician, Matthew Guthrie, wrote a work on Russian antiquities, which is still the best authority on the subject. Finally, an Englishman named Medox founded the Moscow Theatre; and if his structure was not so magnificent as the one since erected on the same site by the Russian architect of the exterior, Tonn, and the Italian architect of the interior, Cavos, it was, nevertheless, a very fine building, and was actually commenced and finished in five months.

Mr Medox was a man of mystery. He had travelled much, had seen many countries, and wore a scarlet cloak – a peculiarity which gained him the nickname of 'the Cardinal.' He came to Russia from India, but he had nothing to do with the Indies. From his passport, it appeared that he was of Oxford University, and that he was – not an architect or a manager, but a professor of mathematics. Catherine II knew something of mathematics herself, and she chose Mr Medox to instruct her son Paul in that science. It was probably during this period that the Englishman gained the Empress's favour; but, however that may have been, she certainly behaved with great liberality towards him throughout his Russian career.

When the mathematician resolved to build a theatre, he had, first of all, to solve a problem which has driven millions to despair, and which may be stated as follows: 'Given a scheme; it is required to find the money necessary for carrying it out.' But Mr Medox, who had studied at Oxford, and travelled in India, and who walked about the streets in a red cloak, was not to be baffled. Not having sufficient capital of his own, he proceeded to the government Loan

Office, and borrowed the sum of 130,000 roubles. For this he must certainly have had the consent, if not the direct recommendation, of the Empress; but the writer in the Moscow journal states that the privilege of managing the theatre for ten years was obtained for him by Prince Vassili Mikhailovitch Dolgorouki Crimski (*i.e.* of the Crimea). The new theatre was opened in 1780, the very year in which the other one was burned down, and was called the Petrovski. It is a remarkable fact, that when Medox entered upon the management of it, he scarcely understood the Russian language. Probably the pieces played were translations; for we are told that he himself instructed all the actors, who were, for the most part, peasants belonging to an estate that he had purchased.

The Petrovsky is said to have been admirably adapted for spectacular pieces, and also for masquerades, which were frequented by the highest society. It occupied, as we have said, the ground on which the Opera-house now stands; but at that time the actors and actresses had their lodgings in the wings. It was a large and magnificent building, and each box, as at the present day, had a retiring-room attached to it. The assemblies were held in a large circular hall, furnished with mirrors, which, when lighted up, produced a very brilliant effect. There was also a splendid chandelier, with forty-two lustres; and the price of admission to this attractive place was no more than a rouble. When the Petrovsky Theatre was first opened, an inaugurative piece was produced, at the suggestion of the Empress, under the title of 'The Wanderers', in allusion, we presume, to the ever-changing abode of the Moscow players. We shall not attempt an analysis of the plot. Suffice it to say, that Apollo, Mercury, Thalia, &c, were the principal characters, and that the scenery included a representation of Parnassus, and a grand view of Moscow, with its new theatre.

[51] Natasha Rostova goes to the opera; from *War and Peace* by Count L.N. Tolstoy.

That evening the Rostovs went to the opera, for which Marya Dmitryevna had obtained them a box . . .

Natasha at that moment felt so softened and moved that to love and know that she was loved was not enough for her: she wanted now, now at once to embrace the man she loved, and to speak and hear from him the words of love, of which her heart was full. When she was in the carriage sitting beside her father and pensively watching the lights of the street lamps flitting by the frozen window, she felt even sadder and more in love, and forgot with whom and where she was going. The Rostovs' carriage fell into the line of carriages, and drove up to the theatre, its wheels crunching slowly over the snow. Natasha and Sonya skipped hurriedly out holding up their dresses; the count stepped out supported by the footmen, and all three walked to the corridor for the boxes in the stream of ladies and gentlemen going in and people selling programmes. They could hear the music already through the closed doors.

'Natasha, your hair . . .' whispered Sonya. The box-opener deferentially and hurriedly slipped before the ladies and opened the door of the box. The music became more distinctly audible at the door, and they saw the brightly lighted rows of boxes, with the bare arms and shoulders of the ladies, and the stalls below, noisy, and gay with uniforms. A lady entering the next box looked round at Natasha with an envious, feminine glance. The curtain had not yet risen and they were playing the overture. Natasha smoothing down her skirt went in with Sonya, and sat down looking round at the brightly lighted tiers of boxes facing them. The sensation she had not experienced for a long while – that hundreds of eyes were looking at her bare arms and neck – suddenly came upon her both pleasantly and unpleasantly, calling up a whole swarm of memories, desires, and emotions connected with that sensation . . .

In the front of the stalls, in the very centre, leaning back against the rail stood Dolohov, in a Persian dress, with his huge shock of curly hair combed upwards. He stood in the most conspicuous place in the theatre, well aware that he was attracting the attention of the whole audience, and as much at his ease as though he had been alone in his room. The most brilliant young men in Moscow were all thronging about him, and he was obviously the leading figure among them.

Count Ilya Andreitch, laughing, nudged the blushing Sonya, pointing out her former admirer.

'Did you recognize him?' he asked. 'And where has he dropped from?' said he, turning to Shinshin. 'I thought he had disappeared somewhere?'

'He did disappear,' answered Shinshin. 'He was in the Caucasus, and he ran away from there, and they say he has been acting as minister to some reigning prince in Persia, and there killed the Shah's brother. Well, all the Moscow ladies are wild about him! 'Dolohov the Persian,' that's what does it! Nowadays there's nothing can be done without Dolohov; they do homage to him, invite you to meet him, as if he were a sturgeon,' said Shinshin. 'Dolohov and Anatole Kuragin have taken all the ladies' hearts by storm.'

A tall, handsome woman with a mass of hair and very naked, plump, white arms and shoulders, and a double row of big pearls round her throat, walked into the next box, and was a long while settling into her place and rustling her thick silk gown.

Natasha unconsciously examined that neck and the shoulders, the pearls, the coiffure of this lady, and admired the beauty of the shoulders and the pearls. While Natasha was scrutinizing her a second time, the lady looked round, and meeting the eyes of Count Ilya Andreitch, she nodded and smiled to him. It was the Countess Bezuhov, Pierre's wife. The count, who knew every one in society, bent over and entered into conversation with her.

'Have you been here long?' he began. 'I'm coming; I'm coming to kiss your hand. I have come to town on business and brought my girls with me. They say Semyonovna's acting is superb,' the count went on. 'Count Pyotr Kirillovitch never forgot us. Is he here?'

'Yes, he meant to come,' said Ellen, looking intently at Natasha.

Count Ilya Andreitch sat down again in his place.

'Handsome, isn't she?' he whispered to Natasha.

'Exquisite!' said Natasha. 'One might well fall in love with her!'

At that moment they heard the last chords of the overture, and the tapping of the conductor's stick. Late comers hurried to their seats in the stalls, and the curtain rose.

As soon as the curtain rose, a hush fell on the boxes and stalls, and all the men, old and young, in their frock coats or uniforms, all the women with precious stones on their bare flesh concentrated all their attention with eager curiosity on the stage. Natasha too began to look at it.

The stage consisted of a boarded floor in the middle, with painted cardboard representing trees at the sides, and linen stretched over the boards at the back. In the middle of the stage there were sitting maidens in red bodices and white skirts. An excessively stout woman in a white silk dress was sitting apart on a low bench with green cardboard fixed on the back of it. They were all singing something. When they had finished their song, the woman in white moved towards the prompter's box, and a man, with his stout legs encased in silk tights, with a plume and a dagger, went up to her and began singing and waving his arms.

The man in the tights sang alone, then she sang alone. Then both paused, while the music played, and the man fumbled with the hand of the woman in white, obviously waiting for the bar at which he was to begin singing with her. They sang a duet, and every one in the theatre began clapping and shouting, while the man and woman on the stage, supposed to represent lovers, began bowing with smiles and gesticulations.

After the country, and in her serious mood, Natasha felt it all grotesque and extraordinary. She could not follow the opera; she could not even listen to the music: she saw nothing but painted cardboard and strangely dressed-up men and women, talking, singing, and moving strangely about in the bright light. She knew what it all was meant to represent; but it was all so grotesquely false and unnatural that she felt alternately ashamed and amused at the actors. She looked about her at the faces of the spectators, seeking in them signs of the same irony and bewilderment that she was feeling herself. But all the faces were watching what was passing on the stage, and expressed nothing but an affected – so Natasha thought – rapture. 'I suppose it is meant to be like this!' thought Natasha. She looked alternately at the rows of pomaded masculine heads in the stalls, and at the naked women in the boxes, especially at her next neighbour Ellen, who, quite undressed, sat gazing intently, with a quiet and serene smile, at the stage, and basking in the bright light that flooded the theatre, and the warm air, heated by the crowd. Natasha began gradually to pass into a state of intoxication she had not experienced for a long while. She lost all sense of what she was and where she was and what was going on before her eyes. She gazed and dreamed, and the strangest ideas flashed unexpectedly and disconnectedly into her mind. At one moment the idea occurred to her to leap over the footlights and sing that air the actress was singing; then she felt inclined to hook her fan into an old gentleman sitting near her, or to bend over to Ellen and tickle her.

[52] The Moscow Theatre (now the Bolshoi); from *The Russians at Home. Unpolitical sketches* by Sutherland Edwards.

Tonn's theatre of 1843 opened with Glinka's 'Life for the Tzar', an opera which has since attained great popularity in Russia.

One morning in the winter of 1853, during a rehearsal, the Moscow Theatre again caught fire, and, with the exception of the outer walls, was burnt to the ground. During the year 1854 there was no 'Great Theatre'; but in the spring of 1855 the masons and bricklayers set vigorously to work, and the whole theatre, with all its decorations, was completed in a year and four months. It is true that the builders raised our Covent Garden from its ruins in less than half that time, and that the entire Winter Palace in St Petersburg was erected in twelve months; but to finish the Moscow Theatre, the most finished that exists, in a year and four months (including a winter of nearly six months, during which it is impossible for bricklayers to work), was a very creditable performance.

M. Cavos is not only an architect, he is also an 'acoustician', if we may use the term: in other words, he understands, what does not appear to be understood in London, that to build a music-hall in which the music is either not heard at all, or only to great disadvantage, is far more absurd than to build one unpleasing to the eye, but, nevertheless, 'good for sound', and that there is no necessity for doing either. M. Cavos ridicules the generally-received idea that it is impossible to know beforehand whether a building will or will not be 'good for sound'. He says that certain proportions must be observed, certain distances kept, and certain materials employed (the Moscow Theatre is lined throughout with wood), and that then there can be no doubt about the result. M. Cavos was kind enough to accompany me all over the theatre, from the Emperor's apartments to the upper boxes, and to give me a number of interesting particulars respecting the construction of the *salle*, and the means taken to ensure 'sonority'. 'It is constructed like a musical instrument', he said; and, apparently, he would have been as much astonished to find the Moscow Theatre not thoroughly adapted for operatic performances as Broadwood or Erard might be at discovering that some pianoforte-case, built in accordance with known rules, failed to answer the purpose for which it was intended . . .

Let me now give the dimensions of the Moscow Theatre (the figures were furnished by M. Cavos himself), and

compare them with those of the two largest Opera-houses of
Italy and of our new Covent Garden Theatre:

English feet

Diameter of Ceiling:	La Scala (Milan)	70
" "	San Carlo (Naples)	73
" "	Royal Italian Opera	65
" "	Moscow Theatre	98
Opening of Proscenium:	La Scala	51
" "	San Carlo	58
" "	Royal Italian Opera	50
" "	Moscow	70

At the Moscow Theatre the breadth of the stage is 126 feet:
the depth, 112 feet; and the principal staircase (there are five
altogether) is 126 feet long. At Covent Garden the breadth
of the stage is 88 feet 6 inches; the depth, 90 feet.

There are five rows of boxes at the Moscow Opera-house,
besides an amphitheatre, and a gallery, or 'paradis', which
occupies the whole of the top tier. There are sixteen boxes
on the pit tier, thirty on the grand tier, or bel étage, and
twenty on each of the amphitheatre tiers. Every box in the
theatre has a room, or 'cabinet', attached to it; those on the
bel étage have 'cabinets' which are so many little drawing-
rooms, furnished with sofas, mirrors, and damask hangings.
The usual allowance of chairs for each box is six; but there is
plenty of room for ten or twelve persons, or even more,
according to our Western notions of theatrical comfort.
Each person taking a box is as much the proprietor of it for
the evening as if it were his ordinary residence. It holds as
many as you like to put into it; and, of course, for this very
reason, it is a proof of very bad taste to fill it. In Russian
novels and comedies it is a stock joke to represent merchants
going to the theatre in family parties of twelve; and I have
actually seen a party of more than twelve in one box, which,
as might be expected, was one of the cheapest in the
house . . .

The Emperor has two boxes at the Moscow Theatre: one

for gala nights, in the middle of the *bel étage*, very magnificent, and reaching to the tier above; the other a comparatively quiet affair, on the right of the stage, but, at the same time, the most richly decorated proscenium-box ever seen. Adjoining the latter is a lofty and splendidly furnished drawing-room, leading to a retiring-room. These apartments, to which there is a special staircase and entrance, are always prepared for the Emperor when he is in Moscow. Opposite the ordinary imperial box is one set apart for the ministers of state.

For the general public there are, on the ground-floor, above five hundred stalls. Each stall is a separate armchair, in which you can enjoy as much space as you would desire in any drawing-room. There is a passage down the middle of the 'stalls' – as in the pit of Her Majesty's Theatre, only wider – and there is a passage all round them; so that at any period of the evening you can walk quietly to or from your place without incommoding either yourself or your neighbour.

The price of stalls is regulated by their proximity to the stage, and also by the attractiveness of the performances. When the Italians were playing, the chairs in the front rows let for six roubles (about a pound), the back rows for five and four roubles. A bureau for the sale of tickets, attached to the theatre, is open all day, and during the performances, but no money is taken at the doors; nor on entering the theatre are you required to give up your ticket, or even, as a rule, to show it. Each ticket entitles the holder to a seat, and in order that there may be abundance of room for some two thousand persons no such thing as 'standing room' is recognized. If you do not know the way to your place, there are plenty of attendants to point it out to you; and it is for the place you pay, not for the mere admission. The Russians take their servants with them to the theatre, and in the winter the wide corridors on each tier are full of them. They mount guard at the back of the boxes, perhaps criticizing the music or, more probably by far, the audience, and waiting in readiness to call the carriage at the first nod, and to untie the sheet in which are enclosed the furs and galoshes that their masters and mistresses will put on before venturing from the vestibule down the steps of the portico to their covered sledge.

[53] The Moscow Art Theatre: the first night of Chekhov's *The Seagull*, 1898; from *Anton Tchekhov, Literary and Theatrical Reminiscences* by K.S. Stanislavsky.

In the spring of 1898 the Moscow Popular Art Theatre was founded. We found it hard to get partners for the new venture, for they did not expect any success for it. But Tchekhov responded to the first appeal and became one of the partners. He was interested in all the details of our preparatory work and asked us to write him frequently and in detail. He loved Moscow and wished to come there, but his illness kept him in Yalta, which place Tchekhov called the Devil's Island, comparing himself to Dreyfus. Above all he was interested in the repertory of the future theatre.

He objected most strongly to our production of his *Seagull*. After its failure in Petersburg, he regarded *The Seagull* as a sick but favourite child.

Yet in August 1898 *The Seagull* was included in our Repertory. I do not know how VI. Iv. Nemirovich-Danchenko had succeeded in persuading Tchekhov to consent to it . . .

Then came the anxious day of the opening of the Art Theatre, and its precarious existence during the first two months. The affairs of the theatre did not run smoothly. With the exception of *Fyodor Ivanovich*, which gave us full houses, nothing attracted the public.

All our hopes rested on Hauptmann's *Hannele*. But the Moscow Metropolitan Bishop Vladimir considered that the play was not suitable, and we had to remove it from our repertory.

Our position thus became critical; moreover we based no great hopes on the financial success of *The Seagull*.

We all realized that the fate of our theatre depended on the success of Tchekhov's play. But there appeared a new difficulty, a new anxiety. On the eve of the performance, after the final rehearsal, Marie Tchekhov, Anton's sister, came to the theatre. She was very much upset by the news she had received from Yalta of her brother's health. The idea that *The Seagull*, in the present state of the author's health, might turn out a failure, drove her to despair, and she was afraid of the risk we were taking.

We, too, felt alarmed and began to talk about cancelling the performance, which was equivalent to closing the theatre. It was not easy to pronounce the death sentence on the theatre and to let the players starve. But then, what would the partners say? How would they regard such a decision? Our responsibilities to them were quite obvious. So at eight o'clock of the following evening the curtain rose. The theatre was not crowded.

How the first act passed off, I do not know. I only remember this that all the actors and actresses smelt of valerian drops. I remember that I felt terror-stricken when I sat, during Nina's monologue, with my back to the audience, and surreptitiously holding my leg which trembled nervously.

It seemed as though we were in for failure.

The curtain went down on a funereal silence. The artistes pressed close to each other, in fright, trying to guess the impression which the act had made on the public. Silence of the grave. From behind the scene the scene-shifters and carpenters tried to hear what was going on in the audience. Then came a cry: Olga Knipper trying to suppress hysterical sobs. Silently we moved behind the scenes.

At that very moment the audience burst out into applause. Then the curtain went up. People say that we stood on the stage with our faces half turned to the audience, that we looked queer, that none of us thought of bowing to the public, and that one of us was even squatting on the floor. Evidently we were not aware of what was taking place.

The play was a tremendous success, and the mood on the

stage was the festive mood of Easter night. Everyone was embracing everyone else, not excepting members of the public, who rushed up behind the scenes. One of the artistes was in hysterics; many others, and myself among those, from joy and excitement, danced a wild dance.

Towards the end of the performance the audience requested that a telegram of congratulation should be sent to the author.

From that evening the relations between Anton Tchekhov and the Art Theatre became intimate.

The Tretyakov Gallery

---

[54] Pavel Tretyakov and his collection; from *My Life in Art* by Konstantin Stanislavsky.

The generation to which my parents belonged consisted of people who had already crossed the threshold of culture, and who although they did not receive the benefits of higher education, and in the majority of cases were educated privately, still made much of culture their own, thanks to their innate abilities. They were conscious creators of the new life. Numberless schools, hospitals, asylums, nurseries, learned societies, museums, and art institutions were founded by their money, their initiative, and even their creative effort. For instance, the famous clinics of Moscow, large enough to constitute a city in themselves, were built mostly by the initiative and the money of these men and their heirs. They made money in order to spend it on social and artistic institutions. And all this was done in a spirit of humility, in the silence of their studies.

In illustration, the manufacturer Pavel Tretyakov, who

collected the riches of art galleries and donated them to the city of Moscow. In order to do this, he worked from early morning till late at night in his office and in his factory, and when he came home gave himself up to his gallery and to conversations with young artists in whom he felt the presence of talent. In a year or two the pictures of the young artists would find their way into his gallery, and they themselves would first become well known and then famous. And how humbly he practised his philanthropy! Who would ever recognize the famous Russian Medici in the bashful, timid, tall, and thin figure with the bearded, priest-like face? Instead of taking vacations he would spend his summers in becoming familiar with the pictures and museums of Europe, and in his later years, in accordance with a long-maturing plan, he travelled systematically on foot through all Germany and France and part of Spain.

The Petrovsky Palace

[55] Tatyana's arrival in Moscow: her first view of
the Petrovsky Palace; from *Eugene Onegin* by
Alexander Pushkin.

XXXVI

But now they're near. Already gleaming
before their eyes they see unfold
the towers of whitestone Moscow beaming
with fire from every cross of gold.
Friends, how my heart would leap with pleasure
when suddenly I saw this treasure
of spires and belfries, in a cup
with parks and mansions, open up.
How often would I fall to musing
of Moscow in the mournful days
of absence on my wandering ways!
Moscow . . . how many strains are fusing

in that one sound, for Russian hearts!
what store of riches it parts!

XXXVII

Here stands, with shady park surrounded,
Petrovsky Castle; and the fame
in which so lately it abounded
rings proudly in that sombre name.
Napoleon here, intoxicated
with recent fortune, vainly waited
till Moscow, meekly on its knees,
gave up the ancient Kremlin-keys:
but no, my Moscow never stumbled
nor crawled in suppliant attire.
No feast, no welcome-gifts – with fire
the impatient conqueror was humbled!
From here, deep-sunk in pensive woe,
he gazed out on the threatening glow.

XXXVIII

Farewell, Petrovsky Castle, glimmer
of fallen glory. Well! don't wait,
drive on! And now we see a-shimmer
the pillars of the turnpike-gate;
along Tverskaya Street already
the potholes make the coach unsteady.
Street lamps go flashing by, and stalls,
boys, country women, stately halls,
parks, monasteries, towers and ledges,
Bokharans, orchards, merchants, shacks,
boulevards, chemists, and Cossacks,
peasants, and fashion-shops, and sledges,
lions adorning gateway posts
and, on the crosses, jackdaw-hosts.

[56] Petrovsky Palace in the 1830s; from *Incidents of Travel in the Russian and Turkish Empires* by J.L. Stephens.

I mounted a drosky, and in half an hour was in another world, in the great promenade of Pedroski, the gathering-place of the nobility, where all the rank and fashion of Moscow were vying with each other in style and magnificence. The extensive grounds around the old chateau are handsomely disposed and ornamented with trees, but the great carriage promenade is equal to anything I ever saw. It is a straight road, more than a mile in length, through a thick forest of noble trees. For two hours before dark all the equipages in Moscow paraded up and down this promenade. These equipages were striking and showy without being handsome, and the Russian manner of driving four horses makes a very dashing appearance, the leaders being harnessed with long traces, perhaps twenty feet from the wheel horses, and guided by a lad riding the near leader, the coachman sitting as if nailed to the box, and merely holding the reins. All the rules of good taste, as understood in the capitals of Southern Europe, were set at defiance; and many a seigneur, who thought he was doing the thing in the very best style, had no idea how much his turn-out would have shocked an English whip. But all this extravagance, in my eyes, added much to the effect of the scene; and the star-spangled Muscovite who dashed up and down the promenade on horseback, with two Calmuc Tartars at his heels, attracted more of my attention than the plain gentleman who paced along with his English jockey and quiet elegance of equipment. The stars and decorations of the seigneurs set them off to great advantage; and scores of officers, with their showy uniforms, added brilliancy to the scene, while the footmen made as good an appearance as their masters . . .

It was one of the most striking features in the animating scene at Pedroski to see family groups distributed about, all over the grounds, under the shade of noble trees, with their large brass urn hissing before them, and taking their tea under the passing gaze of thousands of people with as much unconcern as if by their own firesides.

Leaving for a moment the thronged promenade, I turned into a thick forest and entered the old chateau of the great Peter. There all was solitude: the footman and I had the palace to ourselves. I followed him through the whole range of apartments, in which there was an appearance of staid respectability that quite won my heart, neither of them being any better furnished than one of our old-fashioned country-houses. The pomp and show that I saw glittering through the openings in the trees were unknown in the days of the good old Peter; the chateau was silent and deserted; the hand that built it was stiff and cold, and the heart that loved it had ceased to beat; old Peter was in his grave, and his descendants loved better their splendid palaces on the banks of the Neva.

When Moscow was burning, Napoleon fled to this chateau for refuge. I stopped for a moment in the chamber where, by the blaze of the burning city, he dictated his despatches for the capital of France; gave the attendant a ruble, and again mixed with the throng, with whom I rambled up and down the principal promenade, and at eleven o'clock was at my hotel.

The French Invasion, 1812

[57] Kutuzov abandons Moscow to Napoleon –
Governor Rostopchin's despair; from *Oeuvres
Inédites du Comte Rostopchine.*

(Count Feodor Vasilievitch Rostopchin (1763–1826) was
effectively Tsar Paul I's Foreign Minister between 1798 and
1801. He retired in 1801 at Paul's command. Between 1812
and 1814 he was Commander-in-Chief and Governor-General
of Moscow.)

I found Prince Koutouzow warming himself, sitting by the
fire. He was surrounded by generals and aides-de-camp
expecting orders. Some he sent on to Barklay and others
to Benigson, some to Quartermaster Colonel Toll, his favourite, worthy of his protector. With great politeness he
received me and took me aside. We remained together for
half an hour. I then had with this man a most curious
conversation, which showed the baseness, incapacity and
cowardice of our army chief to whom had been entrusted

the salvation of our country. In fact, he did nothing to merit the title of 'Saviour of Russia'. He declared he had decided to fight Napoleon at this very spot.

I explained to him that the terrain behind his position inclined most steeply towards the city and if our lines were pushed back even a little, they would become confused with the enemy entering Moscow's streets; that we would not be able to pull our army back, and that we risked losing it entirely. He went on assuring me one would not force him to abandon the position, but if, unluckily, he were obliged to move backwards, he would go towards Twer. When I explained he might be without food, he murmured, 'But we must cover the North.' He was thinking of the Emperor's residence and paid no attention to two points: if Wittgenstein's troops were destroyed, St Cyr would reach St Petersburg long before him; and secondly, that Napoleon, after occupying Moscow, would not intend in September to march for six weeks, to take St Petersburg at the end of October.

In fact, by following the road to Twer, Koutouzow would have been separated from his reinforcements and the enemy would have mastered the country up to the Black Sea. I asked him if he would not consider moving on to the Kalouga road towards which his reinforcements were marching, to which he answered evasively. The reason why: the troops of the King of Naples had, after the battle of Borodino, taken that direction and he wanted to avoid it. He started gossiping about the battle he was intending to fight, asking me the day after tomorrow to bring along the Archbishop with two miraculous pictures of the Virgin. He said he wanted them to be carried right along the line headed by the clergy, reciting prayers and blessing the troops with holy water. He asked me to send him a few dozen bottles of wine and warned me that the next day nothing would happen because 'he knew Napoleon's tactics. He would stop tonight, rest his troops for a day, use the next for a reconnaissance and would attack me the very next day.'

We returned with him near the fire, where the generals

were arguing. Doctorow, who was to command the left wing, announced that the artillery would not get through on account of the height of the river and the steep face of the hill.

I was talking to Barklay who exclaimed: 'Look at the plan; all I want is to be killed, if one is mad enough to fight where we are.' Benigson, whom I had not seen since the death of the Emperor Paul, came towards me. I mastered the horror which the leader of the executioners of my benefactor inspired in me, and he informed me he did not believe in the battle proposed by Koutouzow, saying that they themselves did not know the number of men they commanded, and that the retreat, which was indispensable, would be followed by the occupation of Moscow by the enemy. The soldiers were lifeless and the officers dispirited: chaos reigned; everyone was handing out advice and disputes were the order of the day . . .

My orderly came to inform me that Milaradowitsch, with our rear guard, had crossed the Arbat Street, and that the enemy's advance guard followed immediately. I immediately mounted my horse and went toward the Rezan Barrier, where near the Yaousa Bridge I found Prince Koutouzow with his escort. I saluted him but did not wish to speak to him. But as he greeted me with '*bonjour*' – which could well be called a sarcasm – he said, '*Je puis vous assurer que je ne m'éloignerai pas de Moscou sans livrer bataille.*' I did not reply, as an answer to a stupidity could only be nonsensical.

Before reaching the bridge I was stopped by riderless and wounded officers. They asked me for money. I emptied my pockets but my gift was hardly in proportion to my wish to help them. They thanked me, their eyes full of tears. So were mine. I was moved seeing mutilated officers reduced to beg, so as not to starve.

It was difficult for me to get through the barrier on account of the great number of troops and carriages anxious to leave the city. As I was crossing the gate three cannon shots were fired to disperse the crowd. These shots were meant to signal the occupation of the town and thus I knew I was its Governor no more. I turned my horse round and with respect saluted this capital city of the Empire where I was born and which I had guarded. My duty was over, my conscience clear; but sorrow oppressed me, and I was reduced to becoming jealous of those Russians killed at the battle of Borodino who could not be witnesses of Napoleon's triumph!

[58] The Abbé Surrugue saves his flock at St Louis des Français; from *Souvenirs d'une Femme sur la Retraite de Russie* by Louise Fusil.

(Louise Fusil (1774–1848) was a French singer and actress, well known in Paris in the 1790s as a singer of *opéra bouffe*. In 1806 she left France to seek her fortune in Russia, first in St Petersburg and then in Moscow, where the French troops found her in 1812. She decided to leave with the French army on 19 October, and participated in the horrors of the Retreat, which her memoirs vividly describe.)

Much has been written about the burning of Moscow.

The details related in many books of what happened inside the city between the departure of the Russians and the arrival of the French are often inaccurate.

Only foreigners, locked up in Moscow, can relate the truth. The most interesting details were given by l'Abbé Surrugue, parish priest of the Catholic Church. His modesty forbade him to reveal how he had relieved the unfortunate. The precincts round the church were large enough to allow small wooden houses to be used by poor foreigners. Whilst Moscow burnt, soldiers pillaged. What was left of the old, the women and the children took refuge in the church. When the soldiers reached it, the Abbé had the doors opened. Dressed in his sacerdotal vestments, holding a crucifix and surrounded by the poor of whom he was the only protector, he advanced full of assurance towards these desperadoes, who backed away respectfully. How sad that there was no painter to record this scene. Many an artist painted fires they had not even seen!

Abbé Surrugue promptly asked for a guard to look after these unfortunate people, a request at once granted.

The Emperor Napoleon insisted that he should meet him and tried everything to induce him to return to France. 'No,' was his answer, 'I will not leave my flock as I may still be useful to it.' Although food was very scarce, some was sent to the Abbé who, as a good shepherd, distributed it.

[59] Stendhal's description of the fire of Moscow; from *Stendhal* by Marie-Henri Beyle.

Whilst dining at the Apraxin Palace, I left my diary there. As I was taking my leave of M.Z. in the courtyard, I noticed that, as well as the fire in the Chinese quarter (Kitai Gorod) which had been raging for several hours, another had begun in our quarters. The blaze was fiery enough. I developed a toothache during this expedition. Out of the kindness of our hearts, we arrested a soldier who had just twice bayonneted a man owning beer; I went so far as to draw my sword, and was even going to run it through the ruffian; but Bourgeois escorted him to the Governor, who released him.

We left the place at 1 o'clock but not before delivering ourselves of various obvious remarks against fires, which hardly produced any great improvement. Back in the Apraxin courtyard, we tested out a pump. I went to bed tortured by my aching teeth ... I slept until 7 o'clock, had my carriage loaded, and ordered it to take up its place behind those of M. Daru.

They were drawn up on the boulevard opposite the Club. There I found Mme Bursay, ready to fling herself at my feet; thus expressing a ridiculous gratitude on her part. I noticed that there was no sign of sincerity in all that she was saying to me, which naturally made my manner appear icy. Notwithstanding, I did render her a considerable service by placing her plump sister-in-law in my open carriage, and suggesting to her that her *droshkys* should follow it. The fire was rapidly spreading towards the house which we had just left. Our carriages waited five to six hours on the boulevard, and, irritated by such inactivity, I went to inspect the fire and stayed for one or two hours at Joinville's. I was full of admiration for the comfort of his furnishings. We drank, with the help of Billet and Busche, three bottles of wine which restored life to us. I read there some pages from *Virginie*, in an English translation which, amidst such general squalor, revived my finer feelings . . .

At 3 o'clock, I returned to our line of carriages and my melancholy colleagues. Amongst the timber warehouses close by, a warehouse of flour and of oats had been found, and I ordered my servants to take some. They put on a great show of activity, seemed to take a great deal, but in fact hardly took any at all. This is how things are generally dealt with in the army, and is one of the reasons for one's frustration. I would willingly tell them all to go to hell, but as they always come to complain I become very impatient and these, my military days, are very unhappy. My impatience is better controlled than many others, but I often allow myself fits of temper. I am jealous of some of my colleagues who, upon being told they are f–g useless, do not lose their tempers. Their voices get louder, and that is all. They wriggle their ears, as Countess Palfy used to describe to me. 'One would indeed be unhappy were one not able to do that,' she would add. She is right; but with a sensitive soul, how can one follow such advice?

About half-past 3, Billet and I went to inspect the house of Count Peter Soltykoff, which might do for H.E. We went to the Kremlin to report this to him, and stopped at General Dumas', who was in command of the crossroads.

General Kirgener had said to Louis in front of me: 'If entrusted with 4,000 men, I would guarantee in six hours to master the fire and it would be stopped.' I was struck by this. (I doubt of its success; unceasingly Rostopchine was arranging for fires to be lit afresh; contained on the right, they would have flamed anew on the left in twenty different places.)

We saw M. Daru arriving from the Kremlin, and the kind Marigeniev, whom we escorted to the Soltykoff palace, which we visited from top to bottom on foot. M.Z. thought the place unsuitable, and so we inspected others on the way to the Club; this latter was decorated in the French style, imposing and locked. In Paris there is nothing to compare with it. The adjoining house was magnificent and huge. Finally we decided to occupy an attractive, well-built, white house.

We were all very tired, I more than others. Since Smolenski I find myself drained of energy, and childishly I had set my heart and energies on finding the right houses.

We settled ourselves into this house which seemed to have belonged to a rich man loving the arts. It was comfortably disposed, full of statuettes and pictures; he had fine books, to wit Buffon, Voltaire (present everywhere here) and the 'Gallery of the Palais Royal'.

Violent attacks of diarrhoea made all of us fear a lack of wine. We were told there was wine to be found in the cellars of the handsome Club which I have already mentioned – I made old man Billet go there, and we got in through a magnificent stable and a garden which would have been beautiful were it not for the ineradicably stunted character – as I see it – of the trees in this country.

We sent our servants to raid this cellar, where they found for us quantities of bad white wine, damask tablecloths and similar napkins, but very worn. These were looted and made into sheets.

Little M. Joly, on the staff of the Quartermaster General, who had joined us to loot away as well, took it on himself to confirm our loot as official presents. He said he would take over the house for the Intendant General and began to moralize: I had to shut him up. My batman was quite drunk. He piled into the carriage the tablecloths, the wine and a violin to which he had helped himself, and a thousand other objects. Two or three of us had a drinking session.

The servants tidied up the house. The fire was a long way away, and enveloped the whole atmosphere under a lofty pall of coppery smoke. We settled ourselves down and at last were going to relax when M.Z. arrived to announce that we should leave. I took the news bravely, but felt weak-kneed. My carriage was quite full; nevertheless, I put into it the wretched diarrhoea-ridden Bonnaire whom I had gathered up out of pity to pay back the good deeds of Biliotti. He is the silliest and most boring mother's darling I know. I helped myself before leaving to a volume of Voltaire's called *Facéties*.

The carriages of François were long in coming. We only got going at 7 o'clock and met a furious M.Z. We went directly towards the fire along part of the boulevard. Little by little as we advanced through the smoke, breathing became harder; finally we passed between smouldering houses. All our efforts were at risk because of the complete lack of discipline and caution. A long line of carriages was engulfing itself in the very heart of the fire to avoid it. This manoeuvre would have had some reason to it if only a small core of the town had been encircled by flames, which was not at all the case. The line of fire ran along one side of the town; one had to get away but there was no need to cross it, only to turn around it, and this being impossible, we were stopped dead in our tracks. We had to turn round. Absorbed as I was by the magnificent spectacle before me, I forgot for a second that I had made my carriage turn before the others. I was harassed, on foot, because my carriage was piled high with the servant's loot and that hunched-up wretch. I thought my carriage lost in the fire. François at the head took off at a gallop. The carriage had incurred no danger, but my servants, like everybody else's, were drunk, and quite capable of nodding off in the middle of the flaming street.

On return, our colleagues found General Kirgener on the boulevard, which greatly pleased me that day. He chided them into a mood of boldness, that is to say, common sense, and showed them that there were two or three ways of getting out. Towards 11 o'clock we were in a queue fighting the baggage-train of the King of Naples for space. We passed before a very fine palace under construction, and I noticed later that we were following Tverskoi Street. We left the town, our way lit by the finest blaze in the world which was in the form of a huge pyramid resembling the prayer of the faithful whose base is on earth and whose spire reaches to heaven. The moon, I think, appeared above the holocaust. It was a magnificent sight but one should have been alone to see it, or in the company of intelligent men. Such was my sad state during the Russian Campaign. It was spoilt for me, as I had to endure it with people who would have belittled the Coliseum and the Bay of Naples.

Our route lay along a fine boulevard towards the Castle of Petrovskoi where his Majesty had made his headquarters. Paf! From my carriage where I had made a corner for myself, I saw in the middle of the road the barouche of M.Z. overbalancing and finally falling into the ditch. The road was only 80 feet wide. Oaths, anger. It was extremely difficult to retrieve it.

Finally we arrived at a bivouac facing the town. There was a marvellous view of the vast pyramid consuming the divans and pianos of Moscow. What rich pleasures they would have given us without that incendiary maniac. This Rostopchine will be judged as a rogue or as a Roman; time will show. Today a notice was found affixed to one of Rostopchine's houses, stating that the value of its contents was so much (a million I believe), etc. etc., but that he had given orders for it to be set on fire so that bandits should not enjoy its use. So far it is a fact his fine palace has not yet been burnt.

At the bivouac we supped on raw fish, figs and wine.

These are the details of one of the most painful, indeed boringly painful, days of my life.

[60] The fate of property abandoned during the French invasion; from *Staraya Moskva* by D.M. Nikoforov.

When Napoleon's troops retreated from Moscow, many foreigners and a small number of Russians followed in the wake of the enemy forces. By order of the Commander-in-Chief, it was decreed that all the property left behind by those who had fled should be auctioned off, and the monies raised by the sales distributed among Moscow's stricken inhabitants. Subsequently it was discovered that many of those whose property had been confiscated had been unjustly accused. Some people had been taken away by force, and others had been in hiding within Russia's borders. Their property was returned to them. Many of those involved in the appropriation of other people's goods were apprehended, and, as may be seen from the notes of Count Rostopchin, suspicion even fell upon the wife of General Ivashkin. On page 239 of 'la Biographie futur du comte Theodore Rostopchine', we find the following remarks made by Count Andrei Feodorovich Rostopchin: 'Le général Iwaschkine, grand-maître de Police de Moscou. Lui et sa femme parlait un frances de tous les diables. Madame était assez avide de sa nature, et quant apres la sortie des Frances de Moscou, on faisait des inventaires d'objects trouvés, ramassés, rapportés des maisons en ruines et que personne ne reclamait, elle ne manquait pas de s'y trouver, et choisissant ce qui était à sa convenance, criait à son mari: "Cher, puis-je?" Et le mari repondait: "Pouvez, ma chère, pouvez".'

[61] Moscow grieves and rejoices after the French invasion; from *Griboyedov's Moscow* by M. Gershenzon.

The letters written to Grigori Korsakov by his loved ones from a burnt-out Moscow paint a vivid picture both of the city after its devastation, and of the emotions experienced by

Muscovites returning to their cinders. Volkov who was, as we already know, Moscow's police chief, returned to take up his duties soon after the French had left the city and brought his wife with him. On 9 November, Sophia Alexandrovna found a moment to write to Grigori. 'I have been back in our unhappy Moscow for five days now. Oh, Grisha my darling, you would not believe what has become of Moscow, it is unrecognizable, and one can not look upon these ruins without weeping. Only the walls of the stone houses are left, and only stoves sticking out of the wooden ones. Imagine what a miracle it was to find Mamma's house still in one piece, and even more miraculous Matushka's wooden one in which we are now living. As for the settlement, it is as if it has never existed – burnt to the ground and our own house and all our goods with it. The village, too, is in ruins, and we are left with nothing.'

'Europe is saved, the nations freed, the tyrant disarmed, and exhausted humanity, like a seafarer after storm and shipwreck suffered on the stern bosom of the ocean, calls for silence and a safe harbour.' Thus wrote an anonymous Moscow columnist at the end of April 1814. Paris was taken, Napoleon was in captivity – Moscow rejoiced. On 13 April, a courier from Petersburg brought the first news of the capture of Paris; on the 17th, Count Vassiliev arrived, sent by Alexander for the express purpose of informing Moscow of the joyful events. A long series of festivities now began in the Senior City. On 23 April, before a huge gathering of people, a service of thanksgiving was held in the Kremlin; during the ensuing three days, bells pealed unceasingly in the city; from morning to night, and on each of the three evenings, there were magnificent illuminations. On the 24th, Moscow's nobility, partly to celebrate the taking of Paris, and partly as an expression of gratitude to the Emperor who had, a short time before, sent 150,000 roubles towards the restoration of the building which housed their Assembly, staged – in this very Assembly – a magnificent ball, at which, among other things, the choir sang, to the accompaniment of an orchestra, a polonaise composed for the occasion:

> Portentous tidings come winging
> From the Neva river shore,
> Joy in our souls anew is singing,
> And Moscow comes alive once more . . .

and so on. On 25 April there was a solemn meeting of the Moscow University – speeches, poems, music etc. On the 26th, Moscow was treated to a masquerade by Posniakov – and here the choir thundered:

> Glory and the Lord be with us, with us!
> The messenger of Tsars is come:
> Russ, spreading eagle wings
> Flew into Paris,
> With leaves of laurel on his brow.

There then came a break in the celebrations which were resumed on 10 May, by a concert at the house of S.S. Apraksin given by the artistes of the Moscow Imperial Theatre: the trio 'He who Gives Alms to the Poor', the aria from *Russalka*, the song 'To the Tsar our Father', etc. On 13 May, Posniakov gave an entertainment at his house in aid of Russian warriors wounded beneath the walls of Paris, during which one of the actresses cunningly contrived to insert one or two couplets about the triumphant entry of Alexander into Paris into the sketch 'Apparitions, or Argue Your Fill But Never Wager'. Finally on 19 May, Moscow's nobility arranged a grandiose celebration at Poltoratsky's house by the Kaluga Gate. Our Maria Ivanovna gave a foretaste of this evening's programme in a letter to her Grisha. By that time it seems, the Korsakovs had recovered from their sorrows and tribulations. On 14 May Maria Ivanovna wrote to her son:

The Almighty has taken pity on his creation, and has at last laid that blackguard low. Here, although Moscow has been burnt to its very bones, we are too happy to lose heart, and celebrate to our very last *kopek*. There was a masquerade at the Assembly, the members donated funds: the merchants paid for the masquerade, Posniakov for the masquerade-theatre. And how amazing that after one and a half years we should be celebrating there where the French also staged their plays – in Posniakov's theatre! This thought was in everyone's mind, and when they sang in honour of the Emperor, I swear that there were few present who did not shed tears of happiness. And on the 18th, we are to attend a delightful occasion where your little sisters will have their chance to shine. All the members of the nobility have joined forces and each has given what he felt like giving, but never less than 200: they collected 25,000. They are going to act a melodrama: Russia is being played by Verochka Viasemskaya, formerly Gagarin, Europe by Lunin's daughter, Glory by Dimitri Alexandrovich Bakhmetev's. The melodrama has been written by Alexei Mikhailovich Pushkin. They've built a shrine into which they have placed a bust of His Imperial Majesty, our Emperor, and nearby stand the peoples of each nation: Sophia (Volkova) – Portugal; Natasha (Rimsky-Korsakov) – England; the Shakhovskaya girl – Turkey; the other Shakhovskaya girl – Germany; Poltoratskaya – Switzerland; one of the Vissotskis – Italy; the other – Sweden. Nobody wanted to take the part of France or Poland. All these *mamselles* sing in harmony – the words are priceless – and each one deposits a garland of flowers. For the people there are roundabouts, theatre shows, fireworks and illuminations.

The Expansion of Moscow

[62] Moscow in the late eighteenth century; from *Essays about Classical Moscow* by Yuri Shamurin.

In the second half of the eighteenth century, Moscow was still a 'big village'. However, every decade saw an increase in the number of large stone structures, works of art which brought the aesthetic culture of Petersburg within reach of Moscow. The baroque of the Empress Elizaveta and the work of Rastrelli gave Moscow several beautiful monuments, churches for the most part, which were lost in a great sea of pre-Petrine wooden houses and wildernesses. Elizaveta's craftsmen, whether perfecting Rastrelli's plans, or surrendering themselves body and soul to his dazzling artistry, provided Moscow with a few churches, a few palaces, which lasted but a short time, and with the Razumovsky house on Pokrovka (which today houses the Fourth Gymnasium).

Parallel to these few beggarly echoes of the splendour of Petersburg architecture, a fairly modest yet nevertheless reasonably independent architectural movement was developing in Moscow. Its centre was the 'architectural command post' of Prince Dimitri Ukhtomsky, established at the Bureau of Building Works. Dimitri Ukhtomsky, the best Moscow architect of Elizaveta's reign, failed to receive a single substantial commission, but even in accomplishing the humdrum tasks which fell to his lot, he succeeded in demonstrating his creative individuality. He built the gates to the Wine and Salt Store (the present day municipal electric power station), restored the Kremlin Armoury after the 1737 fire, built several official buildings which are no longer standing, and the Krasnoe Gate, which, in the words he used to describe his finest creation, wore '*the Order of its composer*'. Dimitri Ukhtomsky gathered about him a 'brigade' of assistant architects and 'kitchen boys', who were simultaneously his helpers and his pupils. The 'brigade' studied Vitruvio and Palladio, and used engravings of the ancient monuments to master the craft of building; and this early love of classicism bears the stamp of Dimitri Ukhtomsky's personality, the first of Russia's architects to value classical architecture.

In the end, V.I. Bajhenov and M.F. Kazakov were the only two masters to emerge from the ranks of Dimitri Ukhtomsky's 'brigade', but the name of one of these two alone is enough to guarantee the Ukhtomsky School the right to a place in the annals of Russian art. In the middle years of the eighteenth century, very little building took place in Moscow; furthermore, all the important palace buildings were built by Moscow architects following plans sent out from Petersburg by Rastrelli. Annenhof, the Golovinsky Palace and the 'Perovsky House', that is Countess Razumovsky's palace in the Perovko district, were all built in this way.

In 1769, V.I. Bajhenov arrived in Moscow, summoned from Petersburg to realize his colossal plan for the construction of the Kremlin Palace. During his visits abroad, Bajhenov had become acquainted with classical trends in the west, but at home in Russia he preferred to build in the spirit of late baroque. His ill-fated and, for us, mysterious existence crushed an enormous talent, the evidence of which is to be found more in his plans than in his completed buildings. In Moscow, Bajhenov built comparatively few things, but among examples of his work may be found several classical structures. The bell-tower of the Church of All Sufferers on Bolshoi Ordinka (1787) belongs in this group, as do the Yiushkov House by the Myasnitsky Gate, now the premises of the School of Drawings and Sculpture, and the classical summerhouse at Tsaritsyn. As a classicist, Bajhenov does not have a large volume of work to his credit. In comparing his classical achievements with his baroque plans, it becomes evident that all his sympathies lay with the baroque and his interest in classicism was merely a tribute to the times.

Bajhenov's failure to carry out the Kremlin Palace project marked his fall; checked at the same time, this promoted Kazakov's advancement. Kazakov drew up plans for adorning the Kremlin with buildings which 'signalled the new taste'. These sketches of Kazakov's have been preserved in the Armoury. He left all of the Kremlin's ancient monuments untouched, and did not alter its old aspect, but added a row of spacious buildings which, set into the Kremlin walls, formed, as it were, a Moscow Acropolis. Here, it was proposed, would be the Senate House, the *Manège*, the Deputy Governor's House, the Archiepiscopal Palace, and so on. Not all of these buildings came to be built. In 1775, Kazakov began work in the Kremlin, on the Metropolitan's House, today's Nicholas Palace. In 1776 he drew up plans for the Senate and launched into work which was to continue until 1784. This culminated in Moscow's largest and most exquisite building, dating from the period which marked the transition from Baroque to classicism.

During the course of the 1780s, building activity in Moscow picked up considerably. Leading members of the nobility began to build themselves vast palaces, and the majority of these were the work of Kazakov. (Already he was not working on his own: around him was gathered a 'team' consisting of his sons and several assistants out of whose ranks Nazarov, Selekhov, and Eghotov were subsequently to emerge.) Classicism was enthroned to rule alone in Moscow in the 1780s. At first, the city's masterbuilders were unable to achieve freedom in their use of classical forms, but the aesthetic of Classicism, its calm, ordered beauty, was easily within their grasp. Almost the first classical residential palace to be built in Moscow was the house of the Governor General on Tverskaya Street. Kazakov worked on it between the years 1782 and 1784 at the behest of Count Tchernishev, who had been appointed Moscow's commander-in-chief. In the list of works which Kazakov prepared for the Emperor Alexander when applying for a pension, he mentions that apart from the main corpus 'also built by me, but designed by someone whose identity is not known', both the plans for the Governor General's house and their execution had been his responsibility. This lack of clarity denotes that the plans, as so often happened in the case of important commissions, had been sent out from Petersburg where they had been drawn up by one or other of the Court architects. It is most probable that the author of this project was Yu. M. Felten who had bequeathed to Petersburg a whole row of handsome buildings adorned with similar pilasters. The Governor General's mansion, the first private palace in Moscow, could not fail to have an effect on Moscow's nobility, and on Kazakov himself. From the 1780s on, Kazakov, although not abandoning Government orders, began for the most part to build gentlemen's residences. To begin with he gave them the appearance of small palaces, but with the years, having mastered the use of classical forms, he created an entirely new style of Moscow house similar to the Razumovsky mansion on Gorkhovskoe Street.

Kazakov, too, succeeded in creating an original type of church, wedded to the character of Moscow Classicism. He found the perfect answer to the problem of reconciling the spirit of Orthodox places of worship with the demands of classical aesthetics, and produced a different solution to that employed by the classicist architects of Petersburg, who created massive churches along Catholic lines. Kazakov discovered modest, more personal formulas.

Empress Elizaveta's enthusiasm for Classicism, and the architectural evolution of Petersburg, tipped the balance: Moscow's long-hidden sympathies were indeed for the genius of classical architecture.

[63] Moscow as a city for private living, in the early nineteenth century; from *Essays about classical Moscow* by Yuri Shamurin.

V.G. Byelinsky gives a powerful, acute, if somewhat satirical portrait of Moscow at the beginning of the nineteenth century in his essay 'Moscow and St Petersburg'.

As a result of the inevitable incursion into Moscow of Europeanism on the one hand, and the wholly surviving element of old-world conservatism on the other, it has emerged as rather an odd city, in which European and Asiatic features combine to dance in a gaudy haze before your eyes. It has spread and stretched over a vast area; what an enormous city you might say . . . ! Yet you only have to take a walk to discover that this sense of space is greatly favoured by the existence of long, exceedingly long, fences. There are no huge buildings; the more substantial houses are not exactly small, but then again, they are not exactly large. They do not boast any particular architectural merit. Still striving faithfully towards the goal of domestic felicity, the genii of the ancient Muscovite kingdom quite clearly meddled in their architectural design. After an hour's walk through Moscow's crooked, slanted streets you will soon realize that this is a patriarchal, a family, city; the houses stand apart, almost every one in possession of its own wide courtyard, surrounded by outbuildings and overgrown with grass.

Narrow, twisting, Tverskaya Street, with its little piazza to one side, winds its way uphill, and the largest and grandest house upon this thoroughfare would, in St Petersburg, be considered extremely modest in size and elegance. Someone accustomed to straight lines and angles might feel a little strange when confronted by one house which has run a few steps into the street, as if to see what is happening there, and another which – prompted by haughtiness or modesty, depending on its appearance – has stepped back a pace or two.

[64] The reconstruction of Moscow after 1812; from *Essays about Classical Moscow* by Yuri Shamurin.

The fire of 1812 made room for expansive ideas on construction. Moscow, rising from the ashes, was to be a city faithful in plan and detail to the principles of the classical school. A commission was formed to watch over city planning: the facades of buildings were examined and approved by government architects, and among those attracted to this weighty task were leading artists of the calibre of Bovy and Gilliardi. And Skalozub was right to assure us in *Woe from Wit* that Moscow's fire 'greatly favoured her adornment' . . .

Domenico Gilliardi began his career as an assistant to his father during the first years of the nineteenth century. The Empress Maria Feodorovna recognized his budding talent, awarded him an allowance, and sent him off on a journey abroad. Gilliardi came home from his travels in 1810 and remained in Moscow until 1831. His work is as important for the Moscow after the great fire of 1812 as Kazakov's contribution is to the end of the eighteenth century. Gilliardi built widely in Moscow – for the most part, private residences.

Created by the finest master-builders of the epoch, Mokhovaya street at its intersection with Nikitskaya survives as a delightful corner of classical Moscow. Here we find one of Gilliardi's most magnificent creations, the old university building dating from mid-way through the first decades of the nineteenth century; the Manège which was built in 1817 and remodelled by Bovy; the university church built by Gilliardi's pupil, E. Turini; the lovely wall of the recently constructed 'new' university; and the classical wall and gates of the Alexander Gardens built to Bovy's design. As a result, this section of Moscow has retained the planning and siting of buildings given it in the beginning of the nineteenth century, and all the architectural concepts of that time and place have been immortalized . . .

The university was Gilliardi's biggest project. It occupies a place apart in the sum of his achievements. With this gigantic official edifice, Gilliardi brushed against that epic, grandiose side of Classicism epitomized by the creations of Petersburg's master-builders. It is true to say that even here we find signs of Moscow's familiar mellowness, but nevertheless the Doric columns on their massive base, the severe unencumbered walls, the weighty squat dome, are all redolent of that grandeur of form and spirit which only the masters of Classicism knew how to achieve.

BEYOND MOSCOW

Kolomenskoye

[65] The Renaissance palace of the Tsars at Kolomenskoye, scene of the terrible massacre following the Copper Revolt, 1662, when 7,000 rioters were killed and 15,000 punished; from *Precursors of Peter the Great* by Princess Zinaïda Shakhovskoye.

For all the evil memories which hung over Kolomenskoye from then on, Alexis Mikhailovitch did not abandon his plan to construct a new palace there. Building started in autumn 1666 and the bulk of the work was completed within a year. The new palace at Kolomenskoye was built of wood like that of Izmailovo, but seems – in contrast to the latter, with its Westernized appearance – to have been based on tales from Russian national folklore. Its absurd but pleasing lines smacked of Moscow's Church of St Basil, and its onion-domed roofs, towers, turrets, innumerable stairways and maze of interconnecting passages all proclaimed the brilliant workmanship of native joiners.

Visiting the fortress of Archangel in 1586, almost a century earlier, a French sailor named Jean Sauvage had marvelled at the incomparable skill of the local carpenters. 'It is a fortress constructed of tree-trunks,' he noted in his journal, 'admitting neither of nails nor hooks, and its builders had no tools save axes. No architect could have done better.' (Saws did not come into general use until the reign of Peter the Great.)

Perhaps the best way to describe the new palace at Kolomenskoye is to compare it with sets for Russian ballets or the opera *Le Coq d'Or*. It was a building which preserved the traditional elements of the present *izba*. The summer of 1668 was devoted to decorating it and adding finishing touches. The palace had two hundred and fifty rooms and three thousand windows. Its carved wooden ornamentation frothed like lace and its roofs were covered with multi-coloured wooden tiles painted in delicate colours and gilded with gold imported from abroad. An unusual note was struck by decorative motifs in copper and tin affixed to both the interior and exterior. Apart from traditional ornamentation, the builders employed new methods such as the coloured ornamentation of walls and ceilings – the first application of this technique to a wooden building.

The interior decoration of the palace was entrusted to a team of Russian painters supervised by Simon Ushakov, the artist who had decorated the Kremlin. The portraitist Saltanov was commissioned to paint portraits of historical figures such as Julius Caesar, Alexander the Great and Darius. Jaques Reitenfels, who visited Kolomenskoye, described it in the following terms: 'The palace is worth seeing, even though it is built of wood. Its decoration, which is astonishingly well-executed, is so remarkable and its profusion of gilding so brilliant that it appears to have emerged from a jewel-box.'

It would have been unlike Alexis Mikhailovitch not to have busied himself with enlarging and improving the existing gardens and orchards at Kolomenskoye. An inventory of 1701 describes them in detail. One particular orchard contained more than four thousand apple trees and several hundred pear trees, and was bordered on all sides by cherry trees and raspberry and blackcurrant bushes. The entire population of five villages and nine hamlets furnished the labour force needed to maintain the estate. Kolomenskoye* was the Tsar's favourite place for receiving foreign ambassadors. Its praises were sung by the Court poet, Simeon Polotski, who likened it to the eighth wonder of the world:

> The world's four quarters are represented there,
> Across the ceiling spreads the celestial vault,
> The four seasons, flowers most marvellous . . .

Kolomenskoye's three thousand mica-covered windows glittered like stars, and, wonder of wonders, Alexis Mikhailovitch's throne resembled that of Solomon himself. It was flanked on either side by two lions made of gilded copper. Stitched into sheepskins painted and dressed 'lion-fashion', these figures were connected by means of a complicated mechanism invented by the craftsman Peter Vissitsky to a pair of bellows operated by a man stationed in a hidden chamber. They rolled their eyes, opened their jaws and roared with life-like ferocity.

* The building has disappeared. All that remain are models, of which one now reposes in the Stchussev Museum of Russian Architecture, Moscow. Another, older example is in the British Museum in London, and during the eighteenth century there used to be a third in the Botanical Gardens at Leyden, Holland.

Archangelskoye

[66] Prince Yusupov's Tartar retreat at Archangelskoye; from *The Russian Journals of Martha and Catherine Wilmot 1803–1808*.

(Catherine Wilmot (1773–1824) and Martha Wilmot (1775–1873) belonged to an Anglo-Irish clan of some distinction, with links to the Establishment. An aunt of theirs had become a friend of the formidable and famous Princess Dashkov during a Continental tour, and invited her to Ireland in the 1770s. Princess Dashkov, who had helped Catherine the Great take power, invited the Wilmot girls in turn to visit her at Troitskoye near Moscow. Martha arrived in 1803, and remained under the spell of the Princess and of Russia for nearly five years. Catherine came out, in effect to cajole Martha to return, but left Russia in 1807 to avoid internment in view of the impending Anglo-Russian War. Martha, after the adventure of a shipwreck off Finland, returned to Ireland in 1808. Princess Dashkov died (of *ennui* or heartbreak) within a year of her departure, but Martha had inspired her to write her remarkable memoirs. Alexander Herzen himself valued the extraordinary frankness and liveliness of the Wilmot diaries.)

Monday 10th [January], 1808

. . . On Saturday we din'd with Prince Yousoupoff* in his Tartar Palace which in no respect that I can find out differs from any other House of equal dimensions. He has added a spacious gallery to his old House which is extremely agreeable, & one descends a winding Staircase to enter it first passing thro' a Library. The Gallery is furnish'd with a variety of beautiful paintings, amongst which 2 of Angelica Kauffmann's performance pleased me the most. (I'm told that that celebrated Artist is dead.)† There are likewise Birds of every description to enliven the Guests, & as the Gallery is enormous their Clatter & Cry produces a good effect of banishing Ceremony & inducing people to go from the Cages of the Parrots to visit the Cockatoo, the Paroqueets, the beautiful but sulky Purple & Yellow Bird, & so on in every gradation to the Melodious Nightingales of which he has a long file of Cages & tells me that they sing *responsively* to each other the Evenings and early in the Mornings, sometimes likewise in the day time but rarely.

From the Gallery one enters a Green House at the end of which is painted a Perspective which has a magnificent effect & in the Center of which is a rotunda for Entertaining Company Surrounded with Orange & leamon Trees of Great height. But it was too cold for us to stay long that day, so we return'd to the lovely Gallery where I have not yet spoken of the Statues, Billiard table, Stoves, Books & Prints lying on tables & every Species of elegance to excite & exhibit the good taste & refinement of the Master of the

---

* Prince Nicholas Youssoupoff (1751–1831), Russian politician and traveller of Tartar origin. Formerly President of the College of Manufacturers and Director of Crown Lands. Later Governor of the Kremlin. Noted for his love of women and the extravagance of his entertainments.
† Angelica Kauffmann, the famous Swiss artist, died in November 1807 at Rome, where she had been living in retirement for many years.

House. But I owe him a grudge for not Shewing me his Tartar retreat, & so I'll tell tales on him. 'tis say'd that in reality he *has* a suite of apartments in the Tartar taste with oil'd paper instead of Glass Windows, but that they are inhabited by fair Dulcineas who are guarded with all the jealous care of the Grand Turk's Seraglio. A young french Woman burst her prison doors last Week, leaving a letter to say she prefer'd freedom of the West to the gloomy Magnificence of the East. His dismay is still the talk of the Town & Tartarian oil'd paper a delicate subject with his Highness.

[67] Prince Yusupov and Moscow aristocracy; from *Podmoskovnaya, Kulturniya Sokrovishcha Rossii* by Yuri Shamurin.

By virtue of his wealth, his 'enlightenment', his noble breeding, and, particularly, his numerous and extremely successful 'gallant adventures', Archangelskoe's first owner, Prince Nikolai Borisovich Yusupov, shone brightly on Moscow's early nineteenth-century horizon. He was numbered among Moscow's most highly cultured grandees, and found particular renown in artistic and scientific circles. Very typically, his life was closely linked to Archangelskoe, and only when viewed in relation to his own biography does the place come alive, and all the fragments of its past acquire meaning . . .

In a letter to P.A. Pletnev, dated 22 July 1831, Pushkin writes, 'my Yusupov has died . . .' The preceding year, in his ode 'To a Great Lord' the poet celebrated Prince Yusupov, his 'noble idleness', his Archangelskoe.

> . . . this palace
> Where the builder's compass, knife and palette
> Obeyed your wise caprice
> And, inspired, vied to make enchantment.

The great ode to Yusupov is far too serious a work to be attributed entirely to kindnesses exhibited towards Pushkin by a well-disposed grandee.

The dawn of the eighteenth century in Russia had seen the birth of a very definite ideal: that of a free, enlightened, individual who drank greedily of life's every gift, unhampered by an interior or exterior restraint. This feeling of freedom, and of being drunk with joy, pervades the work of Batiushkov, and rages within the breast of the youthful Pushkin; yes, and even in maturity, when he had abandoned his epicurean stance, the old ideas often surfaced again. Also, this was not just a literary mood, an artistic dream: the life of the aristocracy, that is to say, of those of its members who disposed of their endless leisure in a pursuit of culture, provided a favourable ground upon which to seed such ideals.

Among his fellow Muscovites, Prince Yusupov was one of the most brilliant exponents of this philosophy. Possessed of inexhaustible resources, incapable, without the aid of a little notebook, of counting up all his properties, he had travelled the length and breadth of Europe, spoken with her leading men, and caroused at Catherine's court and at Versailles where, 'like an inquisitive Scythian at the feet of the Athenian sophists', he had listened to the words of Voltaire, Diderot, and other eighteenth-century luminaries.

In Yusupov, Pushkin recognized a fellow spirit. Although, by that time, the poet could no longer look at life 'turning in a circle' with dispassionate amusement, the old ideals, as yet unvanquished, slumbered deep in his heart, and at times would make themselves heard with even greater force than before. With envy and respect he addresses Yusupov:

> You know life's reasons: oh, happy man
> You live for life itself . . .

At the beginning of the century there was as yet no knowledge of the concept of debt or duty to society, nor of the morality of altruism; everyone 'lived for life', but a very few knew how to lead serious and beautiful existences, and earned the right of the wise man to look life calmly in the face. This right Pushkin and his contemporaries accorded to Yusupov, one of the most erudite men of his time.

. . . as I step across your threshold
I am at once in Catherine's day.
The library, the idols, and the pictures,
The graceful park, all prove to me
That you worship the Muses in the silence,
In noble idleness they are the air you breathe
. . . the power of beauty
By you is keenly felt. With joy you prize
The glitter of *Alabiev*, the charm of Goncharov,
And blithely gathering round you Correggios, Canovas,
You who take no part in the tumult of the world
Will gaze at times from out your window
And, smiling, see how, turning in a circle,
Everything comes round . . .

The entire philosophy of the Russian aristocrat is contained in these lines. As we stroll through the domain at Archangelskoe, they come repeatedly to mind. It is as if those who lived here knew how to satisfy their every spiritual need, and only in this setting may the key to their souls be found . . .

Above all, they wished to be free of other people: free not only of obligations, but of any ties whatsoever; to turn everything – the world, their fellow men – into adjuncts of a beautiful existence, into a means of satisfying their whims. Voltaire survived comfortably alongside harems of serf girls and a sensuality that knew no bounds; Rousseau was revered to the point where his waxen likeness was given pride of place in the library at Archangelskoe, yet it was still possible to use and abuse people as if they were toys; moved to tears by some poignant work of fiction, you could still be a hard-hearted master. Stories about the highly cultured N.B. Yusupov circulated around Moscow for many years. The orgies at Archangelskoe and in his Moscow house, the gallant adventures of his declining years, were on everyone's lips and only increased universal respect. There persists an obstinate rumour that N.B. Yusupov arranged an apartment for himself at Archangelskoe, hung with an incalculable number of portraits, each one commemorating some brief or lasting attachment.

Living life for itself, and retreating into cultural seclusion, are the two things which characterized Moscow's aristocracy. In Archangelskoe this is clearly felt. Two separate worlds are in evidence: a corner of paradise where all is beauty, elegance, and designed to serve the highest concerns; and, beyond its boundaries, Russia – cold, grey, and disorderly. There are no bridges linking the two, you can stay only on one side of the precipice.

Otradnoye

---

[68] Count Alexei Orlov's hospitality at Otradnoye:
his wild 'Armenian'; from *Travels into Poland,
Russia, Sweden and Denmark in 1792* by William
Coxe.

(The Rev. William Coxe (1747–1828), educated at Eton
and King's College and ordained in 1771, became a tutor
to the Duke of Marlborough's sons and chaplain at
Blenheim. In 1775 he was appointed tutor and companion
to the seventeen-year-old George Herbert, son of the Earl
of Pembroke, and with him travelled through Europe,
south to Italy and then north to Scandinavia and Russia,
which they reached in 1778. In 1784 he returned to St
Petersburg as tutor to Samuel Whitbread, son of the
founder of the famous brewery. In 1803 he married
Elinore, the widowed sister of the British Consul-General
in St Petersburg, and again visited the city in 1806. He
wrote many books of biography and history, as well as
short works on Russian problems; and his famous *Travels*

went through six English editions between 1784 and 1803.)

During our stay at Moscow we frequently experienced the hospitality of count Alexèy Orlof, who, in the last war with the Porte, commanded the Russian fleet in the Archipelago, and burnt the Turkish armament in the bay of Tchesme, for which action he has been honoured with the title of Tchesminski. The custom of conferring an additional name for the performance of signal services to the country, was, in imitation of the Romans, usually practised by Constantine and his successors the Greek emperors, who reigned at Constantinople. From that quarter it probably passed to the Russians, who in the earlier times of their history gave appellations of this kind to some of their illustrious leaders. Thus the great-duke Alexander was called Nevski for his victory over the Swedes near the Neva; and his great-grand-son Demetrius Ivanovitch was denominated Donski, for his conquest of the Tartars upon the banks of the Don. This custom, which had long been discontinued, has been lately revived by the present empress. Accordingly Marshal Romanzof received the denomination of Zadunaiski from his victories south of the Danube; prince Dolgorucki that of Crimski for his sucesses in the Crimea; and count Orlof this of Tchesminski from the action in the bay of Tchesme.

The house of count Orlof is situated at the extremity of one of the suburbs, upon an elevated spot, commanding a fine view of the vast city of Moscow and the neighbouring country. A number of separate buildings occupy a large tract of ground. The offices, stables, manage, and other detached structures, are entirely of brick; the foundation and lower story of the dwelling-house are built with the same materials; but the upper part is of wood,* neatly painted of a green colour. We carried a letter of recommendation from prince

---

* Wooden houses are by many persons in this country supposed to be warmer and more wholesome than those of brick and stone, which is the reason why several of the Russian nobility chuse that part of the house, which they inhabit themselves, to be constructed with wood.

Stanislaus Poniatowski, the king of Poland's nephew, to the count, who received us with great frankness and cordiality, and detained us at dinner: he desired us to lay aside all form; adding, that he was a plain man, had a high esteem for the English nation, and should be happy to render us every service in his power during our stay at Moscow. We had the pleasure of dining several times with him, and always met with the most polite reception. The count seemed to live in the true style of old Russian hospitality; kept an open table, abounding with a great variety of Greek wines, which he brought with him from his expedition into the Archipelago. One dish, served on his plentiful board, must be particularly mentioned as extremely delicious, and only inferior to our best venison; it was a quarter of an Astracan sheep, remarkable for the quantity and flavour of the fat.*

We had music during dinner, which indeed generally made a part of the entertainment at the tables of the nobility. We observed also another very usual instance of parade; namely, a great number of retainers and dependents, mixed with servants, but seldom assisting in any menial office: they occasionally stood round their lord's chair, and seemed infinitely pleased whenever they were distinguished by a nod or a smile. In this train there was an Armenian not long arrived from Mount Caucasus, who, agreeably to the custom of his country, inhabited a tent pitched in the garden, and covered with a thick kind of felt. His dress consisted of a long loose robe tied with a sash, large breeches, and boots: his hair was cut, in the manner of the Tartars, in a circular form; his arms were a poignard, and a bow of buffalo's horn strung with the sinews of the same animal. He was extremely attached to his master: when he was first presented, he voluntarily took an oath of fealty, and swore, in the true

* In the court-yard I observed several sheep of this species ranging about the stables, so perfectly tame that they suffered us to stroke them. They are almost as large as fallow deer, but with much shorter legs: they have no horns, long flowing ears, and, instead of tails, a large bunch of fat, sometimes weighing thirty pounds. Mr Pennant has given an engraving of these sheep in his History of Quadrupeds, which he has accompanied with an accurate description.

language of Eastern hyperbole, to attack all the count's enemies; offering, as a proof of the sincerity of this declaration, to cut off his own ears; he also wished that all the sickness, which at any time threatened his master, might be transferred to himself. He examined our clothes, and seemed delighted with pointing out the superiority of his own dress in the article of convenience; he threw himself into different attitudes with uncommon agility, and defied us to follow his example; he danced a Calmuc dance, which consisted in straining every muscle, and writhing his body into various contortions without stirring from the spot: he beckoned us into the garden, took great pleasure in showing us his tent and his arms; and shot several arrows to an amazing height. We were struck with the unartificial character of this Armenian, who seemed like a wild-man just beginning to be civilized.

Kuskovo

[69] Count Sheremetyev's love for Parasha
Kovalevsky, a serf girl at Kuskovo, and their
subsequent marriage in 1800; from *Podmoskovnaya,
Kulturniya Sokrovishcha Rossii* by Yuri Shamurin.

Designated 'His Excellency Count Emperor' on estate reports, Count P.V. Sheremetyev presided at Kuskovo, surrounded by untold riches, like the mightiest of feudal
potentates. He enjoyed himself and provided enjoyment
for the whole of Moscow in his Kuskovo – 'a scaled down
transfer of Eden', according to Prince I.M. Dolgorukov –
and earned the reputation of being a courteous, enlightened,
and virtuous lord. His son, Nikolai Petrovich, having for
many years lived and studied abroad, returned to Kuskovo
as the representative of an already different culture, of a
different outlook on the world, which caused him to shun
the fanciful nature of his father's endeavours. He soon
abandoned Kuskovo, and built himself a new country
house, Ostankino; and yet the last decade of Kuskovo's

flowering – all of its most poetic legends and memories – is bound up with Count N.P. Sheremetyev, and while not escaping his flaws, reflects the very best qualities inherent in one of Russia's most attractive eighteenth-century figures.

There are lives and natures marked by a particular beauty and melancholy which lends them almost the fascination of a work of art: such was the case with N.P. Sheremetyev in whom shone all that was finest about the spirit which animated the eighteenth century. He had received an excellent education, had spent many years abroad attending the University of Leyden and tasting the opulent gaiety of foreign courts. He came to love music, the theatre, all things of beauty, and having at his command immeasurable wealth, was able to bring them all to his Moscow country properties.

That loathing for the brilliance and sensation of court life which, in the eighteenth century, was expressed with such feeling both in the spoken and written word, remained for most people merely a phrase read somewhere in a book. Ethereal dreamers lived sober lives with their feet planted firmly on the ground. N.P. Sheremetyev, friend of Paul I, most brilliant of courtiers, was forever longing to leave Petersburg for Kuskovo. There he fell in love with the actress, his serf Parasha Kovalevsky, and in 1800 he married her. This unprecedented event has been immortalized in a folk song: '*As from the forest late one evening I drove home my cow . . .*' sung to a typical, lilting, late eighteenth-century tune. The naive, ancient melody still lingers in the park at Kuskovo. The words rustle like falling autumn leaves:

> By the Cathedral of Uspensky
> The great bell chimes,
> For soon our sweet Parasha
> Shall be the master's bride.

During P.V. Sheremetyev's day there was already a theatre in existence at Kuskovo, but only when it was taken over by his son did it become a model of its kind. The Kuskovo theatre outshone the one in Moscow which was under the direction of the entrepreneur Maddox, a man who held the monopoly and complained that Count Sheremetyev was robbing him of his audiences.

The company, with its special costume- and wig-makers, was 230 strong. It contained few leading actors but there was a large supporting cast of dancers, musicians, and singers. In the summer, performances took place in the open air. The repertoire consisted of several dramas, some ten comedies, up to twenty ballets, and numerous operas. Together with the singers and dancers in the troupe were actresses or *comédiennes*: they numbered six in all and were attended by French lady teachers for whom 1785 had been the year of reckoning.

In fact, at the outset, the theatre's principal managers and leading personalities were all foreigners, but as time wore on they were replaced by the serfs who had learned under them. Dramatic actresses and opera-singers held privileged positions in the troupe. The actresses, in common with the leading man, Piotr Petrov, and the foreign musicians, were given a generous allowance: every day each received a loaf of white French bread brought especially from Moscow, and on days of fast, ten small carp fished from the lake. The 'dancers' fared much worse; their quarters were heated only if they were ill.

The theatre's repertiore was very varied. They staged Empress Catherine II's *Tsarevich Fevei*, the ballet *Inez de Castro*, (which had as yet never been performed at Court), and on the occasion of Catherine II's visit to Kuskovo, the opera *The Samnites' Wedding*. The scenery was painted partly by Gonzago and partly by the estate's own artists, under the supervision of the architect Alexei Mironov.

Once installed at Kuskovo, Count N.P. Sheremetyev spent the years 1785 and 1786 arranging the 'big' house to his liking, and began to occupy himself with the affairs of the estate.

In 1789 he fell in love with Parasha Kovalevsky who was a member of his choir, and who subsequently became his wife. Her unprecedented, and – for a serf – almost incredible

fate brought her more sorrow than joy. The weak-willed
Count spent many tormented years vacillating between
aristocratic tradition and the dictates of his heart. Having
found favour, Parasha began to live with the actresses and to
be tutored in the art of declamation, acting, dancing, and
music. Eventually she grew to be a gifted opera-singer who
delighted the most refined of critical tastes. The Count's love
for Parasha was instrumental in the development of the
theatre, which was to become his favourite pastime. Vast
sums of money were spent. Parasha, who had been given the
stage name 'Zhemchugova' [from the Russian word for
pearl]*, wore costumes which glittered with gold and precious stones.

Kuskovo is filled with memories of the extraordinary love
affair between the Count and the peasant girl. Their darkened portraits gaze down from the walls of the old house;
beyond its windows, the clipped green avenues and sunlit
limes beckon us towards life. It is hard to believe that the old
days have disappeared without trace, and it seems as if there,
in the lime thickets beyond the faded walls of the hermitage,
strange shadows of the past, its lovely images, still flicker, as
if somewhere its beings are still melting gently away . . .

The story of the Count's passion belongs between the
pages of a novel, or in a theatrical drama of old-world
chivalry. The tormented hero suffers agonies, his fame and
wealth come close to being an oppressive burden, yet ten
years of love have to pass before he grants his beloved serf
her freedom.

At last, having decided to wed, the Count left Kuskovo
where everything reminded him too vividly of the past, and
in 1799 moved to Ostankino. In his last letter to his son he
explains, as if seeking to justify himself, the reasons for his
unusual marriage: 'I nourished the most tender, the most
loving, sentiments towards her. For a long time I observed
her nature and her qualities: I discovered an intellect graced
by virtue, by honesty, humanity, loyalty, truth – by devotion

* Translator's note.

to the holy faith and the most fervent love of God. It was these qualities rather than her beauty which drew me to her, for they are stronger by far than any surface charms, and most rare . . .'

Everything that we have learned about Parasha Kovalevsky can be seen in her charming face. Having spent her youth as the daughter of a country blacksmith, she died a Countess in a magnificent Petersburg palace. The illiterate country girl, after a brief period of study, amazed audiences with the strength of her dramatic gift, playing heroic roles which were quite alien to her character and to that of Kuskovo. She died young, and an almshouse was built in her memory on Sukharevo Square. Confirmed by the portraits which remain, her image lingers in our thoughts as one of complete tenderness and fragility.

In 1799 Kuskovo became deserted. Although everything was preserved in its entirety, and daily reports were dispatched to the Count, stating that all was well, the locks unbroken, the statues still standing, the menagerie still safe from huntsmen, the swans still swimming, and Parasha's father, Ivan Stepanov, in good health, Kuskovo grew silent and gradually fell into decay. The theatre stood locked and sealed, the actors and the scenery were shifted across to Ostankino; the new house which had been built for Parasha was soon demolished.

Ostankino

[70] Count Sheremetyev's palace at Ostankino; from *Travels from St Petersburg in the Year 1805* by G. von Reinbeck.

(Georg von Reinbeck (1766–1849) was born in Berlin, the son of an archdeacon. He left for St Petersburg in 1792 to be a tutor to the Uvarov family, teaching English, German and 'aesthetics'; he also taught at the prestigious Corps des Pages establishment. Owing to ill health, he returned to Germany in 1805, where he became a well-known writer and a much talked-of raconteur about the good old days in St Petersburg.)

On one side opposite to the Sparrow Mountains, lies the estate of Count Scheremetjew already mentioned. It is called Astankina, and has a palace, the interior splendour of which exceeds any thing I ever saw of the kind. The road thither leads through fields and bushes without any thing remarkable to distinguish them; but at its proper entrance, com-

mences a wide avenue which leads to a bridge, on which two
sentry boxes, painted white and black, according to the
emperor Paul's taste, are standing. Here the elegant building, with its flesh coloured walls, and large green cupola,
begins to peep forth from behind the river Liborcha, which
is here of considerable breadth: an archway leads into the
lawn before the dwelling. The main building, with its
colonnades, stands in the backgrounds, and is enclosed
on both sides by the wings. One of these wings contains
the theatre, with a room for rehearsals, and a dressing-
room, having presses all round full of the most beautiful
porcelain. The floors are inlaid, and the curtains all silk,
partly with genuine gold fringes and tassels. In the dressing
room, stand two triumphal cars, richly gilded and lined with
gold and silver stuffs. The theatre is of a tolerable extent,
and fitted up with extraordinary beauty. The decorations
are not inferior to the rest in splendour and taste. The
theatre formed, when I saw it, a ball-room, after the last
entertainment given by the count to the emperor. But its
transformation into a theatre again, is the business of a few
moments only. The seats for the spectators, run amphithea-
trically in a semicircle, and above are private boxes, which
altogether will hold twelve hundred people. The count was
formerly extravagantly attached to dramatic representations, particularly operas, and formed a company for himself from his own people, of whom he chose the handsomest
and cleverest, and had them trained for the purpose in his
own theatrical school. It was unquestionably the most
distinguished company in Russia, and had the lately de-
ceased countess for a member, before her marriage. She had
been the particular object of her count's choice, and retained
his ardent affections till her death, when she left a child a few
days old, who was acknowledged by the emperor, as the
rightful heir to his immense property, which would otherwise have fallen to his nephews, the counts Rasumowsky.

Lofty mahogany folding doors, inlaid with coloured
woods, and adorned with long bolts of bronze, lead from
the theatre into the apartments, where a superfluity of

glittering furniture serves to dazzle the eyes of the beholder, and to display riches rather than taste. The most costly paintings, tables of jasper, of lapis lazuli, and of mosaic, sconces of the purest crystal, the most elegant carpets, the most gaudy tapestry, among which one of *Hautelice* was distinguished, curious clocks and time-pieces in rich bronze and marble cases, statues, vases, groups of ore, and the most beautiful china were all so thronged together in one immense mass, that the individual parts are entirely lost. The prodigious sums which must have been expended on the whole, may be easily conceived, from only knowing the amount of some articles which are by no means the most costly. In one hall, a large rotunda is formed by pillars of porphyry, jasper, and coloured marble, in the middle of which is an alabaster statue of Catherine the Great, which is a striking likeness, and is said to have cost 6,000 rubles: and in the background stands a marble statue of the Goddess of Health, leaning on Hermes, which was found at Athens in 1787, and is in good condition. Notwithstanding the workmanship is nothing extraordinary, it cost 12,000 rubles. The building of this hall, must have cost at the most moderate computation 30,000 rubles. The galleries are crowded with the most superb paintings, among which, are many by Angelica-Kaufmann, and also several master-pieces from the Dutch school.

Tsaritsyno

[71] A visit to Tsaritsyno in 1793; from *A Tour of Russia, Siberia and the Crimea, 1792–1794* by John Parkinson

(John Parkinson (1754–1840), a Fellow of Magdalen College, Oxford, and Rector of Brocklesby in Lincolnshire, accompanied young Edward Wilbraham-Bootle (later the first Lord Skelmersdale) on his Grand Northern Tour of Russia from 1791 to 1794. Astonishingly they visited not only the Caucasus and the Crimea, but penetrated as far as Tobolsk in Siberia.)

Zaritzina is an imperial palace in the Gothic Style which has been building ten years. The Country about it is well wooded and the ground lies exactly as the Gardener could wish. In the particular situation of Zaritzina, a deep valley, very bold on one side and formed by gentle slopes on the other but well wooded on both, winds along, watered formerly by a small stream, which they have now by damming it converted, as at Blenheim, into a broad lake or river. The palace is situated on the side of the water where the ground rises the most abruptly. It consists of several detached buildings dispersed about without forming one general whole which it is by any means possible to analyse, and built in a taste meant to be gothic, but fantastical and quaint beyond any thing of that kind that I ever saw. The Materials are brick and stone, the stone being used for the decorations of all kinds, such as columns, corniches, frames of windows, frames of doors and other embellishments, which are stuck all over in such profusion that we compared the ground on which they were stuck to a larded chicken. These buildings are also crowded together in such manner, that one could fancy it the object of the Architect to shut out as much as possible the beauties of the situation.

The most elaborate and gaudy structure, intended one may suppose to contain the state rooms, has indeed one end towards the water on the brow of the eminence, but it has close to it in the principal front one of those fantastic buildings and on the other a wood. A kind of Colonnade or Screen with a fine triumphal arch in the middle unites the palace with a very large and ugly pile of building round a small court. It was natural to suppose that this would have served for a passage between them. Upon examining it however, though there was an opening, it did not appear wide enough to answer the purpose of a passage . . . A.M. Ismailoff, the Gentleman I believe whom we saw at Mr Dickenson's, has the direction of this imperial bauble, which will not hand down to posterity, if it is as they say her own plan, any very favourable idea of her Majesty's taste. Perhaps if they proceed according to any Model and not altogether according to the whim of some fanciful Architect, the style may be at least as much Moorish as Gothic, the former being often mistaken and substituted for the latter, according to Mr Walpole . . . I grudged the labour and particularly the fine stone which has been thrown away in this motley and tasteless undertaking.

The Troitsko-Sergievo Monastery

[72] The Monastery in the 1790s; from *A Tour of Russia, Siberia and the Crimea, 1792–1794* by John Parkinson.

After breakfast we repaired to the Monastery. While John was looking about for a person to act as our conductor, we stepped into one of the Churches where Mass was saying. Several Monks were placed in a Seat opposite to the sacred doors and a number of Men stood immediately before them whom I took for 'Freres'. We were led from hence by our guide to the Refectory, a long oblong room, at the extremity of which the service was performing in another Church. A Monk into whose hands we were put here, asked us then whether we chose to wait upon the Archbishop, which offer we readily embraced. He received us with great complaisance and good humour; and after having sat conversing with him for at least an hour and a half and drunk a dish of tea, he was so obliging as to conduct us himself to see the Curiosities of the Convent, viz. the principal Church and the apartments where the dresses and plate belonging to it are kept. We found him dressed in a purple silk robe lined with white fur and a red mitre over his grey locks. But when he went out he put on a larger mitre covered with a sort of white veil which hung down behind and was embellished before with a cross of Amethysts. This looked very venerable. Over his silk robe he wore another much thicker and longer and he walked with a staff.

In the church the Relicts of St Sergius, the founder of the Convent, repose in a silver shrine or Coffin which was opened for our inspection. He pointed out the precious stones which embellished [it] as well as the case of gold which covered in part some of the holy pictures. This Church has a gilt cupola in the middle and four domes round it of tin painted green. The Apartments where the sacerdotal dresses and Utensils belonging to the Convent are deposited are a suite of four handsome rooms fitted with Cabinets all round, in which these Articles are laid up and arranged with great good order. They become more and more costly as one advances and of course the most costly things are in the last apartment, in the midst of which stands a large table covered with Bibles and Gospels. The Epitrachilion which Sophia the wife of Vassili Ivanovitch brought from Greece was shewn as a curious piece of antiquity. There were two or three things, epitrachilia I think, worked by the Empress Anne which however the Prelate observed did more credit to her devotion than her skill . . . The Epitrachilia is a long, narrow, oblong [vestment], is fixed round the neck and hangs before . . . The Panagea is a picture of our Saviour's head set round with brilliants in the form of a star. He shewed us one prodigiously rich which he said he used to wear constantly, but not of late, his taste for such things having much abated. The Crosses are often very precious. There were several very rich mitres. He put one, given and in part worked by the Empress Elizabeth, on Bootle's head. . . . The Metropolitan was exceedingly communicative and not the least in a hurry.

When we returned to the house we were presented with a glass of brandy and found a tray set out as usual with dried fish which we were partaking largely, under an idea that nothing more was to follow (Bootle observed, I suppose this is the whole of his dinner), when to our surprise we were invited, if we could make a meagre dinner, to go into the next room and dine. A most excellent meagre dinner it proved, for we had two courses and besides caviare, fish soup, Kissel and stewed barley, we had a variety of fishes dressed in a great variety of ways. Our liquors were Russian Ale, a Levant Wine which was placed on the table, and at the conclusion two glasses of different sweet wines. Thus it is, he said, with great good humour, that we mortify. The Bishops in the Greek Church are never permitted to eat flesh meat. If we do it, said he, we must do it in private. In public it cannot be done without giving great offence. A pretty Turkish Boy, who was taken at Ismail and whom he seemed to treat with great tenderness, waited at table . . .

[Later] we had another long conversation upon a variety of subjects, political, moral and religious . . . Diderot paid him a visit at Petersburgh without any previous introduction. Yet he burst into his room in a loud fit of laughter and the first word he said was 'Non est Deus'. To which the Archbishop replied 'There is nothing new in that; as long since as the time of David, Stultus dixit in cordo suo, non est Deus' . . . Voltaire is the man whom he charges with having induced the Empress to pursue the measures which she has done in regard to the Church. For some time whatever was French has been admired in this country.

He seems to have a great antipathy to the Pope and was sorry that we had begun to relax in England in regard to the Roman Catholics. The Pope he said had made repeated attempts to establish his authority in Russia . . . When Peter the Great was at Paris, the Proposal was made to him for uniting the two Churches, to which he answered that being only a warrior he did not understand these matters, but he would communicate the thing to his Bishops, who he supposed would be able to give the proper answer.

He himself, in conversation with some Romish Ecclesiastic upon the conformity of their two religions, had charmed him by making every concession he could wish with regard to Ceremonies and Doctrine. But when they came to the Pope's authority, he denied that he had any more than himself, being Bishop of Rome in the same manner as he was Bishop of Moscow and no otherwise. This threw the Ecclesiastic into a greater rage than if he had disputed all the Doctrines and all the Ceremonies of the Romish Church.

[73] The Monastery and its treasures visited by Princess Dashkov and the Wilmot sisters in 1806; from *The Russian Journals of Martha and Catherine Wilmot 1803–1808.*

To arrive at Troitza Monastry 58 Versts remain'd to be accomplished. Luckily the entire way almost was shaded by Forests with a continuation of such beautiful residences as I have already describ'd towering amidst their foliage, & what is attendant upon every Russian Residence a Church & seperate Belfry dazzling their gilden Domes & Chaines & Crosses & Balls high above the reach of Green which richly cloaths the expance of Country & only broken by the luxuriance of Harvests waving in yellow plains of Corns, Barley, & every species of wild flower which gives an inexpressible gaiety to the Scene.

We travelled day and night & did not arrive till six o'clock the following Morning at Troitza where, tho' we had one of the little wooden Houses of the Town, we did not attempt to sleep but very patiently had the Carriages converted into beds and slumber'd under the protection of a prodigious Shed, where all the Carts & Horses of every sort of traveller came in without Ceremony & neigh'd & kick'd & stamp'd & flounder'd to their hearts' content! Alas! this is getting a little behind the scenes; & to a British Carcase one must confess the Russian grievances of an Imperial Journey, particularly in the Dog Days, pushes one's great patience beyond the inheritance allotted by the gifts of Job himself, as you would be the first to acknowledge when it came to your endurance! A Carriage full of Cooks & Kitchen Utensils always preceded us, so that in that score we were in excellent train – we had even a Butler & silver side board – but it ought to occupy you more the contemplation of the ancient Monastry, as we open'd our eyes on our quadruped Friends & bed fellows which rose in gothic grandeur amidst its battlements and which once fortified the retreat of Peter the Great when by the wiser counsel of his sister Sophia he refuged himself from the rebellion of the Strelitz.

Tho' Catherine 2nd clipp'd the wings of the angelic Brethren who renouncing the Vanities of the World inhabit this place & deprived them of 70 thousand Peasants, yet (tho' their equivalent from the Crown is trifling) they realize every year twenty thousand Roubles as sure Revenues from Pilgrims who swarm from the 41 Governments of this Imperial Realm to kiss the crumbling bones of Saint Sergius who lies in his *Miraculous Shrine* canopied in golden brocading fringed with Oriental pearl! The Coffin was open'd by two Priests who on the approach of Princess Daschkaw said Masses round the Tomb & presented the Cross which she was desired to kiss, as also a famish'd shrunk black finger of the Saint! As for the body nothing was to be seen but a Swathe of crimson embroidery & a wooden head bearing on it a radiant Crown of precious Stones & trophies hung within its Shrine of Mundane Luxury, of Orders, of Portraits set in brilliants, Diamond Crosses, Imperial Cyphers and worldly baubles crowded as in a Sorcerer's Cell precisely in the very Sanctuary made for the *renunciation* of such luxury 'on pain of being carried to Hell on the wings of the Imperial Eagle' on which they solemnly swear! This is literally the form of their oath on being made a Bishop, to signify which many is the Saint (I suppose I have seen myriads) represented on the walls of the Churches on the feathery pinions of the Eagle wide stretched – for the expedition one may naturally conclude! The present Archbishop Plato, who is esteem'd one of the most Singular men in Russia, is the superior of this Establishment. He is a mixture of everything opposite to the Religion & Constitution of his Country, & yet keeps up to all the outward forms so as to awe the populace like a demi-God. He is thought of so much consequence from his influence & cleverness that he is held in dread at Court & universally esteem'd an Iron Wheel in this political Machine of State.

After having been well Smoked by the incense at this Shrine where daily Miracles are perform'd, a parcel of black cowl'd Monks conducted us to see the Treasures of the Monastry. These are all set out as in a Museum in several rooms, the walls of which are lined with Glass Cases, where all the Robes to the number of at least 500, the Covering of the Communion Table on which the Eucharist cannot stand unless some particles of the reliques of a Martyr be woven in the Web, the Sacred Vessels, & all the penitential offerings of Magdalens, Tzars, Bishops & other Sinners are exhibited in the most wonderful display of Oriental riches & Luxury! Chalices & Communion Services sent by Catherine the 2nd are exquisitely beautiful cut out of Onyzes, all enriched with diamonds in the most dazzling splendour; one is a single blood stone with base & handle of Opal, & others of pure gold & pearl! On the Robes of the Priests I observ'd a little Ticket which I ask'd the meaning of, & they told me 'twas a Memorandum of the number of pounds weight of pearl on the embroidery of each Robe! Sometimes 'twas 8 pounds, Sometimes 10, & Sometimes 12. The Communion Cloths are work'd and fringed with real pearl – & there are several dozen of them – besides the entire Calendar of Saints & a hundred Virgin Marys, their frames irradiated in Emeralds, Amethysts, Rubys, Topazes & Sapphires! In short the treasures of Centurys are collected in surprising profusion, tho' for the Historic documents I cannot say much. A few Sclavonian manuscripts of the Evangelists (500 years old & illuminated in colours) are the only ones existing in their Library.

To relieve our eyes from these dazzling maskings of Idolatry we mounted up the highest Belfry to gaze upon the wide extended beauty of the neighbouring Country, & amongst a thousand picturesque objects the 'Hermitage' of Archbishop Plato struck us as most conspicuously charming. This we afterwards Visited. However to continue our holy spirit of Pilgrimage, the following Morning we bid adieu to this Russian Loretto & after travelling 30 Versts by Cock Crow we encamp'd during the heat of the day in the wooden Village of Kiribiriva in the Government of Wolodimer where we reposed our high Mightinesses for 4 hours in a Barn, while on the borders of the Skirting Wood a fire was kindled under the blue vault of Heaven & our dinners very handsomely dress'd & serv'd in Plate! During the time we had slumber'd on the Hay our Damsels (*Diushkas*) arm'd with green branches against the Flies were waving them over our weary heads, while for my part I fell into a profound sleep.

LIFE, CUSTOMS
AND MORALS
IN MOSCOW

[74] The blessing of the waters, in the sixteenth century; from *The Voyage . . .* by Robert Best.

Every yeere, upon the twelfe day, they use to blesse or sanctifie the river *Moska*, which runneth through the citie of *Moskovia*, after this manner.

First, they make a square hole in the ice about 3. fadoms large every way, which is trimmed about the sides and edges with white boords. Then about 9. of the clocke they come out of the church with procession towards the river in this wise.

First and foremost, there goe certaine yong men with Waxe tapers burning, and one carying a great lanterne. Then follow certaine banners, then the crosse, then the images of our Ladie, of S. Nicholas, and of other Saints, which images men carrie upon their shoulders. After the images follow certaine priests, to the number of 100 or more; after them the Metropolitan, who is led betweene two priests; and after the Metropolitan came the Emperour, with his crowne upon his head; and after his maiestie all his noble men orderly. Thus they folowed the procession unto the water; & when they came unto the hole that was made, the priests set themselves in order round about it. And at one side of the same poole there was a scaffold of boords made, upon which stood a faire chaire, in which the Metropolitan was set, but the Emperours maiestie stood upon the ice.

After this the priests began to sing, to blesse and to sense, and did their service, and so by that time that they had done the water was holy, which being sanctified, the Metropolitane tooke a little thereof in his handes and cast it on the Emperour, likewise upon certaine of the Dukes, and then they returned againe to the church with the priests that sate about the water. But ye preasse [press] that there was about the water when the Emperor was gone was wonderful to behold, for there came about 5000. pots to be filled of that water; for that Muscovite which hath no part of that water thinks himselfe unhappy.

And very many went naked into the water, both men and

women and children. After the prease was a little gone, the Emperours Jennets and horses were brought to drink of the same water, and likewise many other men brought their horses thither to drinke; and by that means they make their horses as holy as themselves.

All these ceremonies being ended, we went to the Emperour to dinner, where we were served in vessels of silver, and in all other points as we had been before time.

[75] Lenten customs in the sixteenth century: Palm Sunday procession; from *The Voyage* . . . by Robert Best.

On Palme Sunday they have a very solemne procession in this manner following:

First, they have a tree of a good bignesse, which is made fast upon two sleds, as though it were growing there, and it is hanged with apples, raisins, figs, and dates, and with many other fruits abundantly. In the midst of the same tree stand 5 boyes in white vestures, which sing in the tree before the procession. After this there folowed certaine yong men with waxe tapers in their hands, burning, and a great lanterne, that all the light should not goe out. After them folowed two with long banners, and 6. with round plates set upon long staves. The plates were of copper, very ful of holes and thinne. Then folowed 6. carying painted images upon their shoulders; after the images follow certaine priests, to the number of 100. or more, with goodly vestures, whereof 10. or 12. are of white damaske, set and imbrodered round about with faire and orient pearles, as great as pease, and among them certaine Saphires and other stones. After them followed the one halfe of the Emperours noble men. Then commeth the Emperours maiestie and the Metropolitane, after this manner:

First, there is a horse, covered with white linnen cloth down to the ground, his eares being made long with the same cloth, like to an asses eares. Upon this horse the

Metropolitane sitteth side long like a woman. In his lappe lieth a faire booke with a crucifix of Goldsmiths worke upon the cover, which he holdeth fast with his left hand, and in his right hand he hath a crosse of gold, with which crosse he ceaseth not to blesse the people as he rideth.

There are to the number of 30. men, which spread abroad their garments before the horse; and as soon as the horse is past over any of them, they take them up againe and run before, and spred them againe, so that the horse doth alway go on some of them. They which spred the garments are all priests sonnes, and for their labours the Emperour giveth unto them new garments.

One of the Emperours noble men leadeth the horse by the head, but the Emperour himselfe, goying on foote, leadeth the horse by the ende of the reine of his bridle with one of his hands, and in the other of his hands he had a braunch of a Palme tree. After this followed the rest of the Emperours Noble men and Gentlemen, with a great number of other people. In this order they went from one church to another within the castle, about the distaunce of two flights shot, and so returned agayne to the Emperours Church, where they made an end of their service. Which being done, the Emperours maiestie and certaine of his noble men went to the Metropolitane his house to dinner, where of delicate fishes and good drinks there was no lacke.

[76] A boxing match and an execution: the song of the Tsar Ivan (the Terrible), the young bodyguardsman, and the bold merchant, by M. Yu. Lermontov; from *Michael Lermontov* by C.E. L'Ami and Alexander Welikotny.

Over the spires of gold encrowned Moscow,
Over the Kremlin's white-stoned battlements;
From the blue mountains, from the distant forests,
On wooden beams and roof-tops wayfaring,
Scattering gray clouds upon the heels of night,

The red dawn rises on the world again.
Gold curls she scatters as she takes her way,
Till, like a beauty tranced before her mirror,
She looks into the limpid sky and smiles.
Ah why, red dawn, hast thou awaked this day?
For what good hope, what joy, hast thou arisen?
The bold prize-fighting crew of Moscow town
Betimes assembled, as it was their wont,
Upon the river for the fistic fete,
Blithely, to prank it for the holiday.
Then came the Tsar with all his glittering train,
Boyars and bodyguards attending brave;
And gave command to stretch a silver chain,
Welded with links of gold, to make the ring.
Full five and twenty sajenes* did they chain
To close the single combat, free to all;
And then ordained the Tsar Ivan Vasilievitch
Loudly to call the challenge to all men:
'Where are ye now, brave lads, where are ye all?
Come forth and entertain the Tsar, our father!
Come, in the chained circle take your place:
Who shall prevail, the Tsar will well reward:
Who faileth, him in heaven will God excuse!'
Then strode the bold Kiribeyevitch to the ring,
Silently bowing low unto his Tsar;
From his great shoulders shedding his velvet cloak,
Right arm akimbo at his side propped up,
The other setting straight his blood-red cap.
Coolly he waits for one to challenge him . . .
Then three times loudly was the call proclaimed –
And not a warrior of them all stepped forth;
Sheepish, they stood and jostled one another.
In the ring, the *oprichnik* strutted to and fro,
Laughing and jesting at his timorous foes.
'Certes, thou'rt grown tame, or lately-thoughtful, perhaps?

---

* *Sajenes*. Seven feet. The ring would therefore be approximately 175 feet square – large by modern standards.

Well, then, I promise for the holiday
I'll let thee go alive with penitence,
And make but sport to please our sire the Tsar.'
Suddenly on two sides swept the crowd apart,
And to the ring stepped forth Stepan Paramonovitch,
The youthful merchant, valiant warrior,
By name well known to all, Kalashnikov.
First to the dreadful Tsar he bowed his head;
Then to the Kremlin white, and holy churches;
Then to all people born of Russian soil.
His falcon eyes, burning within his head,
Unwinking gazed upon the bodyguard;
And then opposing him he placed himself,
Stretching his battle-mitts upon his hands,
Squaring his powerful shoulders, and with one hand
Stroking his long and darkly-curling beard.
Then spake Kiribeyevitch and said to him:
'How now, my good stout lad, confide in me –
Say, of what tribe and family art thou,
And by what name art called? For I would know
For whom 'twill be to serve the requiem,
And over whom to boast my victory.'
To him replied Stepan Paramonovitch:
'Stepan Kalashnikov my name is called,
And of an honest father was I born,
And lived my life according to God's law:
I did not harm nor shame my neighbour's wife,
Nor go marauding at the dark of night,
Hiding myself against God's honest day . . .
And thou, O Guard, hast spoken very truth:
Before tomorrow's sun hath reached his prime,
For one of us a requiem they will sing;
And one of us will boast and take his ease,
Feasting and roistering with his valiant friends.
No! not to turn a jest or please these folk,
Do I confront thee, spawn of infidels!
But for the fight, the last and deadly strife!'
Hearing these words, the bold Kiribeyevitch

Grew pale and bloodless like the autumn snow;
His watchful eyes grew blurred and dim with mist,
And icy chill between his shoulders ran,
A word died soundless on his parted lips . . .
Now silently they break away, and then
The valiant strife begins. Kiribeyevitch
Swings first upon the merchant Kalashnikov,
And smites about the middle of his breast;
His stout ribs cracked beneath the heavy blow,
And swayed and shook Stepan Paramonovitch.
Upon his broad chest hung a copper cross,
Adorned with holy relics brought from Kiev:
Bent was it then and crushed into his breast,
And under it the red blood dripped like dew.
Then in his heart Stepan Paramonovitch prayed:
'What judgement is to come? Whate'er it be,
For God and truth I stand while life shall last!'
He roused himself, prepared, raised up his hand,
Gathered his mighty strength, and struck his foe
Full on the temple with a swinging blow.
Faintly then moaned the Tsar's young bodyguard,
Swayed on his feet and fell, fell dead as stone;
Fell like a log upon the cold white snow,
Down on the snow like some tall woodland pine,
Some pine upon the forest's sandy verge,
Cut down with axes through its pitchy roots.
Then rose the dread Ivan Vasilievitch,
His wrath aroused, stamping upon the earth,
Knitting with rage his thunder-clotted brows;
And bade them seize and bind the merchant bold,
And quickly bring him there before the throne.
Then spake in solemn wrath the anointed Tsar:
'In truth and conscience, thou, make answer now:
Was't with intent, or was't against thy will
Thou smot'st to death even now my liegeman true,
This, my best warrior, Kiribeyevitch?'
'I answer thee, O sire, anointed Tsar:
'Twas purposely and by intent I slew him;

But why, and for what cause – I tell thee not!
That story I shall tell to God alone!
Send me to death, and bring upon the block
My guilty head; but this of thee I ask:
Leave not my infant children and my wife,
My youthful widow and my brothers twain –
Leave not these innocent ones without thy grace.'
'Tis well for thee, bold youth, young merchant's son,
That in good conscience thou hast made reply.
Thy wife, thy children, shall receive my grace,
And from my coffers shall be provided well;
And for thy brothers, from this day I ordain
That in my kingdom they shall trade at will,
Of duty free, no import duties pay.
And this for thee, young lad, do I ordain:
To the high place of death thou goest at once,
And layst thy bold head down upon the block.
I will command them edge the keenest axe,
And dress the executioner brave and fine,
And ring the great bell through the city streets,
So that great Moscow's people all may know
Thou wast not doomed bereft of thy Tsar's grace.'
So came the people to the city square,
While dolefully the moaning Kremlin bell
Spread through great Moscow's streets the evil news.
On the high place of execution, brave
In scarlet shirt with many buttons bright,
Rubbing bare hands, clasping his keen-edged axe,
Briskly the executioner struts and preens,
Waiting the youthful warrior doomed to die;
And the brave youth, the valiant merchant, now
To his dear brothers bids his last farewell.
'O thou my brothers, blood-related friends,
For our last parting let us clasp and kiss.
To Alyona Dmitrievna bow for me:
Tell her – grieve not: and to my children dear
Say naught of me. Bow to our parents' house,
To all our friends, yourselves, and God's dear church.

And pray thou for my erring sinful soul!'
So they have slain Stepan Kalashnikov,
With cruel, shameful death upon the block;
And rolled in blood his doomed unlucky head.

Where three roads meet beyond the Moscow River –
Tula, Razan, Vladimir are they called –
They buried Stepan in the open fields,
And built above a mound of earth and sod,
Setting thereon a cross of maple wood.
There soughing, walk the hunting steppe-land winds
Over his nameless grave, and folk go by:
Old men, who cross themselves, and youths, who stare,
And lovely maids, who bow their heads and grieve:
And dulcimer-players, too, who sing a song!

[77] Court fools and dwarfs; from *The First Romanovs, 1613–1725* by R. Nisbet Bain

In the latter years of his reign, the conscience-stricken Ivan the Terrible could not sleep at night without the ministrations of his *bakharei* [story-tellers], and three of them, all very old men and quite blind, took it in turns, every night, to soothe the tyrant to slumber with their stories. But if the Tsar were in a merry mood, he sent for his fools and jesters, who were the chief delight of 'the pleasure hall.' The official duty of the fools was to provoke laughter by any means, witty or foolish, so long as it was extravagant or extra-ordinary. They acted as a sort of moral safety-valve for the society of the day, which, outwardly grave and reverend, was inwardly bubbling over with artificially repressed animal spirits. The fool, as a fool, had the utmost license of expression, and, cynical or absurd as his wit very often was, in that stifling atmosphere of Byzantine stagnation it had, nevertheless, all the bracing effect of a current of fresh air. The fools were of two kinds – mentally deficient persons, kept as curiosities, like the almost equally amusing dwarfs, negroes, apes and parrots; and humourists of real talent, who were to their audience what comedy and comic literature are to us. The fools of Tsar Michael must have been of the idiotic order, as we hear of them being taken in Holy Week to various monasteries to fast, which would have been unnecessary had they been sensible fools. The fools were of both sexes, and even the abbesses of great monasteries, generally princesses, were not above being entertained by them. Manka, the female fool of Tsar Michael's mother, was very famous, and on her death a memorial hospital was built by her mistress. The usual dress of a jester was a red or yellow *odnoryadka*, an upper sleeveless garment of Tatar cut, with an under-linen caftan, a girdle of red or green cloth, and fox-skin cap, often with pointed ears. The famous Polish jester, Yushka, received from Tsar Michael, in 1626, a black velvet jerkin with a velvet collar, a bright red atlas caftan with a gold collar, and red cloth trousers with copper buttons. Dwarfs, as rare sports of nature, a species of living doll, were also highly prized. They appealed to the coarse inhuman sense of humour of a semi-savage state of society. Tsar Michael had sixteen dwarfs, Tsar Alexius even more, and Peter the Great, when a child, had six Court dwarfs to play with, and delighted in the society of dwarfs to the day of his death. The dwarfs were dressed in very bright colours, to show them off, preferably sky-blue and crimson, with red or yellow shoes. They were kept apart from the fools in rooms of their own, and had charge of the Court parrots. There is a curious petition extant from the dwarf Ivashka, who, during the great plague at Moscow in 1659, when the deserted city was a wilderness of snow-drifts, was left behind in the *Kreml* in charge 'of four parrots and one old one,' which he fed for twenty weeks on almond-cakes, and 'kept alive and well.' 'And as regards my patience and the feeding of the sovereign birds,' wrote the dwarf to the Tsar, 'is it not all known unto the oven-heater Alexander Boshkov, who visited me every day and examined thy sovereign birds.' It is pleasant to learn that Ivashka received the twenty rubles compensation which he had asked for his trouble. We also hear of other curios in the shape of negroes, calmucks, and natural monsters . . . In Tsar Michael's last days, when age, sickness, and the stern admonitions of the clergy tended to turn the thoughts of the gentle and pious monarch more and more away from this world, we hear far less of 'the pleasure halls' and their motley inhabitants, while, during the first twenty years of the reign of his son and successor, the God-fearing Alexius, the inner pastimes of the Court either vanished altogether or put on a semi-clerical garb. The singers, players, and jugglers were banished from Court; the dwarfs and jesters were reserved for only very special occasions; but the Tsar had not the heart to do away with the aged story-tellers, so he kept them at Court in special apartments along with the cripples, the pilgrims, and the very poor, whom every rich Moscovite was bound in those days to maintain as part of his household if he would 'save his soul.' Alexius entertained a whole hospital of these infirm and needy pensioners. They were called 'the upstairs beadsmen,' or 'the upstairs poor,' and the Tsar would often spend whole hours among them, listening to their talk.

[78] Moscow habits; from *The Travels of Olearius in Seventeenth Century Russia* by Adam Olearius.

(Adam Olearius (1603–1671) was born in the German principality of Anhalt and studied at the University of Leipzig. In 1633 he entered the service of Duke Frederick of Holstein, and as secretary to the Holstein embassy he first visited Russia in the same year. He returned to the Russian Court on three further occasions: in 1636, 1639, and 1643. On the last two visits he was offered a position in the Russian service of Tsar Mikhail Feodorovich, but returned to work as court mathematician and librarian to the Duke of Holstein.)

Contentiousness and vile speech

The Russians are in general a very quarrelsome people who assail each other like dogs, with fierce, harsh words. Again and again on the streets one sees such quarrels; the old women shout with such fury that he who is unaccustomed to it expects them at any moment to seize each other's hair. They very rarely come to blows, however; but when they do, they strike with their fists, beating one another with all their might on the sides and genitals. No one has ever seen Russians challenge one another to an exchange of saber blows or bullets, as Germans and other Europeans do. Still, there are cases when the foremost magnates, and even princes, fiercely lash at one another with knouts, while mounted on horses. We heard reliable testimony of this, and we ourselves saw two noblemen so engaged at the entry of the Turkish ambassador.

When their indignation flares and they use swearwords, they do not resort to imprecations involving the sacraments – as unfortunately is often the case with us – consigning to the devil, abusing as a scoundrel, etc. Instead they use many vile and loathsome words, which, if the historical record did not demand it, I should not impart to chaste ears. They have nothing on their tongue more often than 'son of a whore' 'son of a bitch,' 'cur,' 'I fuck your mother,' to which they add 'into the grave,' and similar scandalous speech. Not only adults and old people behave thus, but also little children who do not yet know the name of God, or father, or mother, already have on their lips 'fuck you,' and say it as well to their parents as their parents to them.

Recently, by a public order, this foul and shameful swearing and abuse was severely and strictly forbidden, upon pain of knouting. Certain secretly appointed people were sent to mix with the crowd on the streets and in the markets and, with the help of streltsi and executioners assigned to them, were to seize swearers and punish them on the spot by beating, as an object of public disgust. This habitual and deeply rooted swearing demanded more surveillance than could be provided, however, and caused the observers, judges, and executioners such an intolerable burden of work that they tired of spying out and punishing that which they themselves could not refrain from, and gave it up as a bad job.

Shamelessness

One should not seek great courtesy and good manners among the Russians, for neither is much in evidence. After a meal, they do not refrain, in the presence and hearing of all, from releasing what nature produces, fore and aft. Since they eat a great deal of garlic and onion, it is rather trying to be in their company. Perhaps against their will, these good people fart and belch noisily – as indeed they did intermittently during the secret audiences with us.

Just as they are ignorant of the praiseworthy sciences, they are little interested in memorable events or the history of their fathers and forefathers, and they care little to find out the qualities of foreign peoples. One hears nothing of these subjects in their gatherings. I am not speaking here, however, of the carouses of the great boyars. Most of their conversation is directed to the side of things toward which their nature and base way of life incline: they speak of debauchery, of vile depravity, of lasciviousness, and of immoral conduct committed by themselves and by others. They tell all sorts of shameless fables, and he who can relate the coarsest obscenities and indecencies, accompanied by the most wanton mimicry, is accounted the best companion and is the most sought after. Their dances have the same character, often including voluptuous movements of the body. They say that roving comedians bare their backsides, and I know not what else. The Danish ambassador [Ulfeldt] was entertained by such shameless dances when he was there. He tells in his *Hodeoporicon* of seeing Russian women assume strange poses and make strange signs at the windows of their houses.

So given are they to the lusts of the flesh and fornication that some are addicted to the vile depravity we call sodomy; and not only with boys (as Curtius [*De Rebus Gestis*] tells) but also with men and horses. Such antics provide matter for conversation at their carouses. People caught in such obscene acts are not severely punished. Tavern musicians often sing of such loathsome things, too, in the open streets, while some show them to young people in puppet shows. Their dancing-bear impresarios have comedians with them, who, among other things, arrange farces employing puppets. These comedians tie a blanket around their bodies and spread it above their heads, thus creating a portable theater or stage with which they can run about the streets, and on top of which they can give puppet shows.

'They have divested themselves of every trace of shame and restraint,' says Jakob [Ulfeldt]. In Moscow we ourselves several times saw men and women come out of public baths to cool off, and, as naked as God created them, approach us and call obscenely in broken German to our young people. Idleness strongly prompts them to this kind of dissolute behaviour. Daily you can see hundreds of idlers standing about or strolling in the market place or in the Kremlin. And they are more addicted to drunkenness than any nation in the world. Hieronymus [St Jerome] said, 'A stomach filled with wine craves immediate sexual satisfaction.' After drinking wine to excess they are like unbridled animals, following wherever their passions lead.

Drunkenness

The vice of drunkenness is prevalent among this people in all classes, both secular and ecclesiastical, high and low, men and women, young and old.* To see them lying here and there in the streets, wallowing in filth, is so common that no

---

* Samuel Collins, an Englishman who served as physician to Tsar Aleksei Mikhailovich for nine years, remarked that drunkenness was 'the epidemic distemper not only of Russia but of England also.' Montaigne observed that French envoys to Germany found it necessary to get drunk, i.e. to honor the native custom, if they were to get their business done. These observations provide some needed perspective for the student of seventeenth-century Russia. Nevertheless, the fact that foreigners were impelled to dwell so much on drunkenness among the Russians suggests that they conspicuously outstripped others in this regard.

notice is taken of it. If a coachman comes across any such drunken swine whom he knows, he throws them aboard his wagon and takes them home, where he is paid for the trip. None of them anywhere, anytime, or under any circumstances lets pass an opportunity to have a draught or a drinking bout. They drink mainly vodka, and at get-togethers, or when one person visits another, respect is rendered by serving one or two 'cups of wine,' that is, vodka. The common people, slaves, and peasants are so faithful to the custom that if one of them receives a third cup and a fourth, or even more, from the hand of a gentleman, he continues to drink up, believing that he dare not refuse, until he falls to the ground – and sometimes the soul is given up with the draught.

[79] The operation of a Russian bath-house; from *The Travels of Olearius* . . .

There is an aperture from the stove into the bathroom, which they close with a cover and cow dung or clay. Outside there is another aperture, smaller than the first, through which the smoke escapes. When the stones are sufficiently heated, the inner aperture is opened and the outer shut. Then, depending upon how much [*steam*] one wants, a certain quantity of water, sometimes infused with herbs, is poured onto the stones. In the baths, sweat- and wash-up-benches are arranged around the walls, one above the other, covered with linen cloths and cushions, stuffed with hay, and strewn with flowers and various aromatic grasses, with which the windows are also adorned. Scattered on the floor lie small finely chopped shrubs, which give off a very pleasant odor. A woman or girl is assigned to attend the bathers. When an acquaintance or a cherished guest bathes with them, he is looked after attentively, waited on, and cared for. The mistress of the house or her daughter usually brings or sends into the bath some pieces of radish sprinkled with salt, and also a well-prepared, cool drink. If this is omitted, it is considered a great fault and the mark of a bad reception. After the bath they treat the guest, according to his worthiness, with all sorts of pleasure-giving refreshments . . .

One of the members of our suite, having observed the ways of the Muscovites, their life and character, recently described them in brief in the following verses:

> Churches, ikons, crosses, bells,
> Painted whores and garlic smells,
> Vice and vodka everyplace –
> This is Moscow's daily face.
> To loiter in the market air,
> To bathe in common, bodies bare,
> To sleep by day and gorge by night,
> To belch and fart is their delight.
>
> Thieving, murdering, fornication
> Are so common in this nation,
> No one thinks a brow to raise –
> Such are Moscow's sordid days.

[80] Seventeenth-century Russian notions of music; from *The Present State of Russia* . . . by an Eminent Person residing at the Great Tsar's court at Moscow.

(The 'eminent person' was the Rev. Samuel Collins D.D. (1619–1670), a widely educated and travelled man. He studied first at Corpus Christi College, Cambridge, and then became a Doctor of Medicine at Padua. Through his ambassador in Holland, the Tsar Alexis Mikhailovitch invited Collins to serve in Moscow as his physician, which he did for nine years.)

But I come to their Musick, least I should tyre you with tuning it. You must know they have Musick-Schools, where Children are brought up with great diligence, and in much severity. Their notes are very strange, borrowed, I suppose, of the Greeks, or Sclavonians. Their Gamut has small variety; instead of *Fa, sol, la*, they sing *Ga, ga, ge*, warbling them out, as if they were indeed either gag'd or throttled.

Their Cadences and Closes are so unexpected, that they seem frighted into them, as our Fidlers are when a Constable comes in the midst of a Lesson. Sometimes they will run hard upon a scent, as though they meant to imitate the Italian Recitative Musick. Finally, when they have brought up these children to a perfection, what with Bases, Tenors, Contra-tenors, and Trebles, you shall hear as good a Consort, as ever was sung at *Cats Vespers*. They have but little Instrumental Musick, it being prohibited by the Patriarch in opposition to the Romish Church. And it has also been thought State policy to forbid all Musick or Jollity among the Commons, to prevent Effeminacy. They have bagpipes, and small Fiddles with bellies like Lutes, wherewith they play four or five notes.

As for their Warlike Musick they have Kettle Drums, whose dull sound does well agree with the Russian Satur-nine Genius. And the Trumpet, which I think has not been long used, for they can hardly blow it so well as a Sow-Gelder does his Horn. In their hunting they use brass Bugles, which altogether make an hideous noise. In short, if you would please a Russian with Musick, Get a consort of *Billings-gate* Nightingales, which joyn'd with a flight of screech Owls, a nest of Jackdaws, a pack of hungry Wolves, seven Hogs in a windy day, and as many Cats with their Corrivals [partners, compeers], and let them sing *Lacrymae*, and that will ravish a pair of Russian Luggs, better than all the Musick in *Italy*, light Ayres in *France*, Marches of *England*, or the Gigs of *Scotland*.

[81] Other Muscovite customs; from *The Present State of Russia* . . . by an Eminent Person.

The Russians are a People who differ from all other Nations of the world, in most of their Actions.

Their Shirt they wear over their Drawers, girded under the Navel (to which they think a Girdle adds strength). None, neither male nor female, must go ungirt for fear of being unblest. They whistle not with their lips (that they count prophane) but through the Teeth: a strange way of whistling indeed. When they spit on any thing to wipe it (as Shoes, *etc.*) they do use an action not unlike sneezing. In cases of admiration or incredulity, instead of a shrug, they wave their heads from one shoulder to another. Their very speech and accent also differs from other Nations. 'Tis a grand Sin with them to omit *lotionem Post mictum*. As we use paper in our cacking Office to clear accounts, so *Juan de Rusco* uses a little Spade made of Firrchin shaven, like the Ivory *Spatula's* which Merchants and Scriveners use to fold up letters and smooth them.

In our Clock-Dyals the Finger moves to the Figure: In the Russian *e contra*, the Figures move to the Poynter. One Mr *Holloway*, a very ingenious man, contrived the first Dyal of that fashion; saying, because they acted contrary to all men, 'twas fitting their work should be made suitable. Because the Roman Catholicks kneel at their devotion, they will stand, for they look upon kneeling as an ignoble and barbarous Gesture. Because the Polonians shave their beards, they count it sinful to cut them. Because the Tartar abhors Swines-flesh, they eat it rather than any other flesh, although its food is most *Pogano*, or unclean of any Beast. They count it a great sin for a *Russ* to lye with a Dutch woman or English Woman; but a *venia Piccadillo* for a *Russ* woman to prostitute herself to a Stranger, for they say her issue will be educated in the true ancient Faith, but a *Russ* gets an uncircumcized child of a Stranger. They prefer Rye above Wheat, and stinking Fish above fresh. They count their miles by ninties, and not by hundreds. Their New years day is the first of *September*. From the Creation they reckon 7060 and odd years. To things improbable they easily give credit, but hardly believe what is rational and probable.

In their salutes they kiss the woman's right cheek. Lands of Inheritance are entayl'd upon the youngest Brother.

They write upon their knees, though a table stand before them.

They sow with the needle towards them, and thrust it forward with their fore-finger; it should seem they are bad Taylors.

They know not how to eat Pease and Carrets boyld, but eat them shells and all, like Swine. They do not pick their Pease, but pull them up by the roots, and carry them into the Market to be sold.

They know not the name of *Cornuto*: but of a Cuckold they say, *He lyes under the Bench*.

They will sooner take the word of a man who has a Beard, than the oath of one who is Beardless.

The beauty of Women they place in their fatness, *jaxta illud Italicum, Dio mi faccia grassa, io mi faro bella*. God make me fat, and I'le make my self beautiful.

Their painting is no better than that of our Chimneys in the Summer, *viz*. Red Oaker and Spanish White.

They paint or stain their teeth black, upon the same design that our Ladies wear black patches: Or it may be their teeth being spoil'd by mercurial painting, they make a vertue of necessity, and cry up that for an Ornament which is really a Deformity. Low foreheads and long eyes are in fashion here; to which purpose they strain them up so hard under their Tyres, that they can as ill shut them, as our Ladies lift up their hands to their heads. They have a secret amongst them to stain the very balls of their eyes black. Narrow Feet and slender Wasts are alike ugly in their sight.

A lean Woman they account unwholsom, therefore they who are inclined to leanness, give themselves over to all manner of Epicurism, on purpose to fatten themselves, and lye a bed all day long drinking Russian Brandy (which will fatten extreemly) then they sleep, and afterwards drink again, like Swine design'd to make Bacon.

[82] Security in the Kremlin in the seventeenth century; from *The Present State of Russia . . .* by an Eminent Person.

In the night season the *Czar* will go about and visit his Chancellors Desks, and see what Decrees are pass'd, and what Petitions are unanswer'd. He has his spyes in every corner, and nothing is done or said at any Feast, publick Meeting, Burial or Wedding but he knows it. He has spyes also attending his Armies to watch their motions, and give a true account of their actions: These spyes are Gentlemen of small fortunes, who depend on the Emperours favour, and are sent into Armies, and along with Embassadors, and are present on all publick occasions.

'Tis death for any one to reveal what is spoken in the *Czars* Pallace. I being curious to see the fine buildings for the Flax and Hemp, ask't to what end they were built, but not a Workman durst tell me, though they knew it well enough; but they replied, God and the Emperour know best, this was all I could get from them. The *Czars* children are attended with children of their own bred up with them, and there is none of them but know their distance, and their degrees of bowing to all sorts of persons. None dare speak a word what passes in their Court.

[83] Imperial entertainment; from *Anecdotes et Recueil de Coutumes et de Traits d'Histoire Naturelle Particuliers aux Différens Peuples de la Russie* by J.B. Schérer.

(Jean Benoît Schérer (1741–?) was a historian and a civil servant employed in the office of Foreign Affairs at Versailles, advising on Russian affairs. He published books about America as well as about commerce with Russia, and his six-volume source book entitled *Anecdotes Intéressantes et Secrètes de la Cour de Russie* was published in 1792.)

In 1722 Peter I devised in Moscow an entertainment which it would be difficult to arrange elsewhere. It consisted of sleighs built in the shape, and to the size, of warships. Notable among them were Bacchus' drawn by six young bears, and ridden by Witaschi, the court jester, dressed in a bearskin; those of a Tcherkassian and of the Pope's Patriarchs, harnessed to dogs; that of a Neptune sitting in the middle of a conch shell, between two sea gods; that of the Tsar in the uniform of a ship's captain. This last was a frigate with two thirty-foot decks, with eight cast cannons, twenty-four of wood, and three masts, and it was drawn by sixteen horses. Then there was Catherine I's ship (she herself disguised as a Freesian peasant), which was a great gilded vessel decorated with mirrors; another vessel 100 feet long, to which were tied twenty-four smaller sleighs, loaded with common people; the boat of Menzikoff, dressed as a priest (*abbé*); an armed racing frigate, ridden by Admiral Apraxin, dressed as a burgomaster; the sloop of the foreign ministers in ecclesiastic dress, accompanied by their servants on horseback; a sleigh of musicians, drawn by six pigs; that of the Prince of Moldavia, Cantemir, disguised as a Turk, seated under a canopy, and followed by the Lord Chancellor with Polish music, the Privy Councillor Tolstoi with Turkish music, and Baron Schaffiroff with German music. Sixty sleighs of this sort gave the impression on land of a great fleet.

[84] Moscow society as seen by Catherine the Great; from *The Memoirs of Catherine the Great, 1743–4* edited by Dominique Maroger.

Moscow is the seat of sloth, partly due to its immensity: one wastes a whole day trying to visit someone or getting a message across to them. The nobles who live there are excessively fond of the place and no wonder: they live in idleness and luxury, and become effeminate; it is not houses they own there, but regular estates. Apart from that, the town is full of symbols of fanaticism, churches, miraculous icons, priests, and convents, side by side with thieves and brigands. Nor must one overlook the number of large factories which create an excessive accumulation of workmen . . .

At that time [1750], much more so than now, most of the nobility was reluctant to leave Moscow, a place they all cherished, and where idleness and sloth were the chief vices they indulged in. In Moscow one quite often sees a lady covered with jewels and elegantly dressed, emerging from an immense yard, filled with all possible refuse and mud, adjoining a decrepit hut, in a magnificent carriage, drawn by six horrible hacks, shabbily harnessed, with unkempt grooms wearing handsome liveries which they disgrace by their uncouth appearance. In general, both men and women grow spineless in this large town, busying themselves with trifles, a habit which can destroy the greatest intelligence. Governed only by their whims and fancies, they set aside or largely ignore the laws, and thus never learn to command or else turn into tyrants. The inclination to tyrannize is cultivated here more than in any other inhabited part of the world; it is inculcated from the tenderest age by the cruelty which children observe in their parents' behaviour towards servants, for where is the home that has no traps, chains, whips, and other instruments to penalize the smallest mistake on the part of those whom nature has placed in this unfortunate class which cannot break its chains without committing violence? One is barely allowed to admit that they are men like ourselves and when I say it I risk having stones flung at me; what indeed did I not have to suffer from the voice of a cruel and stupid public when questions about this subject began to be raised in the Legislative Committee? The vulgar gentry who were much more numerous than I had ever believed because I had too much respect for those who surrounded me daily, at once began to suspect that these questions might lead to some amelioration of the present condition of the peasants.

[85] Aristocratic households in the eighteenth and early nineteenth centuries; from *Mémoires du Prince Pierre Dolgoroukow*.

(Prince Pierre Dolgorukov, whose memoirs were published in 1867, was a genealogist and historian of the famous Dolgorukov family.)

The way of life for the nobles in Moscow in wintertime, and on the outskirts in the summer (*v podmoskovnykh*) was less savage and Asiatic than that of their provincial cousins, but this only on the surface: there was more luxury and less cruelty, but nevertheless there was a striking similarity.

Most of Moscow's streets were unpaved; in many, boards were laid across them, and this shook carriages terribly: between the slits deep holes often brought horses down and there were many broken hooves and feet. Lanterns were rare, streets remained dark, and both prudence and vanity promoted the virtues of domesticity as a priority. Even the lesser gentry had a house surrounded by a vast courtyard, an orchard, a kitchen garden; there were as well many wooden buildings to house his servants (*dvornia*) and a Russian bath. If he was of high rank he had *Heyduques* or runners (*verschniki*) to accompany his carriage when visiting in town, or his drives in the country.

As well as chefs and scullions, he had amongst his domestic surfs his baker, pastrycook, a man capable of making mead (*medovar*), not only the ordinary one but camomile mead, cherry mead and raspberry mead. He had a brewer (*pivovar*) and a preparer of *Kvas*, not only the ordinary *Kvas* but potato *Kvas* and blackcurrant (*Kvas smorodinnyi*). As well amongst the serfs were more than one locksmith, carpenter, saddler, tin-plater, carter, farrier, shoesmith, cooper etc . . .

Attached to each house there was a laundry with many a washerwoman, milkmaids to look after the cows, a chicken house and its attendants, an aviary, and a woman entrusted to make fruit alcohols (*nalivki*); and finally a pigeon house to amuse the family.

Even now, the Russian people do not eat pigeons. Half a century ago, such a risk would have meant heresy as the Holy Ghost was represented by a dove. Pigeons are undoubtedly the happiest creatures in all the Russian Empire: they freely fly about, are welcomed everywhere, fed and loved; old Russians had for them a true liking and they spent hours in their pigeon houses. In the vast courtyard of great boyars there often was a special church for themselves and their staff. Many of these churches now are open to the public and have become parish ones. These nobles often had, at a convenient distance from Moscow, land which gave them sheep, fish, logs, groats, and oats for bread and *kvas*, fodder and hay for their horses.

Some wealthy people even had in Moscow, in their vast courtyards, lakes and fishponds. Twenty years ago there still was in Moscow an old general, Frolow, who hired a house with garden and pond, but in the lease there was the following clause: the general could use the garden, but could neither fish nor make hay! (*bez pokosow i bez rybnoi lovli*).

Indoors, the houses were furnished with great diversity; the boyars had golden armchairs which looked odd next to the wooden benches and chairs often covered with carpets, which were the seating arrangements for poorer people. In many homes there were a number of poor cousins of both sexes, housed, fed, badly dressed and often roughly treated: they were called 'connaissances' (*znakomtsy, znakomki*) but they were known outside as *prijiviltsy* or *prijivalki*, a nickname explaining they were the unpublished gazetteers, the gossips, the tellers of news, which they often invented.

At great banquets and on feast days, one saw in palaces choirs and musicians, serfs in fact belonging to the nobles. Preference went to horn music (*Rogovaia muzyka*) with choirs (*pesselniki*). They were nearly always summoned to take part. Dwarfs were a passion, baptized Kalmouks of both sexes as well as buffoons (*schouty*). These, pretending stupidity, often had wit more than their masters and their guests, and often more than once told piquant truths. But if they went too far they were whipped, smacked or caned; these unfortunates minded little. There exists in Russia a proverb not quite forgotten nowadays: 'Insult does not remain attached to the collar' (*brane na vorotou ne visniet*).

In summer and autumn, the boyars moved from Moscow to their country houses. Autumn was the shooting season in the vast forests full of every kind of game. These forests, of which little trace remains now, surrounded the old capital to an unbelievable extent. Shoots were often followed by meals that turned into orgiastic and noisy gaiety (*razgoul*) and could go to unbelievable lengths.

[86] Sex and superstition; from *Travels from St Petersburg in the Year 1805* by G. von Reinbeck.

The stillness which reigns after ten o'clock, in this huge and populous city, is astonishing. Even on the finest evenings there are but a few solitary walkers, in the streets, and scarcely any person sitting at his door. But then commence the nightly adventures, chiefly near the Smithsbridge, the most noted place for French milliners shops. In these warehouses the owner only, and at most the principal assistant, are natives of France; all the other women are partly Russian slaves whom the French milliners purchase in the name of some nobleman, (for none but nobles dare buy slaves in their own name,) partly servant-girls confided to their tuition to learn the millinery business. But all of them without exception, and sometimes the mistress too, are priestesses of *Venus vulgivaga*. Moscow has few professed *Filles de joie*; they cannot thrive, the servant-girls spoil their trade. This is actually the case in the strictest sense of the word. The dissolute conduct of both male and female servants in great houses can hardly be credited.

The Russians are very much addicted to sensual love. A kiss is the salute common to both sexes, among the vulgar, even in the street. Their eyes glisten and their lips quiver lusciously, though it be an old woman they embrace. It is the sex which a Russian chiefly values in a female: still he has a thousand delicate attentions for every woman, independent of any nearer connection. He puts up with a great deal from a female. A man in high life is seldom induced to use any severity against his wife, though she should break through all decorum. 'She is a woman!' is the only exclamation that will escape him. If any one be unable to accomplish any thing by himself in Russia, he need only commission his wife or his daughter; and though she should be neither handsome nor young, she will yet infallibly obtain more, and dares to speak less reservedly than himself. There reigns a sort of spirit of chivalry in favour of the ladies . . .

Superstition pervades all ranks, high as well as low. The Russians believe in their *Domowoys* (house-demons), prognostic, prophecies, fortune-telling by means of coffee, cards, or the melting of tin on the eve of saint's day. The last-mentioned practices are particularly in high favour with lords and ladies; and such as have acquired reputation for skill in them, may depend upon a rich harvest. The chief adepts and professors are females, and frequently Cupid confederates here with Apollo. Many superstitious observances obtain at weddings, christenings, and funerals. Dropping salt, spilling wine or water, every thing is portentous. He who is the involuntary cause of any bad prognostic, often makes the person whom it regards, pass suddenly from the most chearful, to the worst of humours.

[87] Moscow 'ghosts'; from *The Russian Journals of Martha and Catherine Wilmot 1803–1808*.

The effect left upon my imagination is that of having flitted amongst the Ghosts of the Court of Catherine. Moscow is the Imperial terrestrial political Elysium of Russia. All those whose power existed in the reign of Catherine & of Paul & all those who are discarded or conceiv'd to be superannuated by Alexander hold an *ideal* Consequence awarded by

Courtesy alone in this lazy idle magnificent & Asiatic town, for all the effective power has long since pass'd as an inheritance to their successors who rule the Imperial realm at Petersburg & flutter away their hours about the Court.

Nevertheless the Ruffled decorated phantom of Prince Gallitzen, Grand Chamberlain in the time of Catherine, retains its Orders, its Stars & its Ribbons which added to the Weight of four score years & ten bends it double to the ground. It wears its Key of diamonds, its bay & embroidery and all its glittering baubles on its *bones*, & receives the homage of its brother Ghosts who in former days shared with it the honors of State! Another of these gaudy phantoms is Count Ostrowman, Grand Chancellor of the Empire in the Reign of Catherine. The orders of St George, of St Alexander Neffsky, St Wolodimer &c. & c. hang it over in red, blue & different coloured stripes. 83 years have frozen in a Pyramid upon his head, and his gibbering Skeleton rattles in his Coach & eight with out riders, dines with his high Dukes behind his Chair & in fact enacts the same etiquette from courtesy that was awarded him in his most effective days of Imperial favor. Count Alexis Orloff who was Grand Admiral in the time of Catherine is richer than any Prince in Christendom & revels in Asiatic luxury. The hand that strangled Peter III is cover'd with its recompence of brilliants beneath which the portrait of Catherine smiles in eternal Gratitude. This is another of our Moscow Ghosts, & another is General Korsikoff a surviving Favorite who may really be call'd a diamond Vision & who in the midst of wrinkles cherishes the remembrance of that past distinction which drew on him the envy of his Country. Prince Bariatinsky, Prince Nesvitsky, Monsr Rgifsky, and other Conspirators of the year 1762 trundle about their paunches & patriotism, their swords & keys, and all the insignia of their former greatness. In short the Grandees – & in this circle, alas, we only move – are as I said before of another World, and yet the same important Gossip of Court folly, the same Vanity, the same puff'd up pride, the same Ostentation sways them & creates their happiness & unhappiness as if the Grave did not yawn beneath their tottering feet to menace them as it hourly does with an earthly oblivion of their Brocaded existence.

[88] Sledging, skating, eating, chess, at the beginning of the nineteenth century; from *An Historical Account and Description of the City of Moscow . . .* By I. A.M. Sulkowski.

Riding in sledges is one of the greatest pastimes of the Moscovites, which are elegantly ornamented; the horses are dressed with ostrich feathers, and little round bells, which are very harmonious: one horse gallops before those in the sledge, which are kept at a trotting pace equal to the galloping of the other, which has a rider, and is not fastened to the sledge; many thousand rubles depend as wagers upon these races; and, not to prevent the horses from breathing freely, their nostrils are opened.

These races are performed upon the ice on the river Moscow; the place is a mile and a half long, and is surrounded with benches for the accommodation of the spectators. Those trotting horses, which have won the wager, retire with the applause and huzzas of the spectators, and the others are hissed.

Near this place is another prepared for the same purpose, where the waggoners, who are proud of their horses, lay wagers to a great amount.

Skaiting is also a favourite diversion. The whole river is crowded with men and boys, and it is impossible to conceive, without being an eye-witness, with what velocity they perform their different evolutions. Although it is a dangerous amusement, yet it is seldom that any accident happens. The river is crowded with bands of music.

The Moscovites are humane and hospitable, the latter is general in all Russia; every person, either native or stranger, who possesses good qualities, is welcome at any time to a Moscovite's house, and the longer he stays the more welcome he is; in a word, no stranger is at loss for a friend.

The tables of the Moscovites are very luxurious: they dine in general at one or two o'clock. Their lunch consists of fried salmon, sardinias, and very fine cordials.

A well furnished table is the pride of a Moscovite: his name is very soon known, and he is never in want of visitors. Coffee, without milk, is presented immediately after dinner. No tobacco is smoked, as the ladies dislike it. The ladies have a custom, when they meet in the streets, of presenting each other with their paint-boxes, in the same manner as the snuff-boxes are in other countries: this custom is general amongst all ranks of females.

The game of chess is much played, and a Moscovite nobleman cannot exist without cards – he calls this a relaxation of his mind, but which frequently costs him very dear.

[89] Moscow judged by an Anglo-Irish lady in the early nineteenth century as 'Asiatic' and 'medieval'; from *The Russian Journals of Martha and Catherine Wilmot 1803–1808*.

I had best at once whisk you back to Moscow & take you to the top of the highest Tower there to catch a glimpse of the Town which was precisely what Matty & I did about a fortnight ago accompanied by 2 or 3 other Traineaus in one of which was Mr Rowand who took us up to the top of Ivan Veleka from whence the view is most beautiful, most striking & extensive! This Tower is a distinguished feature in the Kremlin which rises amidst its fortifications in the centre of Moscow. All the Arms of the Empire decorate its encircling Walls & the Imperial Eagle extends its golden wings amidst the glittering Chains and Crosses which top its thousand Churches. The River which hangs like a Silver Crescent upon the town irradiates a scene of the most vivid animation! The fiery Horses of Livonia, Arabia & Tartary bound by hundreds round and round the Course, mark'd out with green boughs upon the ice, conducted by Cavaliers in little shells of Traineaus that circle & circle in dazzling rotation, & the Ice Mountains raised to a considerable height compel a swiftness in the motion of those who venture which *flying* alone can explain. The remoter part of the River is cut open in trenches & lines of washerwoman bend over to wring their Cloaths unconscious of the Cold. Baskets as large as Huts appear above the Surface which contain the Winter's Fish plunged to a considerable depth beneath & each proprietor weekly visits his watry Prison provident of the impending Fast. Oh, the beauty of the Russian Sky! Whether one contemplates it by Night or by Day, its loveliness is equally resplendent. So vaulted & so blue, so cloudless & so etherial! You may suppose how fine the outline is which frees the objects from the cerulean dome of Light!

Innumerable circumstances concur to give to Moscow an Asiatic air beyond any Town I ever saw! The Crescent glitters beneath the Cross of every Tower as a triumph to Christianity & mingles among the yellow Globes of Gold which blaze amidst the Sunshine. The gaudy Belfrys open to the day, the metal Copings, stupendous Palaces guarded by roaring Monsters & environ'd by Palisades, Theatres, Arches, Panoramas, Hospitals & Convents interspersed by great extent of private & public Gardens recede in an Amphitheatre from the Fortress & fill the Circle of 26 miles! But above all the Churches painted on the outside in gigantic Saints halo'd in radiant gold! One sees before them myriades of people blessing themselves & prostrating before these daubs of sanctification with an ardour more like idolatry than religion. They then rise & holla'ing to their Horses drive on their Cars heap'd with blocks of ice to the Cellars of the Nobles for the approaching Summer. The Houses are fringed with icicles, the water arrested by the cold & hanging in Streaming Crystal from the Spouts, the feather'd Snow upon the branches of the Trees, the magnificently frosted Beards congeal'd upon the Colour'd Sashes of the Peasants. These & a hundred other such Characteristic Sights fill the Streets & relieve the extended Sheet of Snow which veils an undulating Country & glitters like tissued gems upon the surrounding Hills ancient in Cloister'd Monasterys which distance shadows into the vapoury incertitude of endless perspective & loses in the rising mists of Circling Clouds.

As I conjured you up to the top of Ivan Veleka, so let me spirit you down again amongst us at Troitskoe to repose a little with us in this Feudal State, for if you will have my opinion of the matter Russia is but in the 12th Century. Yes! I know all about the luxury of Moscow & the civilization of Petersburg, but have you ever seen a clumsy romping ignorant Girl of 12 years old with a fine Parisian Cap upon her head? So seems to my eye this Imperial Realm. The cloister'd ignorance not only of the 12th but of the 11th Century is the groundwork of this colossal Region and 5 or 6 Centurys will no doubt produce the same effects here they have on other parts of Europe; but Time must disengage the ligaments which bind the plant before it strengthens & expands into a self supported standard. More sudden means would bend it to the Earth & so of Russian political liberty & civilization! But what business have I to shake my ears over the World, as if I held it in my clutches like an Apple elaborately to prove that the rosy side was sweet & the green side sour? I will take you down stairs into the Hall where dozens of Slaves are waiting with their offerings of Bread and Salt to greet the Princess! When she appears they fall down before her & kiss the ground with that senseless obeisance that stupefaction feels at the approach of superior Power! Her Lenity makes their Lot better perhaps than that of others, but that's saying very little for the System. Each Noble is omnipotent. He may be either an Angel or a Devil!

[90] Moscow seen by a nineteenth-century Russian as 'boring' and 'frivolous'; from *Essays about Classical Moscow* by Yuri Shamurin.

Moscow at the beginning of the nineteenth century is vividly portrayed in Batiushkov's *Walk Through Moscow* (1812).

His testimonial is characteristic of those left by the comparatively few Moscow diarists who succeeded in taking a broad, sweeping view of life in the city:

> I do not think that there exists a single city which bears the faintest resemblance to Moscow. The buildings, and the *mores* of its inhabitants provide us with stark contradictions. Here are luxury and penury, abundance and the most extreme deprivation, piety and atheism, the timeless continuity of our grandfathers' days and an unbelievable frivolity – warring elements which, out of their constant conflicts, create this marvellous, outrageous, gigantic whole which we know by its collective name: Moscow. But indolence is something all can share, an attribute exclusive to this town, and which can be observed primarily in a kind of restless curiosity which possesses its inhabitants, driving them towards a continual search for new distractions. Where, in other towns, people strive more or less to work, in Moscow they rest, and thus are familiar with boredom and all its tortures. Here, our proud boast is hospitality – but, between ourselves, what does this word mean? Very often – curiosity. In other towns you will be invited only after your good side has been discovered, and thereafter will always be welcome. In Moscow they invite you first, and get to know you later. Last winter, music turned everyone's head; all Moscow sang: I think from boredom. At present all Moscow is dancing – from boredom. Here, everyone is in love or trying to fall in love: I am willing to wager that it is from boredom.
>
> Unique, incomparable Moscow is a big provincial city, for what can its title 'capital without a court' mean? It makes its own way towards culture for, in effect, very little occurs that has any influence upon it. Here anyone can play the fool if he so chooses, living and dying a buffoon. London itself is less rich in caricatures of life.

[91] Moscow society after the French invasion –
the world of Griboyedov's *Woe from Wit*; from *The
Russians at Home. Unpolitical Sketches* by
Sutherland Edwards.

Let us now turn to Griboiedoff's *Gore ot Ouma*, of which
an English translation, by Nicolas Bernardaky, has lately
been published.

Gore ot Ouma, being interpreted, means 'Grief from Wit'
– not, exclusively, the wit which shines in epigrams, but
'wit' as the word was understood in the eighteenth century;
and the play, while exhibiting an animated satirical picture
of Moscow fashionable life in 1823, points out the fate
which inevitably awaits a man of honesty and perception
who is surrounded by a society of rogues and fools.
Tchatsky, the hero, is a misanthrope, but, at the same time,
an ardent, enthusiastic young man, who perhaps, under
more favourable circumstances, would not have been a
misanthrope at all; though we suspect that, as Sophia,
the heroine of the piece, observes, 'he is happiest where
men are most ridiculous.' He has very little in common with
Molière's 'Misanthrope,' who, compared with Griboiedoff's hero, is a model of patience. Alceste moralizes,
and delivers lengthened disquisitions, while Tchatsky is a
bitter satirist, and declaims the most elaborate tirades.
They, however, resemble one another in this point, that
each of them tires his mistress – in the case of the French-
man, by continual sermonizing; in that of the Rusian, by
unceasing raillery. There is one very fine idea in the Russian
comedy. The intellectual, warm-hearted Tchatsky is at
length declared to be made by the company of dolts and
knaves against whose vices and meannesses he has in vain
directed his satire – just as the patients of a lunatic asylum
might resolve unanimously that their visiting physician was
insane.

The plot of *Gore ot Ouma* is very simple. Tchatsky,
returning from his travels, finds, after three years' absence
from Moscow, that Sophia, whose affection he had once

enjoyed, no longer cares for him. The high-minded but unpleasantly satirical young traveller, who has too much independence to enter the government service, where cringing and flattery alone can procure him advancement, is supplanted by a model functionary named Moltchaline, who is silent before his superiors, lest by too much talking he may chance to utter some unbecoming remarks; who fawns systematically upon those above him, and makes love to the daughter of the chief of this department, merely as a matter of business. 'My father, on his death-bed,' says the cold-blooded secretary, 'counselled me to ingratiate myself with all I came in contact with – with the owner of the house where I lodge, with my superiors in the service, with the servant who brushed my clothes, with the porter who opened the door, and with the very dog of the porter, that it might not snarl at my heels.' Sophia really loves Moltchaline, while Moltchaline loves Lisa, the *soubrette* of the piece, 'and I,' says Lisa, 'fear love as I do the devil; yet how could any one help loving Petroushka the butler?'

Famoussoff, Sophia's father, is a servile functionary of high rank, who, in his best moments, utters commonplaces of a somewhat florid description; while the homely stupidities pronounced by his friend Skalozoub, a military pedant, are principally remarkable for their *naïveté*. The play altogether belongs to satire rather than to comedy. There is a great deal that is terrible, but not much that is laughable, in Griboiedoff's picture of Moscow society thirty-five years since.

[92] Moscow society after the French invasion – a household of the 1820s; from *Griboyedov's Moscow* by M. Gershenzon.

Maria Ivanovna Rimsky-Korsakov's house, between the years of 1816 and 1823, was in every particular typical of the houses in Griboyedov's Moscow. It was precisely at this time (1818 and 1823) and in the circle to which the Rimsky-Korsakov family belonged, that Griboyedov, on his visits to Moscow, was able to observe Moscow society; and it was during these years that *Woe from Wit* was written. There can be no doubt that Griboyedov and Maria Ivanovna had known each other from childhood, and it is highly probable that when in Moscow he would be received at her house. A few years later, when Griboyedov was still alive (in 1828), the two families were united: Maria Ivanovna's youngest son Sergei married that very same cousin of Griboyedov's, Sophia Alexeyevna, who legend has it was the prototype of Sophia Famusova, just as her father, Griboyedov's uncle, was that of Famusov himself . . .

Let us enter Maria Ivanovna's house: no sooner are we over the threshold than the atmosphere of *Woe from Wit* envelops us.

The house is large, spacious, built on two floors, containing some twenty rooms and with a ballroom in which balls, masquerades and charity concerts attended by hundreds of people take place. The façade is on Strastnoye Square: present-day day Muscovites know the building as the Seventh Gymnasium for boys. The house has a vast complex of outbuildings – an entire village; here we find a separate wing and the various service areas: the stables, the coach-house, quarters for the married servants and for the single. The stables contain six or seven horses, the coach-house carriages and sleighs both for town use and long journeys; inside and outside the house, a great many serfs are to be seen – coachmen and post-boys, laundresses, a chef, a cook, maids. Apart from the family, an assortment of old ladies reside in the house – Maria Timofeyevna and others – and a blind little old man called Piotr Ivanovich; 'my invalid brigade' Maria Ivanovna calls them, not without affection. Fifteen people sit down at table, because almost always of the morning's visitors two or three will stay to lunch. Everyone, to the very last watchman, enjoys a life of freedom and plenty: Maria Ivanovna loves to live herself, and allows others to do so.

Maria Ivanovna rises early, at 7 o'clock, sometimes at 6; only if she has returned late from a ball the night before, will she sleep on until 9. Having said her prayers, she goes into the sitting-room where, in the company of her maid and confidante Duniashka, she takes tea. No sooner has she finished than her ministers arrive with their reports. The chief minister is Yakov Ivanovich Rosenberg: he has been living in the house for many years and answers himself. Yakov Ivanovich's report concerns bills awaiting settlement. Maria Ivanovna is displeased: the expenses are enormous, money is swept out of the house like rubbish, and not a penny is being sent from the country: it is a good thing that there is some income to look forward to, otherwise it would be really too trying: funds exist, yet one sits penniless the entire time. They discuss the sins of the Penza steward. Already January is coming to an end, and still the buckwheat has not been threshed, neither have the oats, and the rye has still to be sold. How much income would that bring in? 200 'quarters'* of rye – 14,000 roubles, 600 'quarters' of other cereals – 6,000 roubles, making 20,000 roubles in all. Andrei Ponamarev would have to be dispatched so that he might sort the entire matter out on the spot: the money was needed, and Grisha had to have some forwarded to him. Yakov Ivanovich is followed by Astay, the head coachman: his every word is prefaced by 'begging your leave to announce' . . . Maria Ivanovna needs patience to hear him out. Having finished with Astafy, Maria Ivanovna goes to visit the housekeeper Annisa, drinks a cup of coffee with her, talks over kitchen and wardrobe matters, and sometimes busies herself there until luncheon, cutting out clothes for her daughters. Natasha has grown so plump that words cannot do justice to her, she has become a real country wench, quite unlike a proper *mamselle*. All her dresses can be thrown out, she has nothing to wear, new ones have to be sewn, and both Sasha and Katia have grown.

* A term used exclusively in measuring grain, and being a quarter of the ancient 'Kad'. Each 'quarter' equals 4 'pood', or 4 × 36 lbs.

[93] Moscow society after the French invasion –
the younger generation grows up; from *Memoirs of
a Revolutionist* by Prince Peter Kropotkin.

(Prince Peter Alekseyevitch Kropotkin (1842–1921) was
known as the 'Anarchist Prince', and his remarkable life
spanned the reigns of Nicholas I to that of Lenin. When he
died, his body was allowed to lie in state in the former Hall
of Columns as a great honorary Marxist. A brilliant journalist, his *Memoirs* rank with those of Herzen for vivid im-
mediacy and sheer adventure, and give a magnificent picture
of the *ancien régime* in Russia, albeit through the eyes of a
dedicated radical and sometime revolutionary.)

Life went on quietly and peacefully – at least for the outsider
– in this Moscow Faubourg Saint-Germain [the Starya
Konyushennaya – the Old Equerries' Quarter]. In the morning nobody was seen in the streets. About midday the
children made their appearance under the guidance of
French tutors and German nurses, who took them out
for a walk on the snow-covered boulevards. Later on in
the day the ladies might be seen in their two-horse sledges,
with a valet standing behind on a small plank fastened at the
end of the runners, or ensconced in an old-fashioned carriage, immense and high, suspended on big curved springs
and dragged by four horses, with a postillion in front and
two valets standing behind. In the evening most of the
houses were brightly illuminated, and, the blinds not being
drawn down, the passer-by could admire the card-players or
the waltzers in the saloons. 'Opinions' were not in vogue in
those days, and we were yet far from the years when in each
one of these houses a struggle began between 'fathers and
sons' – a struggle that usually ended either in a family
tragedy or in a nocturnal visit of the state police. Fifty years
ago nothing of the sort was thought of; all was quiet and
smooth – at least on the surface . . .

Wealth was measured in those times by the number of
'souls' which a landed proprietor owned. So many 'souls'

meant so many male serfs: women did not count. My father, who owned nearly twelve hundred souls, in three different provinces, and who had, in addition to his peasants' holdings, large tracts of land which were cultivated by these peasants, was accounted a rich man. He lived up to his reputation, which meant that his house was open to any number of visitors, and that he kept a very large household.

We were a family of eight, occasionally of ten or twelve; but fifty servants at Moscow, and half as many more in the country, were considered not one too many. Four coachmen to attend a dozen horses, three cooks for the masters and two more for the servants, a dozen men to wait upon us at dinner-time (one man, plate in hand, standing behind each person seated at the table), and girls innumerable in the maid-servants' room, – how could anyone do with less than this?

Besides, the ambition of every landed proprietor was that everything required for his household should be made at home by his own men.

'How nicely your piano is always tuned! I suppose Herr Schimmel must be your tuner?' perhaps a visitor would remark.

To be able to answer, 'I have my own piano-tuner,' was in those times the correct thing.

'What a beautiful pastry!' the guests would exclaim, when a work of art, composed of ices and pastry, appeared toward the end of the dinner. 'Confess, prince, that it comes from Tremblé' (the fashionable pastry-cook).

'It is made by my own confectioner, a pupil of Tremblé, whom I have allowed to show what he can do,' was a reply which elicited general admiration.

To have embroideries, harnesses, furniture – in fact, everything – made by one's own men was the ideal of the rich and respected landed proprietor. As soon as the children of the servants attained the age of ten, they were sent as apprentices to the fashionable shops, where they were obliged to spend five or seven years chiefly in sweeping, in receiving an incredible number of thrashings, and in running about town on errands of all sorts. I must own that few of them became masters of their respective arts. The tailors and the shoemakers were found only skilful enough to make clothes or shoes for the servants, and when a really good pastry was required for a dinner-party it was ordered at Tremblé's, while our own confectioner was beating the drum in the music band.

That band was another of my father's ambitions, and almost every one of his male servants, in addition to other accomplishments, was a bass-viol or a clarinet in the band. Makar, the piano-tuner, *alias* under-butler, was also a flutist; Andrei, the tailor, played the French horn; the confectioner was first put to beat the drum, but he misused his instrument to such a deafening degree that a tremendous trumpet was bought for him, in the hope that his lungs would not have the power to make the same noise as his hands; when, however, this last hope had to be abandoned, he was sent to be a soldier. As to 'spotted Tikhon', in addition to his numerous functions in the household as lamp-cleaner, floor-polisher, and footman, he made himself useful in the band – today as a trombone, tomorrow as a bassoon, and occasionally as second violin . . .

My father liked to have plenty of guests in his house. Our dinner-hour was four, and at seven the family gathered round the *samovar* (tea-urn) for tea. Everyone belonging to our circle could drop in at that hour, and from the time my sister Hélène was again with us there was no lack of visitors, old and young, who took advantage of the privilege. When the windows facing the street showed bright light inside that was enough to let people know that the family was at home and friends would be welcome . . .

Dancing-parties were not infrequent, to say nothing of a couple of obligatory balls every winter. Father's way, in such cases, was to have everything done in a good style, whatever the expense. But at the same time such niggardliness was practised in our house in daily life that if I were to recount it, I should be accused of exaggeration. It is said of a family of pretenders to the throne of France, renowned for their truly regal hunting-parties, that in their everyday life even the tallow candles are minutely counted. The same sort of miserly economy ruled in our house with regard to everything; so much so that when we, the children of the house, grew up, we detested all saving and counting. However, in the Old Equerries' Quarter such a mode of life only raised my father in public esteem. 'The old prince,' it was said, 'seems to be sharp over money at home; but he knows how a nobleman ought to live'

[94] Moscow society after the French invasion – the older generation dies; from *My Past and Thoughts* by Alexander Herzen.

Princess Anna Borisovna's [Meshchersky] house, preserved by some miracle at the time of the fire of 1812, had not been repaired nor redecorated for fifty years: the silk hangings that covered the walls were faded and blackened; the lustres on the chandeliers, discoloured by heat and turned into smoky topazes by time, shook and tinkled, glittering and shining dimly when anyone walked across the room. The heavy, solid mahogany furniture, ornamented with florid carvings that had lost all their gilt, stood gloomily along the walls; chests of drawers with Chinese incrustations, tables with little copper trellis-work, rococo porcelain dolls – all recalled another age and different manners.

Grey-headed flunkeys sat in the outer hall, occupied with quiet dignity in various trifling tasks, or sometimes reading half aloud from a prayer-book or a psalter, the pages of which were darker than its cover. Boys stood at the doors, but they were more like old dwarfs than children – they never laughed nor raised their voices.

A deathly silence reigned in the inner apartments; only, from time to time, there was the mournful cry of a cockatoo, its unhappy, faltering effort to repeat a human word, the bony tap of its beak against its perch, covered with tin, and the disgusting whimper of a little old monkey, shrunken and consumptive, that lived in the great hall, on a little shelf of

the stove with its Dutch tiles. The monkey, dressed like a
débardeur, in full, red trousers, gave the whole room a
peculiar and extremely unpleasant smell. In another big
room hung a multitude of family portraits of all sizes,
shapes, periods, ages, and costumes. These portraits had
a peculiar interest for me, especially from the contrast
between the originals and their semblances. The young
man of twenty with a powdered head, dressed in a light-
green embroidered *caftan*, smiling courteously from the
canvas, was my father. The little girl with dishevelled curls
and a bouquet of roses, her face adorned with a patch,
mercilessly tight-laced into the shape of a wine-glass, and
thrust into enormous petticoats, was the formidable old
Princess Marya Alexeyevna.

The stillness and the stiffness grew more marked as one
approached the princess's room. Old maidservants in white
caps with wide frills moved to and for with little teapots, so
softly that their footsteps were inaudible; from time to time a
grey-headed manservant in a long coat of stout dark-blue
cloth appeared in a doorway, but his footsteps too were as
inaudible, and when he gave some message to the head
parlourmaid, his lips moved without making a sound.

The little, withered, wrinkled, but by no means ugly, old
lady, Princess Anna Borisovna, was usually sitting or reclin-
ing on the big clumsy sofa, propped up with cushions. One
could scarcely distinguish her; everything was white, her
morning dress, her cap, the cushions, the covers on the sofa.
Her waxen white face of lace-like fragility, together with her
faint voice and white dress, gave her an air of something that
had passed away, that was scarcely breathing.

The big English clock on the table with its loud, measured
spondee – tick-tack, tick-tack – seemed marking off the last
quarters of an hour of her life . . .

There were always some old women of every sort, either
habituées of the old princess's house, or encamped there
temporarily, like nomads, ranged along the walls or sitting
in various corners. Half saints and half vagrants, rather
crazy and very devout, sickly and extraordinarily unclean,

these old women trailed from one old-fashioned house to another: in one they were fed, in another presented with an old shawl; from one place they were sent groats and fire-wood, from another cloth and cabbage; and so they some-how made both ends meet. Everywhere they were a nuisance, everywhere they were passed over, everywhere put in the lowest seat, and everywhere received through boredom and emptiness and, most of all, through love of gossip. In the presence of other company these mournful figures were usually silent, looking with envious hatred at each other . . . They sighed, shook their heads, made the sign of the cross, and muttered to themselves the number of their stitches, prayers, and perhaps even words of abuse. On the other hand, *tête à tête* with their *benefactresses* and *patronesses*, they rewarded themselves for their silence by the most treacherous gossip about all the other benefac-tresses who received them, fed them and made them pre-sents.

They were continually begging from the old princess and, in return for her presents, often made without the knowl-edge of her niece, who did not like them to be indulged, brought her holy bread, hard as stone, and unnecessary woollen and knitted articles of their own make, which the old lady afterwards sold for their benefit, regardless of whether the purchaser was willing or not.

Apart from birthdays, name-days, and other holidays the most solemn gathering of kinsmen and friends in Princess Anna Borisovna's house took place on New Year's Eve. On that day she 'elevated' the Iversky Madonna. The holy ikon was carried through all the apartments by chanting monks and priests. The old princess walked under it in front, crossing herself, and after her all the visitors, men and maid servants, old people and children. After this they all con-gratulated her on the approaching New Year, and made her all sorts of trifling presents such as are given to children. She would play with them for a few days and then give them away.

My father used to take me every year to this heathen

ceremony; everything was repeated in exactly the same order, except that some old men and women were missing, and their names were intentionally avoided; only the old lady would say:

'Our Ilya Vasilyevich is no longer here, the Kingdom of Heaven be his! . . . Whom will the Lord summon in the coming year?'

And she would shake her head dubiously.

And the spondees of the English clock would go on measuring out the days, the hours, the minutes, and at last it reached the fatal second. The old lady felt unwell on getting up one day; she walked about the rooms and was no better; her nose began bleeding, and very violently; she was feeble and tired, and lay down fully dressed on her sofa, fell quietly asleep . . . and did not wake up. She was over ninety.

[95] Festivities for the coronation of Tsar Nicholas I: a Russian view; from *Staraya Moskva* by D.M. Nikoforov.

In the *Collected Documents of the Past*, compiled by P.P. Shchukin (Vol. 7, p. 76), we find three excerpts from letters written by Mukhanov from Moscow in 1826:

1) Here all is being made ready for the Coronation: agents sent by the envoys are inspecting various houses, and among them Monsieur de Pontcaret (Marmont's trusted man), viewed the Kirsanov house and was full of admiration, but in the end decided against it because it was too small, and, according to him, not of a size to accommodate the '*trente valets de pieds*' whom the Duke of Ragusa intends to bring with him. Our ladies, with an air of importance, are busy discussing dresses, patterns . . .

2) The envoys tumble over each other in jealous haste to hold dances and suppers, scattering money as if it were sawdust, and exhibiting luxury such as Moscow has never yet seen. A bottle of champagne stands between each place laid at Ragusa's supper table, his house is costing him sixty

thousand, with a further twenty thousand for the annexe, and a special pavilion is being built for the festivities which are to succeed the Coronation. You might be interested to hear that the French soldiers have invented the verb *raguser*, meaning *tromper*, *trahir*, out of his name. Devonshire, who is both deaf and stupid, had twice the number of gilded and powdered lackeys as there are steps on his staircase, for two lackeys stand at attention on each one throughout the entire evening. Little did I think that the enlightened West could find reason to employ such graceless luxury, in which neither beauty nor pleasure are to be found. The revels provided by our fellow countrymen are just as numerous, my father arranges modest evenings.

3) The days here are spent in revelry. You have doubtless received accounts; to your eternal amazement, I will tell you that, for sheer enjoyment, Yusupov's reception outshone all the rest, and in magnificence equalled the ball given by Countess Orloff. In this instance, as in many others, the foreigners had to concede victory to the Russians, which gave pleasure to the Emperor as it did to all of us patriots.

The hope that the enlightened West would not adopt the clumsy device of lining its staircase with live caryatids, proved a vain one. On the contrary, this fashion has spread far and wide and we, eternal followers of foreign invention, display it in its advanced form. Aping the fashionable flower-mania which on the shores of the Mediterranean costs mere pennies, we squander entire fortunes; thus at a certain wedding which took place at the University Church, the decorations on the staircase came to thirty thousand and those upon the supper-table five thousand – all for the space of an hour or so.

[96] Pushkin's opinion of Moscow; from *The Letters of Alexander Pushkin.*

TO ELIZAVETA MIKHAYLOVNA KHITROVO
August 21, 1830. From Moscow to Petersburg
(In French)

How much gratitude I owe you, Madame, for your kindness in giving me some acquaintance with what is going on in Europe! Nobody here receives periodicals from France, and as for political opinion regarding all that has just happened, the English Club has decided that Prince Dmitry Golitsyn was wrong in forbidding écarté by an ordinance. I am condemned to live among these orangutans at the most interesting moment of our century.

TO PETER ALEXANDROVICH PLETNEV
January 13, 1831. From Moscow to Petersburg

My dear fellow, here is my life's plan for you: I am getting married this month; I shall live half a year in Moscow; in the summer I shall come to you. I dislike Moscow life. Here you live, not as you wish but as aunties wish. My mother-in-law is just such an aunty. It's quite a different thing in Petersburg! I'll start living in clover, as a petty bourgeois, independently, and taking no thought of what Maria Alexeyevna will say . . .

TO ELIZAVETA MIKHAYLOVNA KHITROVO
March 26, 1831. From Moscow to Petersburg
(In French)

I hope to be at your feet, Madame, in one or two months at most. I am eagerly looking forward to it. Moscow is the town of Nothingness. On its gates are written: 'Abandon all intelligence, O ye who enter here.' Political news arrives to us late or distorted. For almost the last two weeks we have known nothing with regard to Poland – and there is not the slightest pang of impatience! If only we were quite dissolute, quite foolish, quite frivolous – but nothing of the kind. We are destitute, we are woebegone, and we are stupidly calculating the decline of our revenues . . .

[97] The disaffected spirit – and the dirtiness – of Moscow in the 1830s; from *Narrative of a Visit to the Courts of Russia and Sweden in the Years 1830 and 1831* by Captain C. Colville Frankland RN.

I dined at M. Pouschkin's, and met there some very agreeable and clever Russians, among the rest, M.K—, and the Prince W—. The fair bride did not appear.

There is a liberty of speech, and thought, and action, in Moscow, which does not exist in Petersburgh; this makes it an agreeable place to an Englishman, whose device should be – 'Civil and religious liberty all the world over.'

The fact is, Moscow is a sort of rendezvous for all the retired, discontented, and *renvoyé'd* officers, civil and military, of the empire. It is the nucleus of the Russian opposition. Hence almost all the men of liberal opinions, and those whose politics do not suit those of the day, retire hither, where they may find fault with the Court, the Government, &c. as much as they please, without much fear of interruption. I have no doubt that a great deal more may be learnt in this city of the real state of Russia in one month, than one could gather with the utmost industry in six, in Petersburgh.

The dirtiness of the anti-rooms and corridors and staircases in Moscow is indescribable. The Russians have an odious custom, in common with most Continental nations, of spitting about on the floors, in all directions and at all times. They have likewise a singular trick of taking a little piece of wax from the candles and rolling it up between finger and thumb into a little ball. I have often observed in society half-a-dozen persons, one after the other, walk up to the candles and carry off their little spoil: this is a most ludicrous and unaccountable custom.

In Moscow it is at present the fashion among a certain number of the higher classes to wear enormously long fingernails, like eagles' claws, and these not always very clean.

I must not forget to mention the amazing number of kites and buzzards of all sorts which scavenger the streets of Moscow, as they do likewise at Constantinople; also a disgusting sort of carrion crow, with deformed beak and red breast, which performs the same service.

[98] Lermontov's love for Moscow and scorn for St Petersburg, in *Sashka: a moral tale*; from *Michael Lermontov* by C.E. L'Ami and Alexander Welikotny.

VI

My hero was of Moscow. That is why
I scorn the Neva's fog, and hate and mock it;
There (and I call the world to testify)
Joy is unhealthy to the Russian pocket,
And learning dulls the Russian mind and eye.
There life is empty, silent, stern and gray,
Like the flat foreshore of the Finnish Bay.*
But Moscow's not like that: Till life is over,
I swear, my friends, I shall not cease to love her!
There first in days of hope and gaiety,
I drowned my heart in love and lechery.

VII

Moscow, my home – I love you as a son,
Love like a Russian, strong and fierce and gentle!
Your gray-haired lustre, venerable one,
Your Kremlin, tranquil in its winter mantle!
In vain the foreign sovereign† sought to run
A course with you, O ageless Russian giant,
And measure wits, and of all right defiant,
To cast you down. In vain your citadel
The stranger struck: you shook yourself – he fell!
The world was still . . . Majestically there
You live alone, unmoved, our glory's heir!

* Gulf of Finland.
† The foreign sovereign Napoleon.

VIII

You live! . . . And every stone on every tower
Is sacred lore from age to age passed on.
Once by a turret in an idle hour
I sat in shade, and watched the autumn sun
Play on the moss in many a crannied bower,
When from a nest behind a cornice hid,
Swallows flew out, and up and downward fled,
Circling above, careless of men and me.
And I, so full of passion to be free.
Envied their unknown life, seeing on high
A hope of freedom in the boundless sky.

[99] Slavophiles versus Westerners: Moscow as a symbol; from *My Past and Thoughts* by Alexander Herzen.

It is infinitely sad to set side by side Pushkin's two epistles to Chaadayev, separated not only by their life but by a whole epoch, the life of a whole generation, racing hopefully forward and rudely flung back again. Pushkin as a youth writes to his friend:

'*Comrade, have faith. That dawn will break*
Of deep intoxicating joy;
Russia will spring from out her sleep
And on the fragments of a fallen tyranny
Our names will be recorded,'

but the dawn did not rise; instead Nicholas rose to the throne, and Pushkin writes:

'*Chaadayev, dost thou call to mind*
How in the past, by youthful ardour prompted,
I dreamt to add that fatal name
Unto the rest of those that lie in ruins?
. . . But now within my heart by tempests chastened

Silence and lassitude prevail, unchallenged,
And with a glow of tender inspiration
Upon the stone by friendship sanctified
I write our names . . .'

Nothing in the world was more opposed to the Slavophils than the hopeless pessimism which was Chaadayev's vengeance on Russian life, the deliberate curse wrung out of him by suffering, with which he summed up his melancholy existence and the existence of a whole period of Russian history. He was bound to awaken violent opposition in them; with bitterness and dismal malice he offended all that was dear to them, from Moscow downwards.

'In Moscow,' Chaadayev used to say, 'every foreigner is taken to look at the great cannon and the great bell – the cannon which cannot be fired and the bell which fell down before it was rung. It is an amazing town in which the objects of interest are distinguished by their absurdity; or perhaps that great bell without a tongue is a hieroglyph symbolic of this huge, dumb land, inhabited by a race calling themselves Slavs as though wondering at the possession of human speech.'

Chaadayev and the slavophils alike stood facing the unsolved Sphinx of Russian life, the Sphinx sleeping under the overcoat of the soldier and the watchful eye of the Tsar; they alike were asking: 'What will come of this? To live like this is impossible: the oppressiveness and absurdity of the present situation is obvious and unendurable – where is the way out?'

'There is none,' answered the man of the Petrine epoch of exclusively Western civilization, who in Alexander's reign had believed in the European future of Russia. He sadly pointed to what the efforts of a whole age had led to. Culture had only given new methods of oppression, the church had become a mere shadow under which the police lay hidden; the people still tolerated and endured, the government still crushed and oppressed. 'The history of other nations is the story of their emancipation. Russian history is the development of serfdom and autocracy.'

Peter's upheaval made us into the worst that men can be made into – *enlightened* slaves. We have suffered enough, in this oppressive, troubled moral condition, misunderstood by the people, struck down by the government – it is time to find rest, time to bring peace to one's soul, to find something to lean on . . . this almost meant 'time to die', and Chaadayev thought to find in the Catholic Church the rest promised to all that labour and are heavy laden.

From the point of view of Western civilization in the form in which it found expression at the time of restorations, from the point of view of Petrine Russia, this attitude was completely justified. The Slavophils solved the question in a different way.

Their solution implied a true consciousness of the *living soul* in the people; their instinct was more penetrating than their reasoning. They saw that the existing condition of Russia, however oppressive, was not a *fatal disease*. And while Chaadayev had a faint glimmer of the possibility of saving individuals, but not the people, the Slavophils had a clear perception of the ruin of individuals in the grip of that epoch, and faith in the salvation of the people.

'The way out is with us,' said the Slavophils, 'the way out lies in renouncing the Petersburg period, in going back to the people from whom we have been separated by foreign education and foreign government; let us return to the old ways!'

But history does not turn back; life is rich in materials, and never needs old clothes. All reinstatements, all restorations have always been masquerades. We have seen two; the Legitimists did not go back to the days of Louis XIV nor the Republicans to the 8th of Thermidor. What has once happened is stronger than anything written; no axe can hew it away.

More than this, we have nothing to go back to. The political life of Russia before Peter was ugly, poor and savage, yet it was to this that the Slavophils wanted to return, though they did not admit the fact; how else are we to explain all their antiquarian revivals, their worship of the manners and customs of old days, and their very attempts to return, not to the existing (and excellent) dress of the peasants but to the clumsy, antiquated costumes?

In all Russia no one wears the *murmolka* but the Slavophils. K.S. Aksakov wore a dress so national that people in the street took him for a Persian, as Chaadeyev used to tell for a joke.

They took the return to the people in a very crude sense too, as the majority of Western democrats did also, accepting the people as something complete and finished. They supposed that sharing the prejudices of the people meant being at one with them, that it was a great act of humility to sacrifice their own reason instead of developing reason in the people. This led to an affection of devoutness, the observance of rites which are touching when there is a naïve faith in them and offensive when there is visible premeditation. The best proof of the lack of reality in the Slavophils' return to the people lies in the fact that they did not arouse in them the slightest sympathy. Neither the Byzantine Church nor the Granovitaya Palata* will do anything more for the future development of the Slav world. To go back to the village, to the workmen's guild, to the meeting of the *mir*,† to the Cossack system is a different matter; but we must return to them not in order that they may be fixed fast in immovable Asiatic crystallizations, but to develop and set free the elements on which they were founded, to purify them from all that is extraneous and distorting, from the proud flesh with which they are overgrown – this, of course, is our vocation. But we must make no mistake; all this lies outside the purview of the State: the Moscow period will help here as little as the Petersburg – indeed at no time was it better. The Novgorod‡ bell which used to call the citizens to their ancient moot was merely melted into a cannon by Peter

* Granovitaya Palata, the hall in the Kremlin in which the Tsar and his councillors used to meet before the time of Peter the Great.
† Village council.
‡ Novgorod, the most famous city in the earliest period of Russian history, was to some extent a republic under the rule of its princes from Rurik onwards. It was almost destroyed and was deprived of its liberties by Ivan III in 1471.

but had been taken down from the belfry by Ivan III; serfdom was only confirmed by the census under Peter but had been introduced by Boris Godunov; in the *Ulozheniye** there is no longer any mention of sworn witnesses, and the knout, the rods and the lash made their appearance long before the day of *Spiessruten* and *Fuchteln*.

The mistake of the Slavophils lay in their thinking that Russia once had an individual culture, obscured by various events and finally by the Petersburg epoch. Russia never had this culture and never could have had it.

[100] The *Ryadi*, or bazaars, of Moscow; from *Russia: 1842* by J.G. Kohl.

All liquids, such as beer, wine, &c., are excluded from the commerce of the Gostinnoi Dvor and the Ryädi; also all bulky articles, such as hay and straw, and such things as must be had in all the corners of the city; bread, for example . . .

The fine West European wares, French books, and objects of ornament and luxury, French and English cloths, and Swiss confectionaries, are to be found on the Kusnetzkoi-Most (Smiths bridge). All the inscriptions there announce something foreign, and recommend themselves in the French language. In the print-shops it is easier to find views of London, Paris, Calcutta, and New York, than of St Petersburg or Moscow. I asked in one for some Russian costumes, and was told they were expecting them from Paris. Many more pictures are manufactured at Moscow than in St Petersburg, but they consist exclusively of bad imitations of originals published in London or Paris. It is incredible what numbers of caricatures of cupids and goddesses, celebrated men and women, and other pictures, issue from Moscow for the supply of the interior. Moscow's original genius shows itself only in representations of churches, saints, &c.

* The *Ulozheniye* was the code of laws of Tsar Alexis Mikhaylovich (father of Peter the Great), issued in 1649.

At the foot of the Kremlin, the flower-market of Moscow is held. It is a repetition of what may be seen in spring in the hay-market of St Petersburg, but much prettier. In Moscow it has the appearance of a village of which every house stands in its own garden. Huts of painted wood are filled with cherry-trees in blossom, with roses of all kinds, and all such flowers as will not bear exposure to the open air. Before the door sits the guardian of these fragrant prisoners. The huts stand at a certain distance from one another, surrounded by flower-beds and little shrubberies, every bed containing only one kind of flower. Here is a whole bed of violets, there a painted field of ranunculus; behind are ranged the larger kinds of plants and bushes, in whose branches the birds twitter and chirp as in their native groves. A more agreeable stroll cannot be imagined than among these huts, to look at their contents, and talk with the quiet dealers about their flower trade. On the limits of the colony, a number of vehicles are constantly at work, conveying flowers and shrubs to and from the market, and at one end of it are the waggons of those who visit the place only for the one day, who have no regular stand here, but carry about with them house and garden on four wheels.

Many flowers are sold here, but more are hired only. Many great personages, who are not much in the habit of giving dinners, or wish to make an extra show on some particular occasion, find their account in borrowing rather than buying. Every rose, cherry, and orange-tree has therefore its selling price and its letting price, which amounts, if the plant be a choice one, to several rubles . . .

The number of shops in the Ryädi are not less than twelve hundred: all united under one common roof. Not only the shops, but the passages between, are covered, but the roof is so awkwardly constructed, that in the strongest sunshine people stumble in darkness, and after the slightest shower wade through mud.

It would be difficult, nevertheless, to find a market of a more cheerful character than the Moscow Ryädi, not that it can be said the Russian merchants are more indifferent to gain than others, but they have, notwithstanding their lust of gain, a cheerfulness of temperament wholly wanting to the German and English merchant. The Russians carry on their business in the midst of praying, tea-drinking, ball and draughts, playing laughing, and gossipping. Their appetite is always ready, and nearly as many sellers of edibles are to be met with here as customers, with every thing necessary for breakfast ready prepared, including plates and knives and forks. They play at ball in the narrow passages between their shops, making use of a great leathern ball filled with air, which is struck by the foot. But the favourite game is draughts, which they play before their doors, in the shops, and sometimes in the middle of the street; however, they neither play for money, nor bet; they love their kopeks too well to expose them to such danger.

The whole range of shops are plentifully adorned with pictures of saints nailed to the beams with lamps burning before them, singing birds in cages, and whole flights of pigeons, which nestle under the eaves of the shops, and are cherished and fed by the owners as a kind of sacred bird.

The merchandise is arranged here as elsewhere in masses, not promiscuously; here a range of thirty shops for paper, another range for spices, a third for ornamental articles, a fourth for pictures of saints. In this last article, as might be expected in Moscow the holy, a very large trade is driven. Here are to be found pictures for every place and occasion; for halls, bed-chambers, churches, private chapels, coffee-houses, and ships; big ones for the merchant who likes a large foundation for his faith; small ones for the palaces of the great, where they are half hidden behind the curtains. I was surprised to find among these, some copies of Roman catholic saints; gloriously caricatured, it is true, by Russian artists, but honoured by the Russian traders as the Greek pictures are.

[101] The streets of Moscow in the 1870s; from *Behind the Scenes in Russia* by George Carrington.

No words can give any idea of the filthy and neglected state of a Russian town in spring and summer. In spring, for instance, owing to bad paving and draining, every street is either a water-course or a morass. At Moscow, especially, owing to the nature of the soil, the stones sink and become displaced, and the black mud oozes between them. A horse that has sunk up to the belly in mud, is no uncommon sight in the streets of Moscow. I have frequently been obliged to hire a carriage to take me across the street, and this not from any delicacy about soiling my boots. I have in my time seen bad roads of all descriptions, and on both sides of the world, but I have never seen any roads in town or country so atrociously bad as the streets of Moscow. The pavement, instead of being an improvement, makes them worse, for it rises here in hillocks, and sinks there to form holes full of water or liquid mud. As soon as the mud dries, and turns into dust, many streets resemble the dry beds of mountain torrents, and the carriages rock and roll in them like ships in a storm. The sun is very hot in the early spring, and in consequence of this, and the cold dry wind that prevails, the air is full of dust. One sees little attempt at remedying this evil. There are no water-carts, but one or two enterprising shopkeepers are in the habit of sending out boys with watering-pots. The water supply of Moscow is managed by carts, and one sees at the principal fountains in the town men employed all day long in filling them. In the winter these carts when driven through the streets present a singular appearance, as the water dripping over the sides forms icicles in all kinds of grotesque shapes.

One great cause of the stinks and unhealthy state of the atmosphere in Moscow in spring time is, that all the winter through, people make large use of frozen provisions – meat, fish, and vegetables; now when a sudden thaw comes, with a hot sun, great quantities of these provisions go bad, and are thrown away. Hence, whole streets in which provisions are sold exhale a very fetid smell. The fish that are not sold, and which do not go bad, are returned to the ice cellars to be kept frozen till required. Thus one never knows whether one is eating a fresh fish, or one that has been hawked about the streets for years, or preserved from the time of Peter the Great. The fish are frozen just as they are caught and sent as stiff as logs in cart loads to the towns. The Russians pretend that fish thus frozen is just as good as if it were fresh, and of course they can get no other in the winter; but in my opinion it decidedly lacks flavour, and is moreover unwholesome . . .

Russia is the head-quarters of cholera, and no wonder, considering that in matters of cleanliness and common decency the Russians, as a nation, are yet children. Indeed it is from Russia that the cholera taint has been wafted westward into Europe.

[102] Fresh milk in Moscow in the 1870s; from *Across the Kremlin, or Pictures of Life in Moscow* by G.T. Lowth.

The proceedings of these cows in the early morning in the heart of the city, wandering alone, was a mystery. On inquiring I was told that throughout Moscow various families possess, among their worldly goods, a cow. Vast numbers of the larger houses have considerable spaces enclosed in the rear of their dwellings – gardens, courts, grassy places. Likewise the innumerable cottages in the by-streets have within their gates green plots and outhouses. In very many of these there is a cow. During the summer time, when there is pasture, the first duty to be observed in all these dwellings is to open the gates and let out the cow. If there is delay in this performance a loud warning from the outhouse or the court awakes the servant to it. The cow let out, he may go to bed again. She knows her way by certain streets towards a certain barrier of the city. As she goes other cows join her from other cottages or houses, and by the time they all arrive near the barrier they are a considerable body. Here they find a man blowing a horn, whose business it is to conduct them to some pasture outside the town, to take care of them during the day, to collect them by his horn in the afternoon, and to bring them back to the barrier at a given time. When he has done this his business is over. Each cow knows her way home, and finds it unmolested up to the very heart of the city, the Kremlin. What a simple and convenient method for insuring good and pure and fresh milk to the family! Each *mater-familias* can water it according to her wants or tastes, and she can omit the chalk – a blessed privilege!

[103] Tolstoy in the slums; from *Leo Tolstoy* by Ernest J. Simmons.

Although the poverty and evil Tolstoy observed in the city discouraged him, he felt keenly that he must do something to remedy the situation. Such human misery struck deeply at the roots of his new faith and called into question his own way of life. He first felt the need to inform himself fully of the extent and causes of all this suffering. Frequently he stopped and talked with beggars on the streets; their obviously lying accounts gave him some insight into their psychology but little information concerning the true reasons behind their degradation.

Determined to see the worst the city had to offer, one late December afternoon in 1881 Tolstoy made his way to the Khitrov market, a disreputable section of the town. His well-dressed appearance quickly attracted attention among the throng of ragged, shivering, hungry, importunate human derelicts and they crowded around him. He listened to their tales of desperate circumstances, and in an agony of helplessness he bought them hot drinks and distributed money freely. The news of the ministering angel ran through the street. Each upturned begging face seemed to him more pitiful and degraded than the last. The press of people became great; disorder and a crush ensued. Tolstoy took refuge in Lyapin House, a charitable institution that provided free night lodgings. The sight of these tiers of bunks, each with its impoverished occupant in tatters, further sickened him. Feeling terribly ashamed of himself, he hurried away.

Tolstoy reached home that night, ascended the carpeted stairway, took off his fur coat, and sat down to a five-course dinner served by two lackey in dress clothes with white ties and gloves. And at that moment he understood with his whole being that the existence of tens of thousands of destitute people in Moscow was a crime, not committed once, but again and again; and that he with his luxury not merely tolerated it, but shared in it. He should have given not only hot drinks and small sums of money to those wretched people in the Khitrov market, but the overcoat that he wore and all that he possessed at home. Yet he had not done this, and therefore he felt and would continue to feel that as long as he had any superfluous food, money, and belongings, and someone else had none, then he shared in a constantly repeated crime.

That same evening, after returning from Lyapin House, Tolstoy described his impressions to a friend. With some satisfaction the friend began to explain that poverty was a most natural thing in the city and an inevitable condition of civilization. In the argument that followed Tolstoy, quite unconscious of his rising temper, waved his arms at his friend and with tears in his voice shouted: 'One cannot live so, one cannot live so! It is impossible' His alarmed wife ran into the room, and both she and the friend remonstrated with him for his unnecessary ardour and reminded him that the existence of poverty-stricken people did not justify his spoiling the lives of those around him.

Tolstoy agreed that their criticism was just, but in the depths of his heart he felt that he too was right. When he told his experiences to other friends and acquaintances, they approved of his kind-heartedness, but insisted that the most that wealthy people could do was to attempt to alleviate the misery of the poor by philanthropy.

Perhaps organized philanthropy, Tolstoy thought, was the only answer to the problem of the poor, and he decided to make use of the approaching decennial census (January 1882) for this purpose. His plan was to persuade the numerous census takers to conduct a canvass of the city's poor in the course of their official duties. On the basis of the detailed information thus obtained, a complete list of the most worthy cases would be compiled along with the relevant data necessary to provide the most effective kind of aid. In order to implement the scheme, he intended to use his influence in setting up a large charitable fund.

Tolstoy began the campaign with a stirring newspaper article, 'On the Moscow Census,' in which he outlined his plan and made a forthright appeal for aid. Carried away by his own enthusiasm, he declared towards the end of the article: 'However little may be done, it will be of importance. But why not hope that everything will be done? Why not hope that we will strive so that in Moscow there will not be one person unclothed, not one hungry, not one human being sold for money, not one unfortunate crushed by fate who does not know where to find brotherly aid? It is not surprising that this has not been done, but it is surprising that these things exist side by side with our superfluity of leisure and wealth, and that we can live untroubled knowing that they exist.' He repeated the substance of this plea in the homes of wealthy friends and received promises of financial assistance, but he did not fail to notice among those he solicited the uncomfortable feeling of guilty people and an attitude plainly indicating that his plan was a well-intentioned yet hopeless endeavour.

Tolstoy secured a position as an organizer in the census and asked to have assigned to him one of the worst sections of the city, where was situated Rzhanov House, a series of cheap lodgings that had the reputation of being a den of extreme poverty and vice. His first reaction was one of pained disillusion. He saw that the majority of wretched inhabitants of these cheap lodgings were not at all exceptional, but just such people as those among whom he lived and that their unhappiness depended not on external conditions, but on themselves – a kind of unhappiness that money could not remedy. He was amazed at the contentedness and self-sufficiency of many of these poor people and at their charity to each other. Their conditions of life were appalling, but he did not realize then, as he did later, that they could be helped only by changing their outlook on life. To change another man's outlook on life, however, one must oneself have a better outlook and live in accord with it, and Tolstoy was aware that his own view on life had to be altered before he could really assist these unhappy people.

The many loose women who lived in Rzhanov House gave him deep concern. During his rounds he heard of one mother, a prostitute, who had sold her thirteen-year-old daughter. He visited the mother in the hope of saving the girl, for he thought of speaking to ladies of his acquaintance who took a charitable interest in such cases. The mother and daughter he found living in the direst poverty. After talking with the mother, he reflected on the hard sacrifices she had made to rear the child, and later he understood that in selling her daughter she was not doing anything unmoral but only what she considered best for the child. To save the daughter, one ought long ago to have saved the mother – saved her from a view of life approved by nearly everybody in Russia. If he had thought of that then, he wrote later, he would have realized that the fine ladies whose aid he wished to seek themselves lived without work, serving merely to satisfy sensuality, and deliberately educating their own daughters for such a life. 'One mother leads her daughter to the tavern,' he maintained, 'another leads her to Court or to balls. But both mothers share the same view of life: namely, that a woman must satisfy a man's lust, and for that she must be fed, clothed, and cared for. How, then, will our ladies save this woman and her daughter?'

[104] A conversation between Lev Tolstoy and Maxim Gorky; from *Maxim Gorky on Literature*.

We were walking in Yusupov Park. He [Count Tolstoy] discoursed brilliantly on the morals of the Moscow aristocracy. A big Russian wench was working almost doubled over on a flowerbed, showing her elephantine legs, her enormous, heavy breasts shaking. He looked at her attentively.

'All this splendour and extravagance was supported by caryatides like that. Not merely by the work of muzhiks and peasant wenches, not by quit rent, but literally by the blood of the people. If the aristocracy had not from time to time coupled with mares like this, it would long ago have died out. Strength cannot be expended, as it was by the young men of my day, with impunity. But after sowing their wild oats many of them married peasant lasses and produced good offspring. So here, too, the muzhik strength came to the rescue. It comes in handy everywhere. Half a generation always wastes its strength on its own pleasures, and the other half mixes its blood with the thick blood of the country people, so as to dilute it a little, too. That's good for the race.'

[105] Eating habits in the 1880s; from *Le Volga, Notes sur la Russie* by A. Legrelle.

In the middle of the room is the restaurant's most important piece of furniture. I don't mean the buffet, which is also arranged in the style of an English bar, and where one goes for the preliminary *zakouska*, a slice of bread with caviar and a throatful of more or less powerful alcohol, the essential solid and liquid *apéritif* of all Russian meals. I am referring to the organ, which is the most beautiful adornment to the eyes and ears in any classy *traktir*, which almost constitutes its essence and which, in the nineteenth century, has replaced the musical clocks which in the good old days grand Muscovite lords used to place on their tables on gala days. Here the organ is monumental. It is almost no longer an organ, it is a whole orchestra, and it has in fact been given the title of *Orchestrion*. Thanks to the *Orchestrion*, or *Polyorchestrion*, you have a gastronomic concert while you dine, a digestive table music, just as if you were a German princeling, owner of a 'military chapel'. The conductor's part is played by a boy, whose job, a little like that of an engine driver, is from time to time to feed into the machine a new roll, a huge log with spikes and fixed melodies, taken from the stack where the repertory is heaped . . .

One should not despise Muscovite dishes and cooking. Chicken stock, with a wing of the same bird and a few pieces of finely chopped vegetables, is a treat as delicious as it is nourishing. The cabbage soup, the national *Tchi*, with a slice of beef and thick cream add to taste, reveals a most satisfactory degree of culinary culture in its creator. The cold fish, salmon or sturgeon, is always irreproachably fresh. Partridge and hazel grouse are available all the year round. Giant crayfish are sent from all the rivers in the country, which, at your command, a bath of boiling water will quickly dress in cardinal red. Large or small strawberries, served with an artistic goblet of fresh milk, will round off your meal pleasantly with a pudding *à la Rousseau*. As to the *Okrochka*, a bitter cold soup, one needs the special knowledge of the clever Baron Brisse to fully appreciate its true gastronomic value. The *Pojarski* cutlet is a very sought after dish, which has sanctified the name of the courageous and loyal patriot at least in the kitchen. Alas, how many great men are only kept alive in the memory of posterity thanks to the protection of a cockerel, and where would the name Soubise be today without onion *purée*! Lastly, if you wish to be clear in your mind about *Kvass*, it will be served at your special request. To look at, *Kvass* is reminiscent of British *Porter*. It is very frothy when it is poured. When it is well chilled, it is pleasant and really thirst-quenching, leaving you, however, with a strange aftertaste of prunes and fermented bread.

[106] A visit to Moscow's brothels in the 1890s by medical students; from *A Nervous Breakdown* by Anton Chekhov, translated by Ronald Hingley.

One evening a medical student, called Mayer, and Rybnikov – a pupil at the Moscow Institute of Painting, Sculpture and Architecture – went to see their friend Vasilyev, a law student, and suggested a joint expendition to S. Street. It was some time before Vasilyev would agree to go, but in the end he put his coat on and left with them . . .

Vasilyev lived in one of the side streets off the Tver Boulevard. It was about eleven o'clock when he left home with his friends, it had just begun to snow for the first time that winter, and all nature was under the spell of the fresh snow. The air smelt of snow, snow crunched softly under the feet and everything – the ground, the roofs, the trees, the boulevard benches – was soft, white and fresh, so that the houses looked quite different from the day before. The street lamps shone more brightly, the air was clearer, the carriages' rumble was muffled. In the fresh, light, frosty air, a sensation akin to the feel of white, fluffy, newly fallen snow seemed to obtrude itself on one's consciousness.

The medical student began singing in a pleasing tenor:

> 'Against my will to these sad shores
> An unknown force has drawn me.'

The art student chimed in:

> 'Behold the windmill, now in ruins –'

'Behold the windmill, now in ruins,' repeated the medical student, raising his eyebrows and shaking his head sadly.

After pausing, rubbing his forehead and trying to remember the words, he sang out so loudly and professionally that passers-by looked round at him:

> ''Twas here that I did once encounter
> A love as carefree as my own free self.' . . .

In ten minutes, Vasilyev imagined, he and his friends would knock on a door and creep along dark passages and dark rooms to the women. Taking advantage of the darkness he would strike a match, and suddenly illumine and behold a martyred face and guilty smile. The unknown woman, fair or dark, would surely have her hair down and wear a white nightgown. She would be scared of the light and terribly embarrassed.

'Heavens, what are you doing?' she would say. 'Put that light out.'

It was all very frightening, yet piquant and novel.

The friends turned off Trubny Square into Grachovka Road and quickly entered the side street which Vasilyev knew only by hearsay. He saw the two rows of houses with brightly lit windows and wide open doors, and heard the merry strains of pianos and fiddles fluttering out of all the doors and mingling in a weird medley, as if an unseen orchestra was tuning up in the darkness above the roofs.

He was surprised. 'What a lot of houses!'

'That's nothing,' said the medical student. 'There are ten times as many in London. There are about a hundred thousand of these women there.'

The cabbies sat on their boxes as calmly and unconcernedly as in any other street. Pedestrians walked the pavements as in other streets. No one hurried, no one hid his face in his coat collar, no one shook his head reproachfully. This unconcern, that medley of pianos and fiddles, the bright windows, wide open doors – it all struck a garish, impudent, dashing, devil-may-care note. There was obviously just the same sort of bustle and high spirits, with people's faces and walk expressing just the same offhandedness, at slave markets in the old days.

'Let's begin at the beginning,' said the art student.

The friends entered a narrow passage lit by a lamp with a reflector. When they opened the door a man in a black frock-coat, with an unshaven, flunkeylike face and sleepy eyes, slowly arose from a yellow sofa. The place smelt like a laundry with a dash of vinegar. A door led from the hall into a brightly lit room. In this doorway the medical students and the artist stopped and craned their necks, both peering into the room at once.

'Buona sera, signori and gents.' The art student gave a theatrical bow. 'Rigoletto, Huguenotti, Traviata!'

'Havana, Cucaracha, Pistoletto!' added the medical student, pressing his hat to his breast and bowing low.

Vasilyev stood behind them, also desirous of giving a theatrical bow and saying something nonsensical, but he only smiled, feeling an embarrassment akin to shame, and impatiently awaiting further developments.

In the doorway appeard a small fair girl of seventeen or eighteen, crop-haired and wearing a short blue frock with a white metallic pendant on her breast. 'Don't stand in the doorway,' she said. 'Do take your coats off and come into the lounge.'

Still talking 'Italian,' the medical student and the art student went into the lounge, followed by the irresolute Vasilyev.

'Take off your coats, gentlemen,' said a servant sternly. 'This won't do.'

Besides the blonde there was another girl in the lounge – very tall and stout, foreign-looking, with bare arms. She sat near the piano playing patience on her lap and paying no attention whatever to the guests.

'Where are the other young ladies?' asked the medical student.

'Having tea,' said the blonde. 'Stepan,' she shouted, 'go and tell the girls that some students have arrived.'

Soon afterwards a third girl came in wearing a bright red dress with blue stripes. Her face was heavily and unskilfully made up, her forehead was hidden by her hair, and there was a look of fear in her unblinking gaze. After entering she at once began singing some song in a powerful, crude contralto. After her the fourth girl appeared, and then a fifth.

Vasilyev found nothing novel or interesting in any of this, feeling as if he had seen it all several times before – the lounge, the piano, the mirror with its cheap gilt frame, the pendant, the dress with the blue stripes, the blank, indifferent faces. Of the darkness, the stillness, the secrecy, the guilty smile and all that he had expected and feared to meet here he saw no trace.

Everything was ordinary, prosaic, boring. Only one thing slightly piqued his curiosity – the dreadful and seemingly intentional bad taste evident in the cornices, in the inane pictures, the dresses and that pendant. There was something significant and noteworthy about this lack of taste.

'How cheap and silly it all is!' Vasilyev thought. 'This trumpery that I see before me – what is there in it all to tempt a normal man and make him commit the fearful sin of buying a human being for a rouble? I understand sinning for the sake of glamour, beauty, grace, passion, good taste, but this is different. What's worth sinning for here? But I must stop thinking.'

The fair woman addressed him. 'Hey, you with the beard, treat me to some porter.'

Vasilyev was suddenly embarrassed. 'With pleasure.' He bowed politely. 'But you must excuse me, madame – I er, shan't drink with you, I'm not a drinking man.'

Five minutes later the friends were on their way to another house.

'Now, why did you order porter?' the medical student raged. 'Think you're a millionaire? That's a complete waste of six roubles.'

'Why not give her the pleasure if she wanted it?' Vasilyev riposted.

'The pleasure wasn't hers, it was the Madame's. They tell the girls to ask the customers for a drink, because they're the ones who make the profit.'

'Behold the windmill, now in ruins,' sang the art student.

[107] Moscow's merchants and the arts; from *Diaghileff, his artistic and private life* by Arnold Haskell.

This *fin de siècle* was an exciting period in European painting – a time of feverish activity that called for real discrimination on the part of the amateur, who was often, in the morning, thoroughly ashamed of his enthusiasm of the night before. It had its repercussions in Russia also, and the two great capitals St Petersburg and Moscow reacted in manners entirely different one from the other. The city of Peter was naturally for Europeanization, while Moscow was solidly nationalist, believing in the rejuvenation of Russian art itself. The attitude of each city to the ikon was typical and revealing. St Petersburg looked upon it as a valuable and interesting antiquity – a relic of history; Moscow as something living – an inspiration for the contemporary artist. If St Petersburg looked to France, it was mainly the eighteenth century that held her interest, while Moscow was more venturesome and speculative, and her merchant collectors sought contemporary works for their galleries which are now the basis of the Soviet museums of modern art. This differing outlook of the two great cities was marked almost to the point of hostility.

Diaghileff made frequent visits to Moscow, though he showed no marked preference for either tendency. There he met a remarkable man, in many ways a pioneer in the direction that he himself was to take, and the understanding between them must have had its influence on him.

Sava Mamontoff was a Moscow merchant patron of the arts, but something more than the wealthy man who just signs cheques, and then sits back to await results. He had started as a backer of the private Italian opera, and had then come under the influence of the strong nationalist feeling that was going through Moscow; Stanislavsky had just started his Art Theatre, and was showing Tchekov according to entirely new principles. Everywhere was the desire to express Russian themes in a new manner. Mamontoff turned his mind to Russian opera. He had surrounded himself by a group of young painters, and it was to them that he entrusted the decorative side. This was a bold innovation in the direction that Diaghileff himself was to follow – a landmark in the history of the theatre. For the first time scenery and costume designing was entrusted to easel artists, who were within a short time to sweep away the specialists with their stereotyped ideas and their heavy built-up sets, and to substitute youth, colour, and freshness. Painting took its place in the theatre, and the scene with its costumes, carefully graduated patches of colour, became a living canvas. The opera convention, handled by such a master producer as Sanine, was no longer ridiculous – it was given a truth of its own that has persisted to-day in well-produced Russian opera, in marked contrast to the Italian or the German. The painters took a pride in finding the exact tone for their costumes, often searching the junk shops for antique fabric that would give them their values, as exactly as if they were mixing paint on their palettes.

It is thanks to Mamontoff that such works as *Boris Godounov, Khovantchina, La Pskovitaine, Sadko*, and *Snegourotchka* were recreated, and it is here for the first time that the genius of Chaliapine was revealed. He had previously made his début at the Imperial Theatres, but with no great success, the type of role assigned to him being quite unsuitable. Mamontoff was the first to point out to him the right direction. His interpretation of the role of Ivan the Terrible in Rimsky-Korsakov's *Pskovitaine*, which later Diaghileff was to give on the Continent, wisely renamed *Ivan the Terrible*, was the beginning of his triumphs as a singer-actor.

Diaghileff soon made friends with the artists surrounding Mamontoff, notably, Serov, Korovin, the brothers Vasnetzoff, Maliutine, Vroubel, and others. Of these artist, M.A. Vroubel was the special pride of Moscow, the most versatile artist that Russia has yet produced – painter, sculptor, architect, book illustrator, and scenic artist. His *décors* for the Mamontoff opera were pioneer works in the direction that Bakst was to take. Almost unknown in Western Europe, his tragic story has given him in Russia the romantic glamour of a Van Gogh or a Gauguin, and this glamour has obscured one's view of him as an artist. He had high ideals. 'Is there anything,' he wrote in his youth, 'more tragic than to feel the infinite beauty around one, to see God everywhere, and yet to be conscious of one's own incapacity to express the great things?' He struggled in this atmosphere of doubt; was crude, harsh, powerful, and at times poetical – a queer tormented visionary. Diaghileff knew him well, and appreciated him. His first attack of madness occurred during the fourth *Mir Isskustva* exhibition of 1902. All night he remained in the gallery, with a bottle of champagne for company, repainting his huge canvas of the 'Demon.' The morning of the private view he was found, a gibbering, incoherent being. He remained in an asylum for two years. His last public appearance was at the great Palais Tauride exhibition, where he struck everybody by his volubility and incoherence. He died soon afterwards in an asylum.

Select Bibliography

ALEXANDROV, VICTOR, *The Kremlin*, transl. by Roy Monkcom, London, 1963.

BARING, MAURICE, *What I Saw in Russia, 1905–1906*, London, 1927.

BERTON, KATHLEEN, *Moscow, An Architectural History*, London, 1977.

BEST, ROBERT (interpreter to A. Jenkinson), *The Voyage wherein Osepp Napea, the Moscovite Ambassadour, returned home into his Countrey*, London, 1557.

BEYLE, MARIE-HENRI, *Stendhal*, Journal of 14–15 September 1812, Paris. (Transl. by Laurence Kelly)

BOURKE, RICHARD SOUTHWELL, *6th earl of mayo, St Petersburg and Moscow, a Visit to the Court of the Czar*, Vol. II, London, 1846.

BUXHOEVEDEN, BARONESS SOPHIE, *The Life and Tragedy of Alexandra Feodorovna, Empress of Russia*, London, 1928.

CARRINGTON, GEORGE, B.A., *Behind the Scenes in Russia*, London, 1874.

CAULAINCOURT, GENERAL DE, *Memoirs of General de Caulaincourt, Duke of Vicenza, 1812–13*, ed. by Jean Hanoteau, translated by Hamish Miles, London, 1935.

CHANCELLOR, RICHARD, see Hakluyt.

CHEKHOV, ANTON, *A Nervous Breakdown*, transl. and ed. by Ronald Hingley, Oxford, 1980.

COXE, WILLIAM, *Travels into Poland, Russia, Sweden and Denmark, interspersed with historical relations and political inquiries*, Dublin, 1784.

CUSTINE, MARQUIS ASTOLPHE LOUIS LEONARD DE, *The Empire of the Czar or Observations on the Social, Political and Religious State and Prospects of Russia made during a Journey through that Empire*, Vol. II, London, 1843.

DICEY, EDWARD, *A Month in Russia during the Marriage of the Czarevitch*, London, 1867.

DISBROWE, CHARLOTTE, (ed.) *Original Letters from Russia, 1825–28*, London, 1878.

DOLGORUKOV, PRINCE PIERRE, *Mémoires du Prince Pierre Dolgoroukow*, Geneva, 1867. (Transl. by Marina Berry)

DOSTOEVSKY, FEODOR, *Feodor Dostoievsky 1877, the Diary of a Writer*, London, 1949.

EDWARDS, SUTHERLAND, *The Russians at Home. Unpolitical Sketches*, London, 1861.

FABRICIUS, M.P., *Le Kremlin de Moscou, Esquisses et Tableaux*, Moscow, 1883. (Transl. by Marina Berry)

FLETCHER, GILES, THE ELDER, *Of the Russe Common wealth*, London, 1591.

FRANKLAND, CAPTAIN, C. COLVILLE, R.N., *Narrative of a Visit to the Courts of Russia and Sweden in the Years 1830 and 1831*, Vol. II, London, 1832.

FUSIL, LOUISE, *Souvenirs d'une Femme sur la Retraite de Russie*, ed. by Emile-Paule, Paris, 1910. (Transl. by Marie Noële Kelly)

GERSHENZON, M., *Griboyedov's Moscow*, Moscow and Berlin, 1922. (Transl. by Sophie Lund)

GOLOVKIN, COMTE FEODOR, *La Cour et le Règne de Paul Ier*, Paris, 1905 (Transl. by Laurence Kelly)

GORKY, MAXIM, *Maxim Gorky on Literature*, transl. by Ivy Litvinov, Moscow, no date

HAKLUYT, RICHARD, *Voyages and Documents of Richard Hakluyt, 1553*, Oxford – extract by Richard Chancellor.

HASKELL, ARNOLD, *Diaghileff, his artistic and private life*, London, 1935.

HERZEN, ALEXANDER, *My Past and Thoughts*, transl. from the German by Constance Garnett and Humphrey Higgens, London, 1968.

HOARE, SIR SAMUEL JOHN GURNEY, LL.D., M.P., *The Fourth Seal: the end of a Russian Chapter*, London, 1930.

HORSEY, SIR JEROME, *A Relacion or Memoriall Abstracted out of Sir Jerom Horsey His Travels Imploiements Services and Negociacions*, London, 1856.

KERSHAW, N., *Russian Heroic Poetry*, Cambridge, 1932.

KOHL, JOHANN GEORGE, *Russia: St Petersburg, Moscow, Kharkoff, Riga, Odessa, the German Provinces on the Baltic, the Steppes, the Crimea, and the Interior of the Empire*, London, 1842.

KORB, JOHANN GEORG, *Diary of Austrian Secretary of Legation at the Court of Czar Peter the Great*, transl. from the original Latin and ed. by Count MacDonnell, London, 1863.

KROPOTKIN, PRINCE PETER, *Memoirs of a Revolutionist*, London, 1899.

L'AMI, C.E., and WELIKOTNY, ALEXANDER, *Michael Lermontov*, Manitoba, 1967.

LEGRELLE, A., *Le Volga, Notes sur la Russie*, Paris, 1877. (Transl. by Marina Berry)

LOWTH, G.T., *Across the Kremlin, or Pictures of Life in Moscow*, London, 1868.

MAGARSHACK, DAVID, *Chekhov, A Life*, London, 1952.

MAROGER, DOMNIQUE, (ed.) *The Memoirs of Catherine the Great, 1743–4*, transl. from the French by Moura Budberg, London, 1955.

MASSA DE HAARLEM, ISAAC, *Histoire des Guerres de la Moscovie (1601–1610)*. Brussels, 1866. (Transl. by Marina Berry)

MERIMEE, PROSPER, *Episode de l'histoire de Russie: Le Faux Démétrius*, Paris, 1889. (Transl. by Marie Noële Kelly)

MIEGE, GUY, *A Relation of Three Embassies from his Sacred Majestie Charles II to the Great Duke of Muscovie . . . Performed by the Right Noble the Earl of Carlisle in the Years 1663 and 1664*, London, 1669.

MITCHELL, THOMAS, C.B., *Russian Pictures*, London, 1889.

MOLTKE, FIELD-MARSHAL COUNT HELMUTH VON, *Letters from Russia*, transl. by Robina Napier, London, 1878.

NIKOFOROV, D.M., *Staraya Moskva*, Moscow, 1902. (Transl. by Sophie Lund)

NISBET BAIN, R., *The First Romanovs, 1613–1725*, London, 1905.

OLEARIUS, ADAM, *The Travels of Olearius in Seventeenth Century Russia*, transl. and ed. by Samuel H. Baron, California, 1967.

PALEOLOGUE, MAURICE, *An Ambassador's Memoirs, 1914–1917*, transl. by F.A. Holt, London, 1924–25.

PARKINSON, JOHN, *A Tour of Russia, Siberia and the Crimea, 1792–1794*, ed. by William Collier, London, 1971.

PUSHKIN, ALEXANDER, *Eugene Onegin*, transl. by Charles Johnston, London, 1977.

— *The Letters of Alexander Pushkin*, transl. by J. Thomas Shaw, Wisconsin, 1967.

REINBECK, G. VON, *Travels from St Petersburg in the Year 1805*, in a series of letters transl. from German, London, 1807.

ROSTOPCHIN, COUNT FEODOR VASILIEVITCH, *Oeuvres Inédites du Comte Rostopchine*, Paris, 1894. (Transl. by Marie Noële Kelly)

SCHERER, JEAN BENOIT, *Anecdotes et Recueil de Coutumes et de Traits d'Historie Naturelle Particuliers aux Différens Peuples de la Russie par un Voyageur qui a Sejourné Treize Ans dans cet Empire*, London, 1792. (Transl. by Marina Berry)

SCHUYLER, EUGENE, *Peter the Great, Emperor of Russia*, Vol. I, London, 1884.

SHAKHOVSKOYE, PRINCESS ZINAÏDA, *La Vie Quotidienne à Moscou au XVIIe Siècle*, Paris, 1963. (Transl. by Marina Berry)

— *Precursors of Peter the Great*, transl. from the French by J. Maxwell Brownjohn, London, 1964.

SHAMURIN, YURI, *Podmoskovnaya, Kulturniya Sokrovishcha Rossii*, Moscow, 1914. (Transl. by Sophie Lund)

— *Essays about Classical Moscow*, Moscow, 1914. (Transl. by Sophie Lund)

SHCHERBATOV, PRINCE MIKHAIL MIKHAILOVITCH, *On the Corruption of Morals in Russia*, transl. and ed. by A. Lentin, M.A., Ph.D., Cambridge, 1969.

SIMMONS, ERNEST, J., *Pushkin*, Oxford, 1937.

— *Leo Tolstoy*, London, 1949.

STANISLAVSKY, K.S., *Anton Tchekhov, Literary and Theatrical Reminiscences*, transl. and ed. by S.S. Koteliansky, London, 1927.

— *My Life in Art*, transl. by J.J. Robbins, London, 1967.

STEPHENS, J.L., *Incidents of Travel in the Russian and Turkish Empires*, Vol. II, London, 1839.

SULKOWSKI, L.A.M., *An Historical Account and Description of the City of Moscow, so justly celebrated for its antiquity and magnificent buildings, the Religion, Customs and Manners of its Inhabitants*, London, 1813.

The Present State of Russia, in a Letter to a Friend at London; written by an Eminent Person residing at the Great Tzar's Court at Mosco for the space of nine years, London, 1671.

TOLSTOY, COUNT L.N., *War And Peace*, transl. by Constance Garnett, Modern history edition, New York, no date.

ULAM, ADAM B., *Lenin and the Bolsheviks*, London, 1966.

WALISZEWSKI, K., *Peter the Great*, Vol. I, transl. from the French by Lady Mary Lloyd, London, 1898.

WILMOT, MARTHA AND CATHERINE, *The Russian Journals of Martha and Catherine Wilmot. Being an account of two Irish ladies of their adventures in Russia as guests of the celebrated Princess Daschkaw, containing vivid descriptions of contemporary court life and society, and lively anecdotes of many interesting historical characters, 1803–1808*, ed. the Marchioness of Londonderry and H.M. Hyde, London, 1934.

Index